NOVELL
NETWARE

PRISMA Computer Courses are structured, practical guides to mastering the most popular computer programs. PRISMA books are course books, giving step-by-step instructions, which take the user through basic skills to advanced functions in easy to follow, manageable stages.

Now available:

dBase IV
Excel 4.0 for Windows
Lotus 1-2-3 2.4
MS-DOS 3.3 to 5.0
UNIX
Windows 3.0 and 3.1
WordPerfect 5.1
WordPerfect for Windows

Peter Freese, Heinrich Tofall and Werner Wehmeier

NOVELL NETWARE

PRISMA COMPUTER COURSE

Prisma Computer Courses first published in Great Britain 1993 by

McCarta Ltd
P.O. Box 2996
London N5 2TA London

Translation: George Hall
Production: LINE UP text productions

© Rowohlt Taschenbuch Verlag GmbH, Reinbek bei Hamburg
For the English translation
© 1993 Uitgeverij Het Spectrum B.V. Utrecht

No part of this book may be reproduced in any form, by print, photoprint, microfilm or any other means without written permission from the publisher.

ISBN 1 85365 321 7

British Library Cataloguing-in-Publication Data.
A catalogue record for this book is available from the British Library.

Contents

	Foreword	9
1	PC networks	11
1.1	The use of PC networks	11
1.2	The network standard configuration	12
1.3	The network users	14
2	Beginning in the network	16
2.1	Starting up a workstation in the network	16
2.2	Logging in to, and out of, the network	20
2.3	Assigning and altering a password	26
2.4	Displaying information about the workstation	28
2.5	Displaying directories	30
2.6	Displaying information about files	36
2.7	Displaying information about a fileserver	40
2.8	Displaying the users who are logged in	46
3	File management in the network	48
3.1	Working with directories	48
3.2	Examining and altering access rights for directories	55
3.3	Working with files	68
3.4	Displaying and altering file attributes and access rights	83
4	Supervisor tasks	97
4.1	Control of access by the supervisor	97
4.2	User management	98
4.2.1	User group management	100
4.2.2	User management	108
4.2.3	User accounts	122
4.2.4	Activating a different server	125
4.2.5	File Server Information	126
4.3	Specifying the user work environment	128
5	Installing applications in the network	141
5.1	Applications and their suitability for a network	142

5.2	Examples of applications for several workstations	143
5.2.1	The dBASE IV database program	143
5.2.2	The Word 5.5 word processor	148
5.2.3	The Windows graphical user interface	156
5.3	Multiplan as an example of a network application	161
6	Printing	166
6.1	Printers in the network	166
6.2	Printing from applications on a network printer	167
6.3	Installing print routines in the network	195
6.4	Control and operation of network print routines	225
6.5	Activating a print server	241
6.6	Logging out a remote network printer from the print server	248
7	Communication within the network	251
7.1	Sending messages in the network	252
7.2	Accepting or refusing messages	260
7.3	An example of electronic post: Pegasus Mail	261
8	Archiving and protecting data	270
8.1	Forms of data protection	270
8.2	Saving data using NBACKUP	272
8.3	Restoring data using NBACKUP	280
9	Adapting workstations to the network	286
9.1	Creating and using startup files	286
9.2	Compiling and using menus	292
10	The installation	298
10.1	Installation of Novell NetWare on the fileserver	298
10.2	Creating a NetWare shell for the workstations	309
11	Utility programs and commands	312
11.1	Menu-driven utility programs	312

11.2	Utility programs on the command line	. 314
11.3	Console commands	. 320
11.4	List of the login script commands	. 325
11.5	List of login script variables	. 334
11.6	List of the configuration commands for SHELL.CFG	. 336
	Index	. 342

Foreword

In companies, ever-increasing use is being made of stand-alone personal computers instead of multi-user systems. Relatively little technical application is required to link these computers to one another via a server to form a network. The following factors have determined this development:

- Most programs can also be run in a network nowadays.
- The workstation can be used either as a network computer or as a stand-alone computer, according to choice.
- A network is not much more expensive than a multi-user system.
- The average user can easily learn the network functions relevant to his/her work.

Just as MS-DOS has, in essence, become the standard operating system for the personal computer, Novell NetWare has developed into the standard for networks.

This book provides an extensive introduction to the use and application of the Novell NetWare network operating system. This information enables you to comprehend and employ the procedures of PC networks which use this operating system, from both the point of view of the normal user and that of the network manager. The topics discussed are supplemented by many practical examples and explanatory figures.

- The first two chapters deal with the basic principles. This will enable you, as a normal user, to execute the first activities within the network.
- In chapter 3, working with directories and files are discussed in combination with the operating access restrictions which apply in Novell NetWare.
- Chapter 4 outlines the function of the network manager for user groups and individual users in the network.

- In chapter 5, the use of applications in the network is described with reference to the standard programs, dBASE, MS Word, MS Multiplan and Windows.
- Network printers are dealt with extensively in chapter 6.
- Chapter 7 discusses communication possibilities.
- Chapter 8 deals with the safeguarding of programs and data.
- Chapter 9 provides additional information concerning the formulation of your workstation's start procedure.
- The installation of Novell NetWare on a fileserver is discussed in Chapter 10.
- Chapter 11 provides a survey of utility programs and Novell NetWare commands.

1 PC networks

1.1 The use of PC networks

Many tasks in a company can be carried out by means of a personal computer, such as book-keeping, the formulation of engineering drawings and correspondence. When these kinds of office activities reach such proportions that they can no longer be executed by one staff member, the demand for more computer capacity becomes valid. When the task assignment becomes extended, many employees not only have to use the same programs, they also have to work with the same data.

In order to meet these demands, a firm may purchase a multi-user system (a computer system for several users). However, it is also possible to link several personal computers to one another via a server to form a network. The advantage of a network over a multi-user system lies in the possibility of choosing one of the following methods of working:

1. Common usage:
   All connected workstations can address a common data file on the server at the same time. Individual records can be processed separately. Special programs for common usage operate the data addressing.

2. Partial stand-alone usage:
   The workstations work independently of the network to a certain extent. Programs and data are stored on the network server. All workstations are able to make simultaneous use of the programs. The data are processed locally; data stored on the server, however, can be loaded by each station.

3. Completely stand-alone usage:
   The workstations run entirely independently of the network. The network link is not used. The programs and data are managed on local disks.

In the case of common usage, several users may work with, for instance, the same customer file at the same time but not with data from the same customer. While a user is working with the data from one customer, these data are inaccessible to other users. However, they become available again immediately after use.

In the case of partial stand-alone usage, different users may activate the same program in a network, a word processing program for example. Using this program, the users are able to create and edit files themselves. By defining the rights of access for each user, overwriting someone else's file (perhaps due to the accidental choice of the same file name) can be prevented.

However, files can be exchanged with other workstations via the server. Accordingly, a user may create a text document and save it in a specified directory. A second user may then retrieve this file from the directory, modify it and save it once more. Subsequently, the first user can retrieve the document again and edit it further. Information is required to carry out this kind of procedure. This can be supplied using the network communication system.

Another possibility for partial stand-alone usage is that data from the network server are transported to the workstation harddisk and subsequently edited using a program which is not active in the network.

In the case of total stand-alone usage, a workstation can be used as an independent personal computer. The user at this station does not have to log in (register him/herself) in the network. Only programs and data which are stored on the workstation harddisk are used.

1.2 The network standard configuration

Server and workstations. For the points of reference in this book, we have chosen the following widely-used configuration from the various possible combinations of devices:

- The server is an IBM-compatible personal computer; the Novell NetWare operating system is installed on the harddisk. The server is used in the *dedicated mode*. This means that the server in the network executes exclusively operating and storage functions, and cannot be used as a workstation.
- All connected workstations are also IBM-compatible personal computers which run under the MS-DOS operating system.
- Each workstation is equipped with a network card. This is an electronic component which is inserted in one of the free slots of the computer. The network card has a contact point by which the computer can be linked to the server by means of a cable.

The workstations. The workstations may possess their own diskdrives and harddisks, but that is not absolutely necessary. Harddisks are necessary if large amounts of data have to be stored in the buffer, or if other data from outside the network are required in addition to the data and programs stored on the server. Diskdrives are necessary if data are stored on diskettes or have to be exchanged by means of diskettes. If workstations which do not have their own harddisk are used in a network, the network cards must possess an extra switch element (boot PROM) in order to activate the workstation.

Network system software. The basic reference point of this book is the Novell NetWare network operating system version 3.11, based on the 2*xx*, 3.0 and 3.1 versions. Versions 3.0 and 3.1 were subject to small irregularities which have been eliminated from the current version.

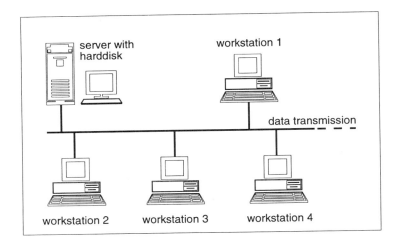

1.3 The network users

The network user is anyone who is entitled to work in a certain network. This entitlement is attained by specifying a name, the *user name*, at any workstation of the network. This procedure is called *logging in*.

Certain rights of access in a well-organized network are acquired by defining the name. These rights may be compared to rights in an office where many locked desks and filing cabinets are situated. The rights of the staff to open these desks and cabinets and to examine or modify the data are exactly specified in many cases, for various reasons. Normally, only the manager is entitled to inspect all dossiers. Heads of department have the rights appropriate to their department, and staff members are assigned individual rights.

The rights in a Novell NetWare network are similar, but apply to files and directories. Anyone only having to execute a few tasks at the workstation requires comparatively few rights to files and directories. Rights to directory and file groups are necessary to manage groups. The system manager or *Supervisor* of the entire network posseses all rights for all directories and files. This produces the following hierarchy:

- The system manager *(Supervisor)* receives all rights for all directories and all files. He allocates the specific rights to the other users.
- The *Workgroup Manager* receives the rights for the directory groups, for instance, the SALES directory group. He can regulate the rights of individual users for the subdirectories and files or file groups.
- The normal user receives certain rights, relevant to his/her requirements, in a few directories or files.

2 Beginning in the network

2.1 Starting up a workstation in the network

Each workstation running under the MS-DOS operating system must be started up as a stand-alone computer (this is called *booting* in computer terminology). During this process, important parts of the MS-DOS operating system are loaded into the station memory and certain individual system settings are applied. Subsequently, the connection to the network must be made. Depending on the workstation configuration, the following start procedures are possible:

- from the built-in harddisk
- using a diskette
- via the server.

Starting up from a harddisk. When a workstation has a harddisk, this is normally used to start up the workstation independently of the network. If this is also the case with your workstation, you only need to switch on the computer (and the monitor if it has its own power supply) and wait until the starting procedure is completed.

Caution: A harddisk can be used to start up a computer if the necessary operating system programs have been installed (IO.SYS or IBMBIO.COM, MSDOS.SYS or IBMDOS.COM and COMMAND.COM). In addition, the configuration file, CONFIG.SYS and the automatic starting file, AUTOEXEC.BAT, should be formulated for the individual settings. Generally, the computer dealer will have done this already, but you can also do it yourself at a later date. Consult the MS-DOS manual for the necessary information.

Starting up with a diskette. If your workstation has diskdrives, you can start it up by means of a special start diskette. Switch the station on and insert the dis-

Starting up a workstation in the network

kette in the default drive (normally drive A:). Wait until the start procedure has ended.

Caution: The operating system programs mentioned above must be located on the diskette, along with the configuration file and the automatic starting file. Chapter 9 discusses how to create a diskette like this.

Starting up via the server. As mentioned, workstations without diskdrives and harddisks can also run in a network. If you have this kind of workstation, you only have to switch on the network and wait until the start procedure has taken place.

Caution: When starting up a computer without drives, the most important operating system programs and, if necessary, the configuration and starting files, must be read in from the server harddisk. For this, a separate switch element (boot PROM) must be installed on the network card of the work station. This element ensures that the required programs are retrieved from the server harddisk during the start procedure. A boot PROM can also be used with devices possessing drives, but it is only possible to reduce waiting during the start procedure by using diskdrives. The operating system programs and files must be compressed in the NET$DOS.SYS in the LOGIN directory on the server harddisk. Section 9.1 outlines how to make this kind of file.

Establishing the connection to the network. The physical connection between the workstation and the network is made via the network *shell*. In principle, this shell consists of the programs, IPX.COM and NETX.COM (the latter program is called NET3.COM, NET4.COM or NET5COM, according to the MS-DOS version). Both programs must be located on the harddisk, start diskette or server. The programs can be activated one by one: firstly IPX and then NETX. Normally however, both activation commands are included in the automatic starting file. The connection is then made automatically.

Caution: If you wish to be able to choose whether to use a computer with a harddisk either in a network or independently, you should not include both program activation commands in the automatic starting file. Instead, you should create a separate starting file (see the example below).

If required, the network shell can be adapted to your own configuration by means of the SHELL.CFG file. This file, if present, is processed after the activation of the IPX and NETX shell files, in the same way as the CONFIG.SYS configuration file under MS-DOS. The SHELL.CFG is a simple text file which you can create by means of the DOS command COPY CON or using an editor. In chapter 6, we shall describe several commands which are important for the configuration of network printers in the SHELL.CFG file. Section 11.6 provides a survey of all configuration commands.

Switching to the server drive. The physical connection to the network has been made. Before you can log in as a user, you must switch to the server harddisk. In the case of NET3 to NET5, you can address the server by means of the letter F:. It is possible to do this using the keyboard, but it is more convenient to include the command in the automatic starting file, so that the switch to the appropriate drive is performed automatically.

Example 1:
A workstation with a diskdrive is started up using a diskette. Subsequently, the connection to the network must be made.

(1) When the computer has been started up, the first shell program, IPX.COM is retrieved from the diskette.
(2) Message from the shell program.
(3) Another message concerning the workstation devices. NE1000 indicates that the Ethernet network card is recognized. The addresses of the network card in the workstation working memory are displayed.

Starting up a workstation in the network 19

```
A:\>ipx                                                              (1)
Novell IPX/SPX  v3.10 (911121)                                       (2)
(C) Copyright 1985, 1991 Novell Inc.  All Rights Reserved.
LAN Option: NetWare NE1000  v3.02EC (900831)                         (3)
Hardware Configuration: IRQ = 3, I/O Base = 300h, no DMA or RAM

A:\>netx                                                             (4)
NetWare V3.21 - Workstation Shell (910729)
(C) Copyright 1991 Novell, Inc.  All Rights Reserved.
Running on DOS V6.00                                                 (5)
Attached to server SERVER1                                           (6)
01-11-93    08:15:32

A:\>f:                                                               (7)
F:\LOGIN>
```

(4) The second shell program is also retrieved from diskette.

(5) The message indicates that the connection of the network to the workstation takes place under the MS-DOS operating system.

(6) The connection of the workstation to the SERVER1 server has been made. The date and time are also shown. If no connection is made, the message *A File Server could not be found* is displayed.

(7) The server harddisk is activated. The LOGIN directory containing the logging in program is shown.

Example 2:

When the workstation has been started up from a built-in harddisk, the connection to the network must initially be made using the keyboard. The shell programs are located in the NETWARE subdirectory on the harddisk. In addition, a starting file (batch file) which automatically makes the connection must be started up.

(1) The first shell program is started up from the NETWARE directory on the harddisk. The message indicates that the program has already been activated. Otherwise a message appears, identical to that in example 1.

```
C:\NETWARE>ipx                                                         (1)
IPX/SPX already loaded.

C:\NETWARE>netx                                                        (2)
NetWare V3.21 - Workstation Shell (910729)
(C) Copyright 1991 Novell, Inc.  All Rights Reserved.

Running on DOS V6.00

Attached to server SERVER1
01-11-93    08:04:50
C:\NETWARE>f:

F:\LOGIN>


C:\>type netstart.bat                                                  (3)
@echo off                                                              (4)
cls                                                                    (5)
path=;                                                                 (6)
c:\netware\ipx                                                         (7)
c:\netware\netx
f:

C:\>
```

(2) The second program is activated and control switches to drive F:. The messages are identical to those in example 1.

(3) You can make an automatic connection using the batch file shown. You only need to enter the name of the file: *netstart*. The last three commands may also be located in the automatic starting file AUTOEXEC.BAT. In that case, the connection to the network is made immediately after the computer is switched on.

(4) This and the other commands in the batch file are not shown during execution.

(5) The contents of the screen are removed.

(6) The prior path indication is removed.

(7) Both shell programs are started up and the server drive becomes active.

2.2 Logging in to, and out of, the network

Logging in to a fileserver. When the physical connection between the workstation and the fileserver has been made, the user must register in the fileserver under his/her user name in order to be able to work in the network. This is called *logging in* in computer terminology. The user is included in the server system management when he/she logs in. This means that the specific user rights are then allocated and a time account is opened. If the work environment makes it necessary, each user may be assigned a password. This must then be entered as a second login condition.

Entering the user name. The examples in the previous section illustrated the activation of the LOGIN system directory after the workstation had been started up and the switch to the server harddisk had been made. This directory contains the LOGIN.EXE login program. You must activate this program along with your user name to implement the login procedure, for instance:

```
F:\LOGIN>login cook
```

The command may be typed in both capital and small letters. There must be a space between the program and the user name. It is also possible to activate the program without specifying a user name at the same time. The system will then ask you enter the user name:

```
F:\LOGIN>login
Enter your login name: cook
```

Entering the password. If you have been assigned a password, you should specify it now:

```
Enter your password:
```

You may type the password in both small and capital letters. The characters comprising the password are not shown on the screen for security reasons.

After logging in. When you have entered all login data, the following procedures will be instigated, depending on the network operating system settings:

- Certain settings will be made for your workstation, such as the assignment of user rights and valid directories.
- System messages will be shown.
- Either
  ➤ an applications menu will be displayed, or
  ➤ an application will be activated immediately, or
  ➤ a switch will be made to the level of the network operating system.

The settings are regulated using a system and user login script. This consists of text files containing the necessary commands and messages. Just as in the case of the automatic starting file AUTOEXEC.BAT under DOS, these commands are read and executed one by one during the login procedure.

Settings which apply to all users are regulated by means of the system login script. The user login script applies to one specific user. The creation and usage of login scripts and menus will be discussed in chapters 4 and 9.

Logging out. When you end a network session, or interrupt it for a lengthy period of time, you must leave the fileserver in the proper manner. If the user menu contains the *Log out* option, you only need to activate it. Otherwise you must give the following command behind the system prompt:

```
LOGOUT [fileserver]
```

fileserver   If you have logged in to several fileservers, specify the name of the fileserver where you wish to log out.

The network operating system is active when the system prompt is visible, for instance F:\> or F:\USER\SALES\WS4>. If a diskdrive is active at this moment without there being a diskette in the drive, the request to insert a diskette may appear on the screen. In that case, insert any formatted diskette in the drive and repeat the command.

Logging in to, and out of, the network

Caution: You can only be certain that all opened files will be closed if you log out in the proper way. In order to prevent non-authorized persons making use of your programs and data, you should always log out when you leave the workstation.

Example 3:

When a workstation has been started up and a connection has been made to the network, the Supervisor must log in by specifying his/her name and password to the fileserver.

```
F:\LOGIN>login supervisor                                              (1)
Enter your password:                                                   (2)
SERVER1/SUPERVISOR: Access to server denied.                           (3)
You are attached to server SERVER1.                                    (4)

F:\LOGIN>login supervisor                                              (5)
Enter your password:
Good morning, SUPERVISOR  01-11-1993  8:30                             (6)
Drive  A:   maps to a local disk.                                      (7)
Drive  F: = SERVER1/SYS:  \SYSTEM                                      (8)
Drive  G: = SERVER1/SYS:  \WORD-DAT
-----
SEARCH1:  = L:. [SERVER1/SYS:  \PUBLIC]                                (9)
SEARCH3:  = X:. [SERVER1/SYS:  \PUBLIC\IBM_PC\MSDOS\V6.00]
SEARCH9:  = R:. [SERVER1/SYS:  \WORD5]

F:\SYSTEM>logout                                                       (10)
SUPERVISOR logged out from server SERVER1 connection 11.               (11)
Login time:   Monday November 01, 1993  8:30 am
Logout time:  Monday November 01, 1993  8:30 am

F:\LOGIN>
```

(1) The name *supervisor* is entered along with the *login* program command.
(2) The system requests the password.
(3) The password has not been entered correctly. Accordingly, the system does not allow access to the fileserver.
(4) The physical connection is not severed.
(5) The login procedure is repeated.
(6) When the password has been entered correctly, system messages will appear. These depend on the system login script. The messages shown in the example may differ slightly from those on your screen.
(7) Unless otherwise specified in the automatic start-

ing file, the letters A to E are assigned to the local drives in the workstations. You can address a diskdrive or harddisk on your workstation in the same way as under MS-DOS, thus as a letter with a colon. Due to shortage of space, only the indication of the first drive A: has been included in the figure shown.

(8) Subsequently, F: indicates the first server harddisk. This and the following drive indications do not, however, refer to physical drives; they refer to logical areas (directories) on the harddisk. In the example, the letter F is assigned the \SYSTEM directory and G the \WORD-DAT directory. If you specify one of these letters along with a colon, the corresponding directory on the server harddisk is addressed.

Caution: During the installation of Novell NetWare, the server harddisk can be divided into a maximum of 32 physical areas (volumes). The name of the first volume is always SYS:. This name is displayed immediately behind the server name in the example.

(9) The drive indications may be compared to the path names under MS-DOS. This enables you to retrieve programs in other directories, such as MS-DOS 5 and the WORD 5 word processor shown in the example.
(10) The supervisor uses this command to log out.
(11) The logout is confirmed. The time and date of the logout are then shown.

Logging in to several fileservers. Different fileservers may be active in larger networks. The following command enables a user to log in to various fileservers at the same time, if the user name is valid:

```
ATTACH [fileserver[/user name]]
```

ATTACH the command to create the link
fileserver the name of the other fileserver
user name a valid user name must be given

Logging in to, and out of, the network

Caution: If you wish to log in to a certain server, use the command *LOGIN [server name[/user name]]*.

Instead of using the ATTACH command, you can also use the menu-operated utility program FCONSOLE. In that case, select the *Change File Server* option. The names of the servers to which you may be logged in are displayed in the subsequent window. By means of the Ins key, you can display a list of servers to which your work station is physically connected. You can select another server using the cursor keys and Enter. The program will then ask for a user name and a password if necessary.

This program may also be used to log out. In this case, select the name of the active server and press Del.

You can also activate another fileserver if you wish to work with a server to which you have already logged in. To do this, select the name of the server you wish to activate and press the Enter key (see section 4.2).

Login security. The user name not only has a function in the system management, it is also directed towards network access security. If you cannot specify a valid user name, you will not gain access to the system. Since the user name is shown on the screen during the login procedure, adequate security is only attained by assigning a password. Whether a password is essential or not depends on the work environment. This necessity may occur, for instance, if several people are working with rather sensitive information in the network. The system manager must always be allocated a password, even if the network is open to all users. This guarantees that the supervisor can log in at any moment if non-authorized manoeuvres are being carried out in the network. The following section outlines how to assign and alter a password.

2.3 Assigning and altering a password

If your work environment makes it necessary to have a password, this requirement is initially determined by the system manager when dealing with your user data. The system manager may allocate a certain name, but you may receive permission to alter this. The system manager can also determine the length of your password. (Compare the login restrictions in chapter 4.)

If you are allowed to alter your password, or if the system asks you to do this, proceed as follows:

- Activate the SYSCON utility program by typing *SYSCON* behind the system prompt.
- Select the *User Information* option from the menu.
- Select the user name in the subsequent window. If you are the system manager and you wish to alter your password, select SUPERVISOR here.
- Select the *Change Password* option in the next window.
- Type a new password. You will have to type it again to confirm it.

Instead of using the SYSCON utility program, you can use the following command to assign or alter your own password:

```
SETPASS
```

You will then have to specify the password twice.

The password is allocated to the active user. If you are the system manager, and wish to assign passwords to other users, it is more convenient to make use of the SYSCON utility program.

Example 4:
The password for the user COOK is to be altered using the SYSCON menu.

Assigning and altering a password 27

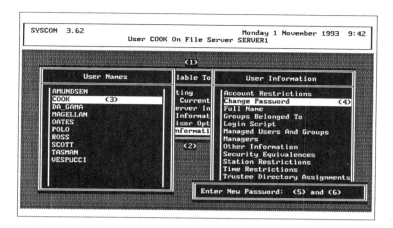

(1) The command SYSCON is typed behind the system prompt. The SYSCON main menu, *Available Topics*, then appears.
(2) The *User Information* option is activated (move the cursor bar to the required option using the cursor keys and then press Enter). The names of all users are shown in the following window, *User Names*.
(3) The appropriate user is selected from the list. A new menu appears displaying the available user data.
(4) The *Change Password* menu option is activated. The password must be typed in the subsequent window.
(5) Text box for the password. Normally, the password is five characters long. The system manager may alter this, ranging from a minimum of one character to a maximum of twenty. (See also the login restrictions in chapter 4.)
(6) *Retype New Password* means that the system is asking you to confirm the new password by typing it once again.

Example 5:
The same alteration must be made using the SETPASS command.

28 *Beginning in the network*

```
F:\USER\COOK>setpass                                        (1)
Enter new password for SERVER1/COOK:                        (2)
Retype new password for SERVER1/COOK:                       (3)

The new password on SERVER1/COOK has been used previously,  (4)
password not changed.


F:\USER\COOK>setpass                                        (5)
Enter new password for SERVER1/COOK:
Retype new password for SERVER1/COOK:

The password for SERVER1/COOK has been changed.

F:\USER\COOK>_
```

(1) The alteration command is given behind the system prompt.
(2) The new password is typed behind the program prompt.
(3) The password must be repeated and thus confirmed.
(4) The message indicates that the password will not be accepted - *(has been used previously)*. In this case, the user does not have the right to use the same password again. The program refuses to change the password - *(not changed)*.
(5) Repetition of the same procedure with a different password. The system accepts the input and states that the alteration has been carried out - *(has been changed)*.

2.4 Displaying information about the workstation

During the first activities in the network, or when you are working as a user or system manager at different workstations, it may be useful to request the following information concerning the workstation at which you are working:

Displaying information about the workstation

- the user name
- the server name
- the link number
- the Novell NetWare version
- the date and time of logging in.

By applying a simple parameter, you can request the workstation rights.
The following operating system command enables you to request information about the position of your workstation in the network:

WHOAMI [/A]

WHOAMI Who am I?
/A (ALL) In addition to the standard messages, the following user rights are displayed:
➤ the position in relation to the rights of other users or groups
➤ group membership
➤ effective rights of access to certain directories.

Example 6:
Extensive information is to be requested about the OFFICE logged-in workstation.

```
F:\>whoami /a                                                    (1)
You are user OFFICE attached to server SERVER1, connection 14.
Server SERVER1 is running NetWare v3.11 (250 user).
Login time: Monday November 1 1993  9:59 am

You are security equivalent to the following:                    (2)
    EVERYONE (Group)
    MANAGEMENT (Group)
    WORD5 (Group)
You are a member of the following groups:                        (3)
    EVERYONE
    MANAGEMENT
    WORD5
[         ]   SYS:                                               (4)
[ R     F ]   SYS:LOGIN
[ R     F ]   SYS:PUBLIC
[   C     ]   SYS:MAIL
[ RWCEMF  ]   SYS:MAIL\19000001
[ R     F ]   SYS:WORD5
[SRWCEMFA]    SYS:USER\OFFICE
Server SERVER1 is not in a Domain.

F:\>
```

(1) Here, the command is given with the parameter /A for ALL. This ensures that all messages are shown in full. Without this parameter, only the first three lines of the message are shown. The first line displays the user and server names (OFFICE and SERVER1) and the link number. The second line displays the Novell NetWare version, and the third line shows the date and time of logging in.
(2) The user has the same rights as the groups mentioned.
(3) The user is a member of the groups mentioned.
(4) The user has effective rights of access to certain directories. The names of the these directories are located behind the volume name SYS: and the rights are indicated by letters between square brackets. Chapter 3 explains the significance of these letters.

2.5 Displaying directories

The server harddisk organization. In principle, the server harddisk has the same layout as a harddisk under MS-DOS. Directories are created in which programs and files are stored. Directories may be subdivided into subdirectories and these may also be subdivided into subsubdirectories and so on. The directory commands commonly used under MS-DOS can also be given with Novell NetWare. However, there is a big difference. The security system enables the system manager to protect directories and files against inspection and alteration. For this reason, unlike under MS-DOS, a user cannot address all directories and the data stored there without the relevant rights of access.

The active directory after login. In section 2.2 we have already indicated what happens after logging in. As soon as the system messages have been displayed, an application is started or a menu is activated. The system prompt may appear. Unless the network manager has made other specifications, the main directory for the user will appear on the harddisk of the server

F:\>. The directory *F:\SYSTEM>* will appear for the supervisor. It is also possible that a certain home directory which has been assigned to the user will be shown. In addition, the system may be regulated so that a menu can be exited by pressing the *Esc* key, after which the home directory appears.

Caution: If you wish to put the following description into practice, you must also be able to switch to the network operating system.

Displaying the directory tree of the server harddisk.
The following command produces a display of the directory tree of the server harddisk. TREE is the equivalent command under MS-DOS.

```
LISTDIR [\directory] [/A]
```

LISTDIR   Display directory tree.
\directory   A particular directory can be specified here. Otherwise you will receive a survey of the current directory. The first character must be the backslash (\). If you wish to gain a display of the root directory, a backslash alone is sufficient. The backslash must be placed in front of each specified subdirectory.
/A (ALL)   This parameter produces the entire structure with all subdirectories along with the time and date of creation, and the rights.

Example 7:
The names of all subdirectories of the root directory on the server harddisk are to be displayed on the screen.

(1) The command is given with the backslash parameter to produce a survey of the root directory. In this case, the command would have produced the required result without the backslash since the root directory is the current directory.
(2) The subdirectories of the SERVER1 server in the volume SYS: are displayed. In fact, the root direc-

tory contains more subdirectories but these are not displayed because the user has no rights for these.

```
F:\>listdir \                                                    (1)

Sub-directories of SERVER1/SYS:                                  (2)
Directory
-----------------------------------------------------------------
->LOGIN
->PUBLIC
->MAIL
->WORD5
->DBASE
->WORD-DAT
->DBAS-DAT
->DBNETCTL.300
->WINDOWS
->USER
->MP4
->MP4-DAT
12 sub-directories found

F:\>
```

Example 8:
The complete directory tree, beginning at the root directory, is to be displayed along with all available data.

```
F:\>listdir \ /a                                                 (1)

The sub-directory structure of SERVER1/SYS:                      (2)
Date      Time    Inherited    Effective     Directory
-----------------------------------------------------------------
2-14-93   1:10p   [SRWCEMFA]   [ R    F ]   ->LOGIN
2-14-93   1:10p   [SRWCEMFA]   [ R    F ]   ->PUBLIC             (3)
2-14-93   1:48p   [SRWCEMFA]   [ R    F ]   ->   IBM_PC
2-14-93   1:49p   [SRWCEMFA]   [ R    F ]   ->      MSDOS
2-14-93   1:49p   [SRWCEMFA]   [ R    F ]   ->         V5.00
2-14-93   1:49p   [SRWCEMFA]   [ R    F ]   ->         V3.21
2-14-93   1:49p   [SRWCEMFA]   [ R    F ]   ->         V6.00
2-14-93   1:10p   [        ]   [   C   ]   ->MAIL
2-14-93   3:33p   [SRWCEMFA]   [ RWCEMF ]   ->  19000001
2-14-93   2:55p   [SRWCEMFA]   [ R    F ]   ->WORD5
2-14-93   2:57p   [SRWCEMFA]   [        ]   ->USER               (4)
2-14-93   3:30p   [SRWCEMFA]   [SRWCEMFA]   ->   OFFICE
2-14-93   3:30p   [SRWCEMFA]   [SRWCEMFA]   ->   W55
...
28 sub-directories found                                         (5)

F:\>
```

(1) The command contains the parameter /a for /ALL. In other words, all available data must be displayed.

(2) The system indicates that it will display the directory structure which is accessible to the user, thus all relevant directories and subdirectories. In addition, the time and date of creation and the assigned rights will be shown. Chapter 3 provides more information about the rights.
(3) The PUBLIC directory is subdivided into three further hierarchical levels: IBM_PC, MSDOS and the level with the MS-DOS operating system in versions 4, 3.21 and 5.
(4) The USER directory contains the home directory of the user who is logged in. In this case, the name is the same as the user: OFFICE. The home directory further contains the W55 subdirectory.
(5) 28 subdirectories are displayed. They are not all shown in the figure.

Activating other directories. Using the same commands as under MS-DOS, you can switch back and forth between directories and examine the files contained:

```
CD [\directory]
```

CD This is an abbreviation for *Change Directory:*.

\directory A specific directory should be registered here, otherwise the current directory remains active. If you wish to move one level higher (to the parent directory), enter two dots behind the CD command. Enter one extra dot for each level upwards you wish to move.

To display the contents of a directory:

```
DIR (directory)
```

More information can be gained by specifying the NDIR command from Novell NetWare (see section 2.6).

Example 9:
The contents of a directory are to be displayed. Subsequently, a switch to other directories is to take place.

```
F:\USER\OFFICE>dir                                          (1)

 Volume in drive F is SYS
 Volume Serial Number is 0900-7CD9
 Directory of F:\USER\OFFICE

SCREEN     UID         13416 01-08-92   14:50
MP         INI           514 14-08-92   10:59
EPPAGE     DBS         50214 15-08-92   10:36
JOHN       TXT          2048 25-02-93   14:09
MW         INI           268 25-02-93   14:09
W55        <DIR>              14-02-93   15:30             (2)
        6 file(s)        66460 bytes
                      19636224 bytes free

F:\USER\OFFICE>cd w55                                       (3)

F:\USER\OFFICE\W55>cd ...                                   (4)

F:\USER>_
```

(1) The contents of the \USER\OFFICE subdirectory are displayed along with the data normally shown under MS-DOS: file name (a maximum of 8 characters), extension (a maximum of 3 characters), the size in characters (bytes), date and time of creation.
(2) Six files are shown. In fact, there are only five files; the sixth is a subdirectory of this directory. In addition, the total number of bytes of the displayed files is shown, along with the remaining free space on the server harddisk.
(3) Switch to the W55 directory.
(4) Switch to the directory which is two levels higher.

Displaying drives and pathnames. Depending on the information in the login script, a number of drives can be shown after logging in (compare the example in section 2.2). As you know, logical drives are abbreviations consisting of a letter with a colon. Because special characters are not permitted, only 26 letters are available. These can be used to represent the following drives:

■ local diskdrives and harddisks

- directories on the server
- pathnames.

If, for example, your workstation is equippped with a diskdrive and a harddisk, you can address these normally as A: (diskdrive) and C: (harddisk). In Novell NetWare, the letters A to E are reserved for local drives unless special specifications are made in the configuration file CONFIG.SYS (see chapter 9). Chapter 3 discusses how to specify logical drives.

Using the other letters, it is possible to define directories on the server harddisk and drives and pathnames (searches) for directories. In this, directories are defined in ascending order from the letter F onwards, and pathnames in descending order from the letter Z. In general, F: is used to represent the root directory of the server. If you activate a logical drive, the corresponding directory is activated; thus F: activates the root directory on the server harddisk, for example.

A meaningful organization places programs in directories with a corresponding name. The word processor, WORD 5, is thus stored in the WORD5 directory. If you wish to activate a program like this from a different directory, you must specify the entire pathname unless other specifications have been made.

Imagine that WORD is to be activated from the \USER\OFFICE directory. The command is then as follows:*word5\word*. However, if the directory has been included in a continuous valid path, the program can be activated from any directory without having to enter the entire pathname. In that case, the command *word* will suffice in this example. Continuous valid pathnames (searches) are defined by means of abbreviations in Novell NetWare, just like logical drives. It is possible to define separate logical drives for each user.

The following command displays a list of all available logical drives:

MAP

Example 10:
The list of available logical drives is to be displayed for the OFFICE user.

```
F:\>map                                                        (1)

Drive  A:   maps to a local disk.                              (2)
Drive  B:   maps to a local disk.
Drive  C:   maps to a local disk.
Drive  D:   maps to a local disk.
Drive  E:   maps to a local disk.
Drive  F: = SERVER1/SYS:   \                                   (3)
Drive  G: = SERVER1/SYS:   \WORD-DAT
Drive  H: = SERVER1/SYS:   \DBASE
Drive  I: = SERVER1/SYS:   \DBAS-DAT
Drive  J: = SERVER1/SYS:   \DBASE\VOORBLD
Drive  K: = SERVER1/SYS:   \DBASE\SQLHOME
Drive  L: = SERVER1/SYS:   \WINDOWS
      -----
SEARCH3:  = Z:. [SERVER1/SYS:   \PUBLIC]                       (4)
SEARCH4:  = Y:. [SERVER1/SYS:   \PUBLIC\IBM_PC\MSDOS\V6.00]
SEARCH5:  = X:. [SERVER1/SYS:   \DBASE]
SEARCH6:  = W:. [SERVER1/SYS:   \DBNETCTL.300]
SEARCH8:  = U:. [SERVER1/SYS:   \WINDOWS]
SEARCH9:  = T:. [SERVER1/SYS:   \WORD5]

F:\>
```

(1) Command to display the list.
(2) The first five letters are reserved for local drives for this user. The local drives do not all have to be present.
(3) The letters F to L are defined for directories. Using F: for example, the user can switch directly to the SERVER1/SYS:\ root directory.
(4) These letters have been specified for the pathnames. These can be used to activate, for instance, the external programs MS-DOS 5, dBASE, Windows and Word 5 directly from all directories accessible to the user.

2.6 Displaying information about files

In section 2.5, we have seen that it is possible to apply the well-known MS-DOS command DIR to display information about subdirectories and files in a certain directory. However, this information is often insufficient. The following information is displayed by means of the Novell NetWare command NDIR:

For directories:
- directory name
- rights which can be passed on to subdirectories (inherited)
- effective available rights
- name of the creator
- date and time of creation or copy.

For files:
- file name
- size in bytes
- date and time of previous modification
- file attributes (flags)
- name of the creator.

In addition, the total number of bytes of the files is shown, along with the disk space occupied in terms of bytes and memory blocks.

This command enables you to display certain data by means of supplementary options:

```
NDIR [\directory] [options] [[REVERSE] SORT [options]]
```

NDIR Displays the contents of the directory.
\directory You can enter a specific directory here. A backslash must be placed in front of the directory.
options The following options to select data are possible:
  ➤ display files according to date of previous access: ACCESS BEF(ORE)/AFT(ER) 02-28-93
  ➤ display files according to archiving date: ARCHIVE BEF(ORE)/AFT(ER) 02-28-93
  ➤ display files according to attributes: ATTRIBUTE=RW (reading and writing)

➤ display according to creation date: CRE-
ATE BEF(ORE)/AFT(ER) 02-28-93
➤ display according to user name:
OWNER=office
➤ display according to size: SIZE
GR(EATER THAN) 2048 [=, !=, GR,
LE(SS)]
➤ display according to date of previous
modification: UPDATE
BEF(ORE)/AFT(ER) 02-28-93

[REVERSE] SORT [options]

This option makes it possible to display sorted data (REVERSE sorts in reverse order of sequence); the options are as above.

Example 11:

All data in the root directory which are available to the OFFICE user are to be displayed.

```
F:\>ndir                                                                    (1)
SERVER1/SYS:                                                                (2)

                Inherited        Effective
Directories:    Rights           Rights         Owner       Created/Copied
-----------------------------------------------------------------------------
DBAS-DAT        [SRWCEMFA]       [SRWCEMFA]     SUPERVISOR   2-14-93  2:56p
DBASE           [SRWCEMFA]       [SRWCEMFA]     SUPERVISOR   2-14-93  2:55p
DBNETCTL    300 [SRWCEMFA]       [SRWCEMFA]     SUPERVISOR   2-14-93  2:56p
LOGIN           [SRWCEMFA]       [-R----F-]     SUPERVISOR   2-14-93  1:10p
MAIL            [--------]       [---C----]     SUPERVISOR   2-14-93  1:10p
MP4             [SRWCEMFA]       [-R----F-]     SUPERVISOR   2-14-93  3:43p
MP4-DAT         [SRWCEMFA]       [SRWCEMFA]     SUPERVISOR   2-14-93  3:45p
PUBLIC          [SRWCEMFA]       [-R----F-]     SUPERVISOR   2-14-93  1:10p
USER            [SRWCEMFA]       [--------]     SUPERVISOR   2-14-93  2:57p
WINDOWS         [SRWCEMFA]       [-RWCEMFA]     SUPERVISOR   2-14-93  2:57p
WORD-DAT        [SRWCEMFA]       [SRWCEMFA]     SUPERVISOR   2-14-93  2:56p
WORDS           [SRWCEMFA]       [-R----F-]     SUPERVISOR   2-14-93  2:55p

          0 total bytes in       0 files                                   (3)
          0 total bytes in       0 blocks

F:\>
```

(1) The command is specified in the root directory, which makes it unnecessary to add a path.
(2) The system shows the required information. The Effective Rights column clearly indicates that the user has only read (R) and find (F) permission in

Displaying information about files

various directories. He/she has no rights in the USER directory. All directories have been created by the supervisor.

(3) Since no files in the root directory have been displayed, the total size of the files is 0.

Example 12:
From the root directory, only the data concerning the home directory of the OFFICE user are to be shown.

```
F:\>ndir \user\office                                                    (1)
SERVER1/SYS:USER\OFFICE                                                  (2)

Files:        Size     Last Updated          Flags              Owner    (3)
--------   ----------  --------------   -------------------   ----------
EPPAGE  DBS   50,214   8-15-92 10:36a  [Rw-A--------------]  SUPERVISOR
JOHN    BAK    2,048   2-25-93  2:00p  [Rw-A--------------]  SUPERVISOR
JOHN    TXT    2,048   2-25-93  2:09p  [Rw-A--------------]  SUPERVISOR
MP      INI      514   8-14-92 10:59a  [Rw----------------]  SUPERVISOR
MW      INI      268   2-25-93  2:09p  [Rw-A--------------]  SUPERVISOR
SCREEN  VID   13,416   8-01-92  2:50p  [Rw----------------]  SUPERVISOR

              Inherited    Effective                                     (4)
Directories:  Rights       Rights       Owner      Created/Copied
------------  -----------  -----------  ---------  -----------------
W55           [SRWCEMFA]   [SRWCEMFA]   SUPERVISOR  2-14-93  3:30p
      68,508 bytes in   6 files                                          (5)
     106,496 bytes in  13 blocks

F:\>
```

(1) The command is given in the root directory with the pathname of the required subdirectory as an additional specification. The same effect is achieved by giving the command in the required subdirectory without the addition.
(2) The full name of the subdirectory is displayed.
(3) Six files are stored in the directory. The screen shows the file names, the sizes of the files and the date and time of the previous modifications. Further, the file attributes are shown in the Flags column: the user may read and write all files. An archiving attribute has been placed at four files, which means that the file has been newly created or modified (see section 3.4).
(4) The directory contains a file called W55. These data are displayed separately, as in the previous example.

(5) The total values of the sizes of the files in bytes. The second value indicates the memory blocks which are occupied on the server harddisk. Since one block consists of 8192 bytes, the number of bytes used for each file consists of a multiple of this amount, even if the file actually consists of less than this.

2.7 Displaying information about a fileserver

Displaying the current fileserver. When you have started up the workstation and the connection to the network has been made (see section 2.1), you can request the following information concerning the active network fileserver, prior to the login procedure:

- the names of the known servers in the network
- the network number
- the node-address (the server address number)
- the activity status.

This information may be important if, for example, there are several servers active in the network and you wish to know the name of a certain server. If you know this, you can log in directly on a specific server.

This information is displayed using the following command:

SLIST

Example 13:
Prior to login on a server, the server data of the network are checked.

(1) When the connection to the network has been made and drive F: has been activated, the F:\LOGIN> directory is displayed. The SLIST command is given in this directory.

Displaying information about a fileserver

```
F:\LOGIN>slist                                               (1)
Known NetWare File Servers   Network   Node Address Status   (2)
--------------------------   -------   ------------ ------
SERVER1                      [    1][              1]Default

Total of 1 file servers found

F:\LOGIN>login server1/office                                (3)
```

(2) Only the SERVER1 server is known in this network. This is active in network 1 and has the node-address 1; this is the first station in the network. The server is the default server for this network (Status Default).

(3) If several servers are displayed, the user can specify the required server in this command (see section 2.2).

Displaying information about the server harddisk.
By means of two menu-operated programs and various commands, it is possible to display data concerning the storage capacity of the server harddisk and the amount already in use. The quantity of information is not always identical. The example below illustrates this.

In the FILER menu-operated utility program, you can request information about the active volume (the physical area on the harddisk). Proceed as follows:

(1) Type the command: FILER after the system prompt.
(2) In the subsequent *Available Topics* menu, activate the *Volume Information* option.
(3) A window appears displaying the available data.
(4) End the display by pressing Esc twice.

Example 14:
Information is to be displayed concerning capacity and the maximum number and available number of directory entries of the active volume on the server harddisk.

Beginning in the network

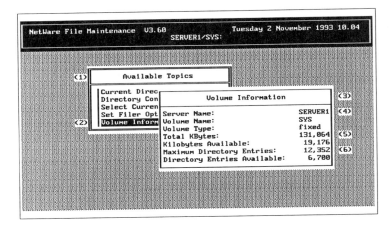

(1) When the program has been started up using the FILER command, the *Available Topics* menu appears. The double border of the window indicates that actions (input, selections) can be performed in this window. No action is possible in a window with a single border. They only provide information.

(2) The *Volume Information* menu option is highlighted by means of the cursor keys and activated by pressing Enter.

(3) A window appears containing information about the volume.

(4) The name of the server (SERVER1) and the active volume (SYS) are shown; In addition, it is stated that the corresponding volume is a physical drive (fixed).

(5) The total capacity is 131 064 Kb, the capacity still available is 19 176 Kb.

(6) The disk can contain a maximum of 12 352 directories; there are still 6700 available.

Using the menu-operated VOLINFO utility program, you can request information about all volumes which are located on the server harddisk. Proceed as follows:

1. Type the command VOLINFO after the system prompt.

Displaying information about a fileserver 43

2. A window containing various fields will appear. A volume with information about capacity is shown in each field, as outlined in the previous example.
3. If you wish to acquire information about a different server in the network, activate the *Change Servers* option in the *Available Options* menu.
4. If there are more volumes on the server than there are information windows, you can use the *Next Page* and *Previous Page* options to display the rest of the information.
5. You can use the *Update Interval* option to specify the time after which the data is to be updated. This ranges from 1 to 3600 seconds. The default setting is 5 seconds.
6. End the display by pressing Esc several times or press the key combination Alt-F10.

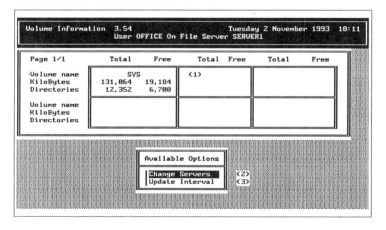

(1) Display fields for the information concerning capacity. There is only one server active in this network. Accordingly, only these data are shown.
(2) Activate this menu option if you wish to select one of the available servers in the network.
(3) This menu option enables you to specify the interval at which the information about capacity is to be updated.

Displaying volume space allocation. The following command enables you to display the way in which the available space of a volume on the server harddisk has been allocated. This is similar to the DOS command CHKDSK, but does not work on local drives.

CHKVOL [[server_name/]volume]

CHKVOL Request display of volume division.
server_name/ Specify the required server name here.
volume Specify the name of the required volume here. If you do not specify a name here, you will receive a display of the current volume. Using an asterisk (*) you will receive a display of all volumes.

Example 15:
A display is to be given of the SYS: volume on SERVER1.

```
F:\>chkvol                                                    (1)

Statistics for fixed volume SERVER1/SYS:

Total volume space:                  131,064  K Bytes         (2)
Space used by files:                 111,880  K Bytes         (3)
Space in use by deleted files:        15,368  K Bytes         (4)
Space available from deleted files:   15,368  K Bytes         (5)
Space remaining on volume:            19,184  K Bytes         (6)
Space available to OFFICE:            19,184  K Bytes         (7)

F:\>
```

(1) The command is given without parameters. This means that the command will deal with the current server.
(2) The total storage capacity of the volume.
(3) The space occupied by files.
(4) The space occupied by deleted files.
(5) The storage capacity which will be made available when the deleted files are definitively removed.
(6) The remaining capacity on the volume.
(7) The maximum space available to the OFFICE user.

Displaying information about a fileserver

Displaying a directory. The following command produces a display of the used and available space of a directory and of the entire server harddisk:

```
CHKDIR [\directory]
```

CHKDIR Display the directory.
\directory Specify here the required directory path.

Example 16:
Display the maximum available, the used and the free storage space for the root directory, for the \USER\OFFICE home directory and for the entire server harddisk.

```
F:\>chkdir                                                          (1)

Directory Space Limitation Information For:
SERVER1/SYS:

    Maximum       In Use     Available
    131,064 K    111,880 K    19,184 K   Volume Size                 (2)
                 108,536 K    19,184 K   \


F:\>chkdir \user\office                                             (3)

Directory Space Limitation Information For:
SERVER1/SYS:USER\OFFICE

    Maximum       In Use     Available
    131,064 K    111,880 K    19,184 K   Volume Size
                     128 K    19,184 K   \USER\OFFICE

F:\>
```

(1) The command is given in the root directory. Since no additional parameters are specified, a display of the root directory is given.
(2) The maximum capacity of the entire server harddisk is 131 064 Kb. 111 880 Kb are in use and 19 184 Kb are still available. 108 536 Kb are in use in the root directory and the available space (19 184 Kb) is also available in the root directory.
(3) This command produces a display of the specified directory. The information about total capacity is identical to the information above. 128 Kb are in use in the subdirectory and the total free space is also available in this directory.

2.8 Displaying the users who are logged in

The following command enables you to obtain a list of all users who are currently logged in on the network. The name of the user who gives the command is marked with an asterisk. This means that you can also request which user is logged in at the station where the command was given.

```
USERLIST [fileserver/user_name] [/A]
```

USERLIST Display a list of logged-in users.
fileserver Specify the name of the required fileserver.
/user_name Specify a user name when you only wish to receive information about a certain user.
/A This option requests the network address (under *Network*) and the address of the workstation *(Node Address)* of the logged-in user.

Example 17:
Only one user is initially logged in on the network. This user is to be displayed, along with the date and time of logging in. Subsequently, a second user logs in. Then all users who are logged in are to be displayed with all available information.

```
F:\>userlist                                                              (1)

User Information for Server SERVER1                                       (2)
Connection  User Name         Login Time
----------  ---------------   --------------------
    14      * OFFICE          11-02-1993  9:59 am


F:\>userlist /a                                                           (3)

User Information for Server SERVER1
Connection  User Name   Network      Node Address   Login Time
----------  ---------   --------     ------------   -------------------
     1      AMUNDSEN    [1B03D6DE] [  1B21F1D2] 11-02-1993  10:03 am
    14      * OFFICE    [1B03D6DE] [  1B225C2C] 11-02-1993   9:59 am

F:\>
```

Displaying the users who are logged in

(1) The command is given from the workstation at which the OFFICE user is logged in.
(2) The OFFICE user is marked with an asterisk. He/she logged in on 5-8-93 at 9.59 am. The internal user number (Connection) is 14.
(3) The second user AMUNDSEN, with the internal user number 1, has logged in at 10.03 am. The /A option produces, in addition, the network address and the workstation address. The network address is identical for all stations in this network.

3 File management in the network

3.1 Working with directories

The organization of the server harddisk. We have seen in chapter 2 that the server harddisk under Novell NetWare is, in principle, organized in the same way as a harddisk under MS-DOS. For practical reasons, a user divides the space on the disk into directories; the files in these directories are stored on a basis of logical points of departure. It is advisable to store programs in directories other than those used to store data, since this enables programs to be adapted more easily and the data to be categorized and stored in a more orderly fashion. If necessary, directories can be divided into subdirectories, which in turn can also be subdivided. The number of directory levels is only actually restricted by the inconvenient use of a lengthy directory path.

Rights for working with directories. In contrast to working under MS-DOS, it is not possible to examine, create or delete directories under Novell NetWare unless you possess the appropriate rights. Accordingly, you must first check which effective rights you have in the directories which are accessible to you, prior to carrying out the examples outlined in this chapter on your own workstation. The effective access rights for a directory are based on the rights which have been assigned to you for this directory and for the entire directory branch. These rights, however, may be restricted by an *Inherited Rights Mask* (see section 3.2). You can request your effective rights for a directory by giving the command RIGHTS.

Example 18:
The effective access rights for the AMUNDSEN user in the active \USER\AMUNDSEN directory are to be displayed.

Working with directories

```
F:\USER\AMUNDSEN>rights                                          (1)
SERVER1/SYS:USER\AMUNDSEN                                        (2)
Your Effective Rights for this directory are [SRWCEMFA]          (3)
    You have Supervisor Rights to Directory.    (S)              (4)
  * May Read from File.                         (R)              (5)
  * May Write to File.                          (W)              (6)
    May Create Subdirectories and Files.        (C)              (7)
    May Erase Directory.                        (E)              (8)
    May Modify Directory.                       (M)              (9)
    May Scan for Files.                         (F)             (10)
    May Change Access Control.                  (A)             (11)

* Has no effect on directory.

    Entries in Directory May Inherit [SRWCEMFA] rights.    (12)
    You have ALL RIGHTS to Directory Entry.

F:\USER\AMUNDSEN>_
```

(1) The AMUNDSEN user has a subdirectory of the same name. The command to display the rights is given from this directory.

(2) The full path including the server name (SERVER1), the volume (SYS) and both directory levels (\USER\AMUNDSEN) are given.

(3) The effective rights for this directory are indicated by [SRWCEMFA]. Since, in this case, all possible letters are included between the brackets, the user has all rights for this directory. Subsequently, the significance of the letters is explained.

(4) The user has all rights for this directory and all its subdirectories. He/she may assign these rights either entirely or partially to the subdirectories. This right contains all other rights.

(5) The user may open and read files. This right has no effect on the directory.

(6) The user may open and edit files. This right has no effect on the directory.

(7) The user may create subdirectories of this directory and save files.

(8) The user may erase this directory and its subdirectories, and the files which are stored in these.

(9) The user may alter name of the directory and the subdirectories it contains and the directory attributes.

(10) The user may search for files and subdirectories in

the directory. This allows the user to examine the names of files and subdirectories.
(11) The user may alter the rights for this directory and all its subdirectories, excepting the S right (Supervisor). These rights may be passed on to other users.
(12) There are no restricted inheritance rights. They can be inherited by all subdirectories.

Restricting the rights by means of attributes. A user's effective rights can also be restricted by attributes. These have higher priority. For instance, if you have the effective right to alter the name of a directory, you will not be able to do this if the Rename Inhibit attribute has been set. Working with attributes will be described in section 3.4.

Planning the directory structure. Before making a new directory or subdirectory, you must specify its position. To do this, display the accessible directory structure using the commands LISTDIR, CD and DIR. If you are the system manager, it is advisable to formulate a plan for the entire directory structure on the server harddisk.

Example 19:
The directory structure of the SYS: volume of the SERVER1 server harddisk is to be organized as follows:

(1) There are six subdirectories in the root directory F:\. However, the system manager has created only the USER and PROGRAM subdirectories. The user and the system manager have no influence at all upon the SYSTEM, LOGIN, MAIL and PUBLIC subdirectories. These are automatically created when Novell NetWare is installed. These directories contain important system files for the Novell NetWare operating system and files which must be accessible to all users. For this reason, these directories cannot be deleted, and it is not possible to alter their names.

Working with directories 51

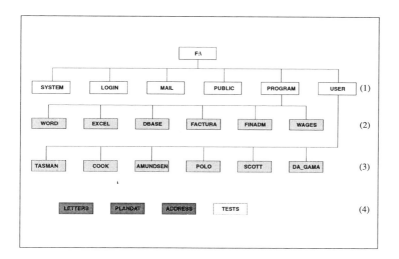

The SYSTEM directory contains the Novell NetWare system programs which are only accessible to the system manager.

The LOGIN directory contains the programs which regulate the user logging-in process (see section 2.2).

In the MAIL directory, a separate subdirectory is created for each user, with system data which are specific for that particular user, such as the relevant login script.

The PUBLIC directory contains the utility programs and data which are accessible to each user, just as the external programs of the MS-DOS operating system.

(2) The PROGRAM directory contains six subdirectories for applications. Only program files are located in these, no data files.

(3) Six user directories have been created in the USER directory. The users can manage their data in these or in subdirectories of these.

(4) The AMUNDSEN subdirectory has three subdirectories which function as work directories. Data can be stored in these on a basis of logical criteria. A fourth directory called TESTS has been added to

the figure shown; this directory will be created in example 20.

Creating a directory. You can create a new subdirectory using the following command. The command is identical to its equivalent in MS-DOS:

```
MD dir_name
```

MD   Abbreviation of Make Directory.
dir_name Specify the name of the new directory here.

Altering the name of a directory. The following command enables you to alter the name of a directory at a lower level (this command does not exist in MS-DOS):

```
RENDIR [drive:]old_name new_name
```

RENDIR   Abbreviation of Rename Directory.
drive: The command can be applied to a directory on a different drive, for instance A: or B:. However, the drive letter may only be specified with the old name.
old_name The current directory name.
new_name The new directory name.

Caution: The command cannot be applied to the current directory. It can only be applied to a subdirectory of the current directory.

Removing a directory. The following command, which is identical to the MS-DOS command of the same name, enables you to delete a directory. The directory which is to be removed must be empty. If there are still files or subdirectories in the directory, you will have to remove them first, otherwise the system will display an error message:

```
RD dir_name
```

RD   Abbreviation of Remove Directory.

Working with directories

dir_name Specify here the name of the directory to be removed.

Example 20:
In the \USER\AMUNDSEN active directory, a work directory called TESTS is to be made. The directory will subsequently be given a different name, TESTDAT. Then the TESTDAT directory will be removed.

```
F:\USER\AMUNDSEN>md tests                                     (1)

F:\USER\AMUNDSEN>cd tests                                     (2)

F:\USER\AMUNDSEN\TESTS>rendir tests testdat                   (3)
The path specification (directory name) was incorrect.
F:\USER\AMUNDSEN\TESTS>cd..                                   (4)

F:\USER\AMUNDSEN>rendir tests testdat                         (5)
Directory renamed to TESTDAT.

F:\USER\AMUNDSEN>cd testdat                                   (6)

F:\USER\AMUNDSEN\TESTDAT>cd..                                 (7)

F:\USER\AMUNDSEN>rd testdat                                   (8)

F:\USER\AMUNDSEN>_
```

(1) This command creates the TESTS subdirectory in the \USER\AMUNDSEN directory.
(2) The new directory is activated.
(3) This command attempts to alter the name of the active directory. However, this is not successful since the command can only be applied to derived subdirectories.
(4) Switch to the parent directory.
(5) The command to alter the name of the directory can now be implemented correctly.
(6) The renamed directory is activated.
(7) Switch to the parent directory.
(8) The renamed directory is removed. This is possible in this case since the directory is empty and it is derived from the active directory.

Assigning a directory name to a drive letter. You have probably realized that it is rather laborious to have to type lengthy directory names. Novell NetWare enables you to replace directory names with drive letters while you are working at your workstation, or even for longer periods of time. In section 2.5, you have already become familiar with the command to display the drive allocation. The same command enables you to assign a drive letter to a directory:

```
MAP [DEL] [driveletter:[=directory_name]]
```

MAP Assign a drive letter. If you give the command without parameters, the list of the available allocations is displayed (compare section 2.5).
DEL An assigned drive indication is deleted.
driveletter A letter of the alphabet.
directory_name Specify the name of the directory along with the names of the server and the volume.

Caution: If you wish to make a permanent assignment, you must include the command in the login script (see chapter 4). The same command enables you to create search drives. This corresponds to the MS-DOS command PATH.

Under Novell NetWare, you can define a maximum of 16 search drives. To define the search paths, specify the term SEARCH# for *driveletter*, where # represents a number between 1 and 16.

Example 21:
A drive letter is to be assigned to the USER\AMUNDSEN\DATA directory, making it easier to switch to it.

(1) The command attempts to assign the directory to the drive letter Q:. However, this is unsuccessful since Q: has already been assigned to a search drive. It is possible to overwrite this assignment. This opportunity is not employed (N).
(2) The list of the available assignments is shown (in

our example, that is only a fragment). The letter K: has not yet been allocated.
(3) The assignation of the letter K: is successful. Now the directory can be activated by specifying K:.

```
F:\USER\AMUNDSEN>map q:=server1/sys:user\amundsen\data         (1)
Drive Q is in use as a search drive.
Do you want to reassign this search drive? (Y/N) N

F:\USER\AMUNDSEN>map                                           (2)

Drive  K: = SERVER1/SYS:   \
Drive  L: = SERVER1/SYS:   \WINDOWS
-----
SEARCH1: = P:. [SERVER1/SYS:   \PUBLIC]
SEARCH2: = Q:. [SERVER1/SYS:   \PUBLIC\IBM_PC\MSDOS\V6.00]


F:\>map k:=server1/sys:user\amundsen\data                      (3)
Drive  K: = SERVER1/SYS:   \USER\AMUNDSEN\DATA
F:\>k:
K:\USER\AMUNDSEN\DATA>_
```

3.2 Examining and altering access rights for directories

In section 3.1, we have seen that a network user must have certain rights
for directories, for instance the F (File Scan) right in order to display the contents of a directory. We shall discuss the following issues in this section:

- How does a user acquire directory rights?
- How can a user find out which rights he/she has?
- How can rights be altered?
- Which effect do rights have?

How does a user acquire directory rights?

When a user has been registerd in a network, the user name is fixed. This name is used to log in on the network. But the user is unable to undertake any action initially because he/she has no access rights for directories. The Novell NetWare access rights are called

Trustee Rights. These indicate which tasks the user may execute with directories and files. The rights for files are described in section 3.4.

The access rights are assigned by the network manager who has the following options:

■ He/she assigns access rights for a directory to the user directly.

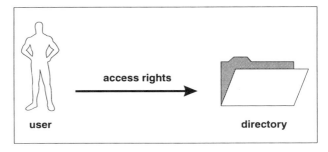

■ He/she includes the user in a user group which has rights for a directory.

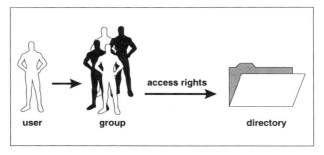

■ He/she specifies that the user is equal to another user or user group with rights for a directory.

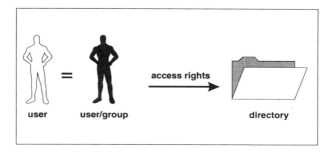

The different allocation possibilities can also be combined to produce the effective rights of a user for a directory. See chapter 4 for more information and examples.

How can a user find out which rights he/she has?

The access rights for one or more directories can be displayed by various commands depending on the application. If you prefer menu-operated utility programs, you can gain most information by means of the FILER program. You can apply the commands in the following ways:

List of the effective rights of a user in all directories accessible to him/her. Using the command WHOAMI /ALL, you can display the position of your workstation in the network along with your rights in all directories which are accessible to you. This command is described in section 2.4.

List of the names and rights of all trustees in a directory. The following command enables you to display the names and rights of all trustees (individual users or groups) who have access rights in a certain directory:

```
TLIST [directory/drive:]
```

TLIST Abbreviation of Trustee List.
directory/drive: If you wish a list of the rights in the active directory, you do not need to specify anything here. Otherwise,

specify the name of the directory or the appropriate drive letter.

Example 22:
A list is to be displayed of the names and rights of all trustees who have been assigned to the \USER\AMUNDSEN directory and the DBASE directory.

```
F:\USER\AMUNDSEN>tlist                                          (1)

SERVER1/SYS:USER\AMUNDSEN                                       (2)
User trustees:
    AMUNDSEN              [SRWCEMFA] Roald Amundsen
No group trustees.

F:\USER\AMUNDSEN>cd\dbase                                       (3)


F:\DBASE>tlist                                                  (4)

SERVER1/SYS:DBASE
No user trustees.                                               (5)
Group trustees:
    DBASE                 [SRWCEMFA]

F:\DBASE>_
```

(1) The data of the active directory are to be shown. Accordingly, the command is given without options or parameters.
(2) Only the AMUNDSEN user is shown to have all rights for this directory. The full name is displayed in addition to the rights. Groups have no rights in this directory.
(3) The DBASE directory with dBASE programs is activated.
(4) The command to display the trustees is given in this directory.
(5) No individual user has access rights for this directory; only the DBASE group has (all) access rights.

Displaying the effective rights in a directory. You can display your effective rights for a specific directory by means of the following command:

Examining and altering access rights for directories

    RIGHTS [directory/drive:]

RIGHTS   Display the rights.
directory/drive: If you wish to display the rights in the currently active directory, you do not need to specify anything here. Otherwise specify the name of the directory or the relevant drive letter.

Example 23:
You wish to examine the effective rights in the currently active directory. (Compare example 18 in section 3.1.)

List of the rights in a directory structure. Using the LISTDIR command, you can display the underlying directory structure along with the effective rights and the Inherited Rights Mask. This command has been dealt with in section 2.5.

Displaying directory rights using a utility program. The access rights which you have in a directory can also be displayed by means of the menu-operated FILER utility program. Proceed as follows:

1. Start up the FILER program in the currently active directory by giving the command of the same name. (If you wish to activate the program from another directory, you must first select the required directory via the *Select Current Directory* menu option.)
2. Activate the *Current Directory Information* menu option.

Example 24:
The access right for the \USER\AMUNDSEN\DATA\DATA1 directory are to be displayed using the FILER utility program.

File management in the network

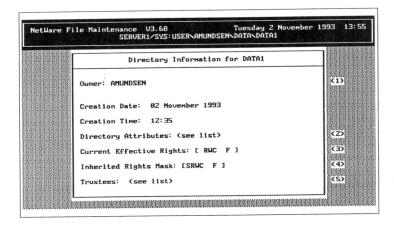

(1) The name of the owner of the directory, the date and time of creation are displayed.
(2) You can display a list of directory attributes via this menu option (highlight using the cursor keys and press Enter).
(3) Display of the effective rights. In this case, they cannot be altered.
(4) Survey of the Inherited Rights Mask. These rights may be altered (see the remarks below concerning FILER).
(5) If several users or user groups have access rights for this directory, this line is shown. It is possible to display a list of entitled users by activating this line (highlight using the cursor keys and press Enter).

How can rights be altered?

The assignation of trustee rights by the network manager is sufficient for most applications. However, there are situations in which a user might wish to make a (sub)directory available with restricted rights to other users. For instance, a user could create a directory to store and exchange work files for him/herself and other users. Since files only need to be retrieved and saved, the users of these only receive the C (Create) and F (File Scan) access rights. The other rights are removed for security reasons.

If a subdirectory is created in this directory, this subdirectory inherits the restricted rights via the *Inherited Rights Mask*. However, this need not remain so. The network manager can extend the rights by assigning new trustee rights.

Restricting rights using the Inherited Rights Mask.
The following command enables you to restrict the rights for a subdirectory and for all derived directories. In order to execute this command, you must have either the A (Access Control) right or the S (Supervisor) right. Otherwise the system message *Not Changed* will appear:

```
ALLOW [directory] [rights]
```

ALLOW   If you do not specify any rights behind the command, all names of all subdirectories and files which are in the current directory are shown, along with their rights.

directory   It is only possible to alter the rights in a lower (derived) directory. You may need to switch to a higher directory in order to change the required rights.

rights   Specify the letters here for the corresponding rights (see example 18 in section 3.1). The different rights must be separated from one another by a space.

It is also possible to restrict rights by means of the FILER utility program instead of using the ALLOW command.

Option 1:
Activate the *Inherited Rights Mask* line. That is line number (4) in example 24. A list of rights is subsequently displayed. You can add rights to the list using the *Ins* key and you can remove them using the *Del* key.

Option 2:
Activate the *Directory Contents* option in the main menu of the FILER program. Select and activate the required

directory in the subsequent window. The *Subdirectory Options* menu appears. Activate the *View/Set Directory Information* menu option. The following window allows you to add or remove one of the inherited rights displayed.

Example 25:
The USER\AMUNDSEN directory has a subdirectory called STORE, as is shown in the figure below. This subdirectory has a subdirectory called STOREDEP. The logged-in user has the A (Access Control) right. In both directories, all rights excepting C (Create) and F (File Scan) are to be removed. The restriction is to be carried out by means of the inheritance mask.

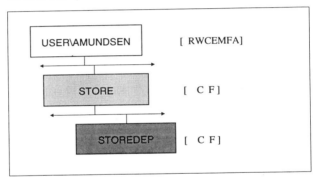

```
F:\USER\AMUNDSEN>listdir/a                                              (1)

The sub-directory structure of SERVER1/SYS:USER/AMUNDSEN
Date     Time    Inherited    Effective    Directory
-----------------------------------------------------------
11-03-93  11:42a  [SRWCEMFA]  [ RWCEMFA]  ->STORE               (2)
11-02-93  11:44a  [SRWCEMFA]  [ RWCEMFA]  -> STOREDEP
2 sub-directories found

F:\USER\AMUNDSEN>allow store  f c                                       (3)
    Directories:
       STORE                              [S  C  F ]                    (4)

F:\USER\AMUNDSEN>listdir/a                                              (5)

The sub-directory structure of SERVER1/SYS:USER/AMUNDSEN
Date     Time    Inherited    Effective    Directory
-----------------------------------------------------------
11-03-93  11:42a  [S  C  F ]  [   C  F ]  ->STORE               (6)
11-03-93  11:44a  [SRWCEMFA]  [   C  F ]  -> STOREDEP           (7)
2 sub-directories found

F:\USER\AMUNDSEN>_
```

Examining and altering access rights for directories 63

(1) This command displays the directory structure along with the rights to be altered.
(2) In the STORE and STOREDEP directories, all rights are effectively available except the S (Supervisor) right. The Inherited Rights Mask is complete. This means that all available effective rights are inherited.
(3) This command is used to remove all rights from the STORE directory excepting the C and F rights.
(4) The result is that the C and F rights and the S right are displayed. This means that the S right cannot be removed from an inherited rights mask using this command.
(5) Command to display the new rights.
(6) The effective rights do not contain the S right since this cannot be added using the inherited rights mask, even if the right is displayed in the mask.
(7) The effective rights from the STORE directory are passed on to the STOREDEP directory. However, the inherited rights mask is again complete since it is not restricted by a command. This is also not possible, since the A right is absent.

Note: This command only enables you to restrict rights.

Extending rights. If you wish to add rights, use the SYSCON utility program or the GRANT option. However, you can only add rights using the SYSCON program if you are the network manager. As a user, you are only able to display the rights.

Example 26:
In the STOREDEP directory, the network manager is to use the SYSCON utility program to extend the effective rights by adding R (Read) and M (Modify).

Proceed as network manager as follows:

1. Activate the SYSCON utility program on the command line.
2. Activate the *User Information* menu option by moving to it using the cursor keys and pressing Enter.

3. In the *User Names* window, activate the required user name to which the directory is assigned.
4. Activate the *Trustee Directory Assignments* option in the following menu window.
5. The window containing the directory names and the assigned rights will then appear. If the required directory is not included, you will have to add it: press *Ins* twice. Adopt the names of the server and the volume, for instance SERVER1/ and SYS: by pressing Enter. Then, using Cursor Up and Cursor Down and the Enter key, select the parts of the required directory. Exit the window by pressing *Esc* and adopt the entire directory by pressing Enter.
6. Activate the name of the directory and add the missing right from the following window by pressing Enter.
7. Repeat step 6 until all required rights are located between the square brackets.

The figure below shows the window displayed when the final right has been adopted. The numbers added between brackets refer to the steps described above.

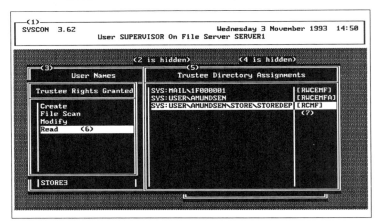

Example 27:
The modified rights are to be displayed.

Examining and altering access rights for directories

```
F:\USER\AMUNDSEN>listdir/a                                              (1)
The sub-directory structure of SERVER1/SYS:USER/AMUNDSEN
Date      Time    Inherited    Effective    Directory
-----------------------------------------------------------
 11-03-93  11:42a  [S  C  F ]  [    C  F ]  ->STORE
 11-03-93  11:44a  [SRWCEMFA]  [ R C MF ]   -> STOREDEP      (2)
2 sub-directories found

F:\USER\AMUNDSEN>cd store                                               (3)

F:\USER\AMUNDSEN\STORE>cd storedep

F:\USER\AMUNDSEN\STORE\STOREDEP>rights                                  (4)
SERVER1/SYS:USER\AMUNDSEN\STORE\STOREDEP
Your Effective Rights for this directory are [ R C MF ]
 * May Read from File.                          (R)
   May Create Subdirectories and Files.         (C)
   May Modify Directory.                        (M)
   May Scan for Files.                          (F)
 * Has no effect on directory.

   Entries in Directory May Inherit [ R C MF ] rights.

F:\USER\AMUNDSEN\STORE\STOREDEP>_
```

(1) Command to display a survey of the directory structure along with the assigned rights.
(2) The restricted rights in the STORE directory are extended in the STOREDEP subdirectory with the M and R rights, as required.
(3) The STORE directory is activated.
(4) The rights in the corresponding directory can also be displayed using the RIGHTS command.

The following command enables you to extend the rights of a user or user group directly. In this case, you must have the S (Supervisor) right or must be logged in as the network manager:

GRANT rights [FOR path] TO [USER/GROUP] name

GRANT   Grant, assign.
rights Specify one or more of the following abbreviations (separated by spaces):
          ALL = all
          N = No Rights
          S = Supervisor
          R = Read
          W = Write
          C = Create
          E = Erase

M = Modify
F = File Scan
A = Access Control

FOR path   Specify here the directory path if the command does not refer to the currently active directory.

TO [USER/GROUP] name
Specify here the name of the user or group to which you wish to assign the right(s).

Example 28:
The rights for the AMUNDSEN user for the USER\AMUNDSEN\DATA\DATA1 directory are to be extended with Create, Read and File Scan.

```
F:\USER\AMUNDSEN>grant c r f for data\data1 to amundsen                (1)

SERVER1/SYS:USER\AMUNDSEN\DATA\DATA1                                   (2)
DATA1                      Rights set to [ R C  F ]
```

(1) The command is given with the directory: only the last two subdirectories of the current directory need be specified (DATA\DATA1). The three rights are separated from one another by spaces.
(2) The message indicates that the rights have only been extended in the DATA1 subdirectory.

What effect do the rights have?
In section 3.1, we mentioned that access rights can be assigned not only to directories but also to files. Directories have a different function than files. Accordingly, the rights for files differ somewhat from those for directories. The effects of the rights for directories and files are as follows:

Effect on directories. In principle: if you do not have sufficient rights for a directory, you cannot examine or activate a directory, not even with an assigned driveletter (MAP).

Examining and altering access rights for directories 67

abbreviation	right	effect
S	Supervisor Rights	You have all rights shown below. The rights cannot be retricted by the Inherited Rights Mask.
R	Read from File	see below
W	Write to File	see below
C	Create Subdirectories and Files	You can create subdirectories and store files in the directory. You require this right to be able to copy files to the directory.
E	Erase Directory	You can remove your subdirectories (only if empty!) and files.
M	Modify Directory	You can alter the names of the directory, the subdirectories and the saved files; the attributes of the directories and files can also be altered.
F	Scan for Files	You can activate the directory and display the files and subdirectories stored there.
A	Change Access Control	You can change the rights in this directory and its subdirectories using the inherited rights mask.

Effect on files. By assigning access rights to files, you can easily lose your grip of the total structure of allocated rights. For this reason, it is advisable to safeguard files by means of attributes (see section 3.3).

abbreviation	right	effect
S	Supervisor Rights	You have all rights for this file.
H	Read from File	You can open the file and read data and copy them.
W	Write to File	You can open and alter the file.
C	Create Subdirectories and Files	see above
E	Erase Files	You can remove the files.
M	Modify Files	You can alter the name and attributes of the file. In order to edit the contents, you require the Write right.
F	Scan for Files	If you do not have this right, you cannot examine the file.
A	Change Access Control	You can remove all rights for the file except the Supervisor right.

3.3 Working with files

In principle, files are handled in the same way in a Novell network as on a independent personal computer running under MS-DOS. You will undoubtedly be able to apply several of the commands discussed below, without much extra information. For these commands, Novell NetWare uses the same method of specification as MS-DOS, with the same effect.

In previous sections, we have seen that access rights for directories and files play an important part in a network. Accordingly, there are additional commands in Novell NetWare which deal with these rights of access.

Creating files. If you are not an experienced MS-DOS user, you will probably wonder how files are created. Normally you only have an indirect influence on the creation of files, since this is carried out by an application program. For instance, if you create a document using a word processor, the text characters are stored in a file. This file is stored on disk under a certain name. It is also possible to create a file without using an application by means of the DOS command COPY CON *file_name*. Then the characters are passed on from the keyboard directly to the file. Consult an MS-DOS manual for more information concerning this command.

Note: If you wish to create files in a directory, you must have the C (Create) right.

Displaying file information. The MS-DOS command DIR displays a list of files stored in a directory. The following information is shown alongside each file: file name, file size, data and time of creation. In addition, the subdirectories of the directory are shown. An example of this is given in section 2.5.

The Novell NetWare command NDIR produces extra and more extensive information. The following information is displayed alongside each file: file name, file size, date and time of previous modification, files attributes (flags) and the name of the owner. The subdirectories of the directory are also shown, in this case along with the rights which you have for these directories. This command is described in the light of two examples in section 2.6.

Extended information about particular files can be gained using the FILER utility program. Proceed as follows:

1. Activate the (sub)directory containing the files about which you wish to be informed (CD *directory* command).

2. Type the name of the FILER command.
3. Activate the *Directory Contents* option in the FILER main menu (select using cursor keys and press Enter). A list with the files and subdirectories stored in the directory will appear.
4. Activate the name of the file about which you wish to be informed. The *File Options* submenu will appear.
5. Activate the *View/Set File Information* option in the submenu. The window containing extended file information will appear on the screen.

The figure below shows the *Directory Contents* of the USER\AMUNDSEN\DATA\DATA1 directory and the display of the *File Options* menu.

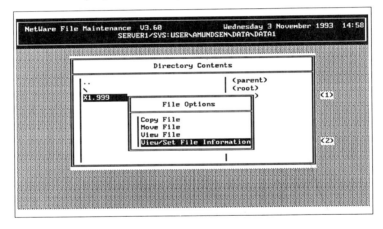

(1) Only the X1.999 file is stored in the directory. The file name is highlighted and the *File Options* menu is activated by pressing Enter.
(2) The *View/Set File Information* menu option is already selected here. The required information is produced by pressing Enter.

The figure below displays information about the X1.999 file:

Working with files

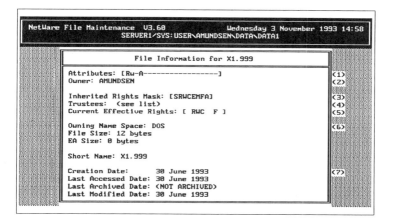

(1) The currently specified attributes (see also section 3.4).
(2) Owner of the file.
(3) Inherited rights mask for the file. All rights have been specified.
(4) The list containing the access rights can be activated via this line.
(5) The effective rights are restricted; for instance, the M (Modify) right is absent. Accordingly, the name and the attributes of the file cannot be altered.
(6) Information about the sort of file: in this case it is a DOS file with a length of 12 characters.
(7) Information about file manipulation: date of creation, date of previous modification, date of previous archiving (the file is not yet archived - see chapter 8).

Note: If you wish to display information concerning the files in a directory, you must have the F (File Scan) right.

Copying files. Just as under MS-DOS, you can also copy files from one disk to another or from one directory to another under Novell NetWare. There are two copy commands and the FILER utility program for doing this. To safeguard data, there is a separate, powerful command (see chapter 8).

The COPY command with which you are familiar from MS-DOS, can also be used in Novell NetWare. The syntax is as follows:

```
COPY source destination
```

COPY Command to copy.
source Specify the name of the source file here. It is also possible to specify a group of files or all files by using the wildcards * and ?. If the source file is located in a different directory or on a different drive, you must place the name of the relevant directory or drive in front of the file name. A backslash (\) must be placed between the names of the directory and the file. The names of directories, files and drives may not be separated from each other by spaces.
destination Specify the name of a different directory or drive here. If the destination is currently active, you do not need to specify anything as the destination. It is possible to alter the file name during copying. To do this, specify the new file name along with the destination directory and drive. The method of specification is identical to that of *source*.

It is also possible to copy files using the following Novell NetWare command. This command also supplies information concerning the source and destination drive, and source and destination directory, during execution. The names of the source and destination file are also displayed.

```
NCOPY source destination
```

NCOPY Novell NetWare copy command.
source See COPY command.
destination See COPY command.

Note: If you wish to copy files to directories on the server harddisk, you must have the C (Create) right in the appropriate directories.

Working with files

Example 29:

In the first of the two subsequent examples, the X1.999 file from the currently active USER\AMUNDSEN\DATA directory is to be copied under the name X3.999 to the DATA1 subdirectory using the COPY command. In the second example, the X1.999 file is to be copied, unchanged, to the DATA1 directory using the NCOPY command.

```
F:\USER\AMUNDSEN\DATA>dir                                              (1)

X1       999          12 30-06-93   12:16
DATA1         <DIR>      30-06-93   12:35

F:\USER\AMUNDSEN\DATA>copy x1.999 data1\x3.999                         (2)
      1 file(s) copied


F:\USER\AMUNDSEN\DATA>ncopy x1.999 data1                               (3)
From  SERVER1/SYS:\USER\AMUNDSEN\DATA
To    SERVER1/SYS:\USER\AMUNDSEN\DATA\DATA1
      X1.999        to X1.999

      1 file copied.

F:\USER\AMUNDSEN\DATA>dir data1                                        (4)

X2       TXT          12 30-06-93   12:16
X1       999          12 30-06-93   12:16
X3       999          12 30-06-93   12:16

F:\USER\AMUNDSEN\DATA>_
```

(1) The contents of the directory are displayed using this command (the disk information from the DIR command is not given here).

(2) This is the normal copy command. Only the X1.999 file name is given as the source, because the source directory is currently active. Since the file name is to be altered, the destination directory is specified along with the new file name, separated from each other by a backslash.

Note: You do not need to specify the entire directory path USER\AMUNDSEN\DATA\DATA1 as the destination.

(3) This is the Novell NetWare copy command. Since the file name is to remain the same, only the destination is specified. The command gives precise in-

formation about the source and destination directories and about the file name.
(4) The contents of the destination directory are displayed as a check (without information about the disk). The X2.TXT file was already located in this directory.

Example 30:
The LETTER1.TXT file in the USER directory is to be copied to the TEST subdirectory using both copy commands, although the C (Create) right is not available there.

```
F:\USER>copy letter1.txt \user\test                                    (1)
Access denied/File creation error-F:\USER\TEST\LETTER1.TXT
        0 file(s) copied

F:\USER>ncopy letter1.txt \user\test                                   (2)
From SERVER1/SYS:USER
To   SERVER1/SYS:USER\TEST
     LETTER1.TXT    to LETTER1.TXT    : DOS - Access denied.
                                      : Failed to create file.

     No files copied.


F:\USER>cd test                                                        (3)

F:\USER\TEST>rights                                                    (4)
SERVER1/SYS:USER\TEST
Your Effective Rights for this directory are [ R      F ]
  * May Read from File.                              (R)
    May Scan for Files.                              (F)
  * Has no effect on directory.
    Entries in Directory May Inherit [ R    F ] rights.

F:\USER\TEST>_
```

(1) The file is to be copied using the normal COPY command. The complete directory path is specified here as the destination. The command states that the USER\TEST directory is not accessible, but gives no explanation of the mistake.
(2) The attempt to copy is repeated using the NCOPY command. This attempt is also unsuccessful, but this time the reason why is given: no files may be created in the directory (*Failed to create file*). The conclusion can be drawn that the C (Create) right is absent.
(3) The destination directory is activated.
(4) The effective rights are displayed. The C right is not present.

It is also possible to copy files using the FILER utility program. Proceed as follows:

1. Type the name of the utility program: FILER.
2. Activate the *Directory Contents* menu option.
3. In the list which then appears, activate the name of the file you wish to copy.
4. Select the *Move File* command in the *File Options* menu (see the first figure in this section).
5. Specify the name of the destination directory in the window. It is also possible to allow the system to construct the destination directory. To do this, press the Ins key and confirm the server and volume name using Enter. You can display a list of directory names for each directory level by pressing the Ins key. Adopt the required names by pressing Enter.

Moving files. There is no separate command to move a file or directory in Novell NetWare. A file is moved by first copying it to the destination directory and then deleting it from the source directory. You may also make use of the FILER utility program. Proceed as follows:

1. Activate the FILER utility program.
2. Activate the *Directory Contents* menu option.
3. Activate, in the subsequent list, the name of the file you wish to move.
4. Select the *Move File* option from the *File Options* menu (see the first figure in this section).
5. Specify the destination directory, just as in the copy command.

Altering the names of files. You can alter the name of a file using the following command which you may know from MS-DOS:

```
REN old_name new_name
```

REN   Abbreviation of RENAME.
old_name Specify the present name of the file here. If the file is located in a different directory

or on another drive, place the name of the directory or drive in front of the file name. A backslash (\) must be placed between the names of the directory and the file. The names of directories, files and drives may not be separated from one another by spaces.

new_name Specify the new name of the file here.

Note: In order to alter the name of a file, you must have the M (modify) right for the corresponding directory. You cannot alter the names of files using the FILER utility program. You can rename directories using the REN-DIR command (see section 3.1).

Example 31:
The name of the X1.999 file is to be changed to X2.TXT. A survey of the rights in the directory is to be displayed first.

```
F:\USER\AMUNDSEN\DATA\DATA1>rights                                    (1)
Your Effective Rights for this directory are [   C MF ]

F:\USER\AMUNDSEN\DATA\DATA1>dir                                       (2)
X1      999        12 30-06-93   12:16

F:\USER\AMUNDSEN\DATA\DATA1>ren x1.999 x2.txt                         (3)

F:\USER\AMUNDSEN\DATA\DATA1>dir                                       (4)
X2      TXT        12 30-06-93   12:16
F:\USER\AMUNDSEN\DATA\DATA1>_
```

(1) The rights for the directory are displayed. The user has the M (Modify) right, which gives the right to change the name of the file. The irrelevant data from this and the following commands are not displayed here.
(2) Display of the present file name.

(3) Alteration of the file name to X2.TXT.
(4) Display of the new file name.

Displaying the contents of files. You can display the contents of files using the FILER utility program. However, this is only useful in the case of files containing legible data, such as text files. Proceed as follows:

1. Activate the FILER utility program.
2. Activate the *Directory Contents* menu option.
3. Activate, in the subsequent list, the name of the file whose contents you wish to examine.
4. Select the *File View* command in the *File Options* menu (see the first figure in this section).

Provisional deletion of files. The well-known MS-DOS commands, DEL and ERASE, can also be used to delete a file in Novell NetWare. And, just as in MS-DOS, the deleted file can no longer be examined or used. However, the file does not immediately disappear from the server harddisk. Novell NetWare provides the possibility of recalling a provisionally deleted file by means of the SALVAGE utility program. The deleted files remain on disk until they are definitively removed using the PURGE command or until the disk is full.

If the disk is full, new files are written over the files which have been deleted the longest in terms of time. Normally, the most recently deleted files are retained on disk in case they need to be recalled. A file is deleted as follows:

```
DEL/ERASE file_name
```

DEL/ERASE   DEL is an abbreviation of DELETE; ERASE is an alternative name for the same command.

file_name   Specify the name here of the file to be deleted. It is also possible to specify a group of files or all files by using the wildcards * and ?. If the file is located in another directory or on another drive, you must specify the name of the corresponding directory or drive in front of the file name. A backslash (\) must be placed between the names of the directory and the file. The names of directories, files and drives may not be separated from one another by spaces.

Note: In order to delete a file, you must have the E (Erase) right.

Example 32:
Initially one file, then a group of files and finally all files are to be removed from the currently active directory.

```
F:\USER\AMUNDSEN\DATA\DATA1>dir                             (1)

X2      TXT       12 30-06-93   12:16
X1      999       12 30-06-93   12:16
X3      999       12 30-06-93   12:16

F:\USER\AMUNDSEN\DATA\DATA1>del x2.txt                      (2)

F:\USER\AMUNDSEN\DATA\DATA1>dir                             (3)

X1      999       12 30-06-93   12:16
X3      999       12 30-06-93   12:16

F:\USER\AMUNDSEN\DATA\DATA1>del *.999                       (4)

F:\USER\AMUNDSEN\DATA\DATA1>del *.*                         (5)
```

(1) List of all file names in the currently active directory. Data and subsequent commands which are not relevant to the display are not shown in the figure.
(2) The X2.TXT file is deleted provisionally.
(3) The deleted file is no longer visible.
(4) This command deletes all files with the 999 extension.
(5) This command deletes all files. Be very careful with this command. For safety reasons you have to repeat this command.

Working with files 79

It is also possible to remove files using the FILER utility program. Proceed as follows:

1. Activate the FILER utility program by typing FILER.
2. Activate the *Directory Contents* menu option.
3. Select the name of the file you wish to delete from the subsequent list.
4. Press Del.
5. In the *Delete Marked File* menu, confirm the *Yes* option by pressing Enter.

Recovering provisionally deleted files. Files which have been provisionally deleted on the server harddisk can be recovered by means of the following utility program, provided no other files have been written over them or the files themselves have not been definitively removed using the PURGE command. Proceed as follows:

1. Give the SALVAGE command in the currently active directory.
2. Activate the *View/Recover Deleted Files* option in the main menu. A list of deleted files is then shown.
3. Activate the name of the file you wish to recover. A window displaying data appears along with the *Recover This File* menu.
4. Confirm the *Yes* option in the menu by pressing Enter.

The following figures indicate the procedures:

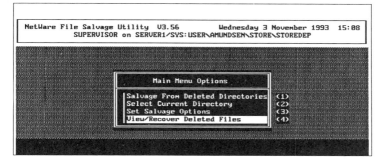

(1) This menu option recovers files from deleted directories provided they have not definitively been removed or overwritten. You may need to possess the rights of the network manager. Files from deleted directories are stored in the DELETED.SAV system file which is normally only accessible to the network manager.

(2) You can use this menu option to select a different directory if the required directory has not been activated at the start of the program.

(3) You can use this menu option to specify the sort criterion on the basis of which deleted files are to be displayed (in the following option).

(4) List of deleted files and the recover menu.

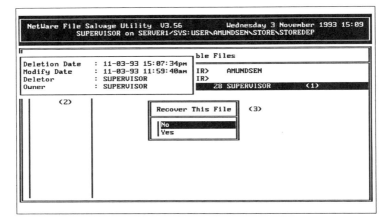

(1) A file to be recovered is marked. Using the F5 function key, it is possible to mark several files for recovery.

(2) The information window for this file, showing date of removal, date of previous modification, the user who has removed the file and the owner of the file.

(3) If you have used F5 to mark several files which are to be recovered, this menu is called *Recover All Marked Files*.

Definitively removing provisionally deleted files. As mentioned, deleted files are not removed from the server harddisk immediately. This may result in large parts of the disk being occupied by useless fragments for some time. If you make use of systematic protection of the data (see chapter 8), you can remove deleted files from the disk without second thoughts. However, you must be sure that you no longer need the files on disk. The following command removes the deleted files from the server harddisk:

```
PURGE [[file_name] [/ALL]]
```

PURGE If you do not specify any parameters here, all deleted files in the currently active directory are removed.

file_name Specify here the name of the file to be removed. It is also possible to specify a group of files or all files by means of the * and ? wildcards. If the file is located in a different directory or on another drive, you must place the name of the appropriate directory or drive in front of the file name. A backslash (\) must be placed between the names of the directory and the file. The names of directories, files and drives may not be separated from one another by spaces.

/ALL All deleted files in the currently active directory and derived subdirectories are removed from the server harddisk. If you give the command in the root directory, all files will be removed from the entire harddisk.

Caution: If you assign the P (Purge) attribute to files, these files are automatically removed from the server harddisk using the DEL/ERASE command. If you assign this attribute to a directory, all the files in the directory are also deleted immediately.

Example 33:

The T1.TXT file is to be deleted and then removed from the server harddisk. Subsequently, various applications of the command with wildcards are to be displayed.

```
F:\USER\AMUNDSEN\STORE\STOREDEP>dir                              (1)

T1      TXT         28 11-03-93   11:59


F:\USER\AMUNDSEN\STORE\STOREDEP>del t1.txt                       (2)


F:\USER\AMUNDSEN\STORE\STOREDEP>purge /all                       (3)

SERVER1/SYS:USER\AMUNDSEN\STORE\STOREDEP

      T1.TXT

Only specified files on SERVER1
have been purged from current directory and its subdirectories.

F:\USER\AMUNDSEN\STORE\STOREDEP>purge t1.txt                     (4)
F:\USER\AMUNDSEN\STORE\STOREDEP>purge *.txt                      (5)
F:\USER\AMUNDSEN\STORE\STOREDEP>purge *.*                        (6)
```

(1) The command to show the directory contents produces one file. Data which are not relevant to the execution of this and subsequent commands are omitted from the figure.
(2) The file is deleted.
(3) This command removes all deleted files in this directory and its subdirectories. In this case, that is only the X1.TXT file which has just been deleted. There are no further subdirectories. The deleted file names are displayed.
(4) Only the X1.TXT deleted file is removed.
(5) All deleted files with the TXT extension are deleted.
(6) All deleted files in the directory are removed. The same effect is achieved by omitting all parameters from the command.

3.4 Displaying and altering file attributes and access rights

File protection. A well-organized security concept is extremely important to prevent damage to, or loss of, data. A consistent protection of data is outlined in chapter 8.

In a network where several users are working with various confidential data, the term 'protection' acquires a slightly different significance. Data must be safeguarded against unauthorized use by means of systematic management of access rights for files and directories. Novell NetWare provides *attributes* and *access rights* to perform this function. Both methods can be applied to directories and files. Although some functions are identical in both concepts, directories are generally equipped with access rights and files with attributes.

Attributes. You can achieve the following effects by means of attributes:

- File data may or may not be altered, depending on the requirements.
- Files may or may not be deleted.
- File names may or may not be altered.
- Files may be regulated for simultaneous use by all users or for only one user.
- Files are (or are not) removed by means of the deletion command from the server harddisk in one go.

Note: In order to alter the attributes, you must have the M (Modify) access right in the directory. If you do not have this right, you will have to accept the restrictions. Attributes have higher priority than access rights. This means that all logged-in users in the network, including the network manager, are subject to the effects of the attributes. However, the network manager can make use of his/her M right in each directory and avoid the restrictions by altering the attributes. The Execute Only attribute is an exception. This cannot be altered by the network manager.

If the attributes of a file are to be altered, the file should not be opened. The attributes Hidden, System, Delete Inhibit, Purge and Rename can also be assigned to directories. They influence all files stored in those directories.

abbreviation	attribute	effect of the attribute
RO	Read Only	The contents of the file may only be read. The attribute cannot be used in combination with the Read Write attribute.
RW	Read Write	The contents of the file may be read and edited. The attribute cannot be used in combination with the Read Only attribute.
S	Shareable	The file may be used by several users simultaneously. This attribute is mostly placed in front of programs with the extensions EXE and COM.
H	Hidden	The file cannot be displayed using the DIR command and thus cannot be be deleted and copied. If the attribute is applied to a directory, these limitations apply to all files in the directory. However, the NDIR command does produce a display of these files.
Sy	System	The effect corresponds to that of Hidden. It is used, for other reasons, for operating system files and directories.

T	Transactional	The file is included in the Novell NetWare transaction system. An action using this file is either executed completely or not at all whenever a disruption occurs.
P	Purge	The file is removed from the server harddisk if it is deleted by means of the DEL/ERASE command. If you assign the attribute to a directory, the files stored in this directory are physically immediately removed whenever they are deleted.
A	Archive Needed	Files with this attribute have been modified since the previous archiving (see chapter 8). The attribute is automatically placed when the file is modified.
RA	Read Audit	This has no effect from Novell NetWare 3 onwards.
WA	Write Audit	This has no effect from Novell NetWare 3 onwards.
C(I)*	Copy Inhibit	Applies to files created on an Apple Macintosh workstation: the files cannot be copied.
D(I)	Delete Inhibit	Files and directories with this attribute cannot be removed. This attribute is placed automatically if the Read Only attribute has been assigned.
R(I)	Rename Inhibit	The names of files and directories with this attribute cannot be altered. This attribute is automatically placed if the Read Only attribute has been assigned.

X	Execute Only	Prevents the copying of files. It can only be assigned by the network manager to files with the EXE and COM extensions (executable files), using the FILER utility program. *Caution:* the attribute cannot be recovered. Prior to placing this attribute, you must certainly make a backup of the file. Some programs do not work flawlessly with this attribute.

*You may only use the first letter in the command, although both letters are shown here.

You can display or modify file attributes by means of the following command or using the FILER utility program:

```
FLAG [[path]file_name] [[+/-] attributes]
```

FLAG   If no parameters are specified, the attributes of all files in the directory are displayed, along with the file names.

path   Specify the required directory here if you wish to examine or modify attributes which are not in the currently active directory.

file_name   Specify the required file here, or the name of a group of files, or all files (using the * wildcard).

[+/-] attributes   Specify the above-mentioned abbreviations to indicate the required attributes. It is possible to specify several attributes at the same time, separated from one another by spaces. When adding an attribute, place a plus sign in front of the abbreviation (although this is not absolutely necessary). When removing an attribute, place a minus sign in front of the abbreviation. If you apply the ALL par-

Displaying and altering file attributes and access rights 87

ameter, all attributes are assigned to the file. If you specify N (Normal), you assign the RW standard attribute to the file.

You can display or modify directory attributes using the FILER utility program or by means of the following command:

```
FLAGDIR [[path]directory] [[+/-] attributes]
```

FLAGDIR Display of modify directory attributes.
path See above (file attributes).
directory_name Specify the directory name here. If you do not specify a directory here, the currently active directory is used.
[+/-] attributes See above (files). Only the attributes *Hidden, System, Delete Inhibit, Purge* and *Rename* can be assigned to directories.

Example 34:
Various attributes are to be assigned and then removed again. The effect of the *Delete Inhibit* attribute is to be shown.

```
F:\USER\AMUNDSEN\STORE\STOREDEP>flag                                    (1)
    T1.TXT          [ Ro - A - - -- - - -- -- -- DI RI ]

F:\USER\AMUNDSEN\STORE\STOREDEP>flag *.* -ro                            (2)
    T1.TXT          [ Rw - A - - -- - - -- -- -- -- ]

F:\USER\AMUNDSEN\STORE\STOREDEP>flag t1.txt ro                          (3)
    T1.TXT          [ Ro - A - - -- - - -- -- -- DI RI ]

F:\USER\AMUNDSEN\STORE\STOREDEP>flag t1.txt p                           (4)
    T1.TXT          [ Ro - A - - -- - - P -- -- -- DI RI ]

F:\USER\AMUNDSEN\STORE\STOREDEP>flag t1.txt -p                          (5)
    T1.TXT          [ Ro - A - - -- - - -- -- -- DI RI ]

F:\USER\AMUNDSEN\STORE\STOREDEP>del t1.txt                              (6)
Access denied

F:\USER\AMUNDSEN\STORE\STOREDEP>flag *.* -d                             (7)
    T1.TXT          [ Ro - A - - -- - - -- -- -- RI ]

F:\USER\AMUNDSEN\STORE\STOREDEP>del t1.txt                              (8)

F:\USER\AMUNDSEN\STORE\STOREDEP>_
```

(1) If no parameters are given, all file names and their attributes are shown. Only the T1.TXT file is located in the directory. At present, this file has the attributes *Read Only* (RO), *Archive* (A) and, in combination with RO, the attributes *Delete Inhibit* (DI) and *Rename Inhibit* (RI).

(2) The *Read Only* attribute is removed (-) from all files (*.*). Instead, the *Delete Inhibit* and *Rename Inhibit* attributes are automatically placed.

(3) The *Read Only* attribute is again specified for the T1.TXT file. See (1) for the effect. The plus sign does not need to be typed.

(4) The *Purge* attribute is assigned to T1.TXT file.

(5) The *Purge* attribute is removed again.

(6) The file is to be deleted. This cannot be done because the *Delete Inhibit* attribute has been assigned.

(7) The *Delete Inhibit* attribute is removed separately. Notice that the command consists of *-d* although the display shows DI.

(8) The file can now be removed.

It is also possible to assign or remove attributes using the FILER utility program. Proceed as follows:

1. Activate the FILER utility program in the required directory.
2. Activate the *Directory Contents* menu option.
3. Activate the name of the required file or of a group of files using F5. The *File Options* menu appears.
4. Activate the *View/Set File Informations* menu options. The file information window appears.
5. Activate the *Attributes* line. A window appears showing the attributes which have already been assigned.
6. Press the Ins key. A window appears showing the other available attributes.
7. Select the attribute which you wish to assign to the file and press Enter.
8. Repeat steps 6 and 7 if you wish to add more attributes.

Displaying and altering file attributes and access rights 89

The figure below displays all windows used to assign attributes.

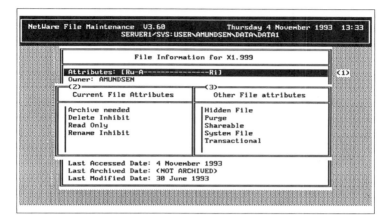

(1) You can examine and modify the attributes via this line.
(2) Window showing the attributes which have already been assigned to the file.
(3) When you have pressed the Ins key, this window appears showing the other available attributes.

To remove attributes using this program, proceed as follows:

1. Implement steps 1 to 5 as indicated above.
2. In the window, select the attribute you wish to remove and press Del.
3. In the *Remove File Attribute* window, select the *Yes* option to confirm the provisional deletion.

The figure below shows the procedure up until the point where you should make the confirmation:

File management in the network

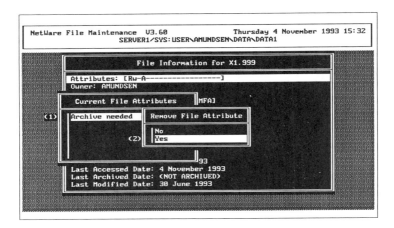

(1) The attribute has been marked and the Del key pressed.
(2) Press Enter to confirm the provisional removal of the attribute.

Note: Program files must be assigned the S (Shareable) and RO (Read Only) attributes when they are to be read by several users simultaneously and may not be altered. Data files which may be altered receive the RW (Read/Write) attribute. They are non-shareable (the S is not assigned). This setting is automatically made during the creation of a file.

Access rights. Users or user groups can be assigned as trustees to files just as to directories. Trustees may receive individual rights for a file, or these rights may be taken from them. Similar restrictions apply to files as to directories. For instance, you cannot delete a file if you do not have the E (Erase) right. In order to assign trustees or rights to a file, you must have the A (Access Control) right. In addition, rights can be removed from the file via the Inherited Rights Mask. You also require the A right in the relevant directory to do this. The following command enables you to display your access rights for a file:

```
RIGHTS file_name
```

Displaying and altering file attributes and access rights 91

> *file_name* Specify the name of a file or a group of files (using the * wildcard).

Example 35:

The logged-in user requests his/her rights for the X1.999 file.

```
F:\USER\AMUNDSEN\DATA\DATA1>dir                                      (1)

X1      999        12 30-06-93   12:16
X3      999        12 30-06-93   12:16

F:\USER\AMUNDSEN\DATA\DATA1>rights x1.999                            (2)
SERVER1/SYS:USER\AMUNDSEN\DATA\DATA1\X1.999                          (3)
Your Effective Rights for this file are [ RWCEMF ]
    May Read from File.                        (R)
    May Write to File.                         (W)
  * May Create Subdirectories and Files.       (C)
    May Erase File.                            (E)
    May Modify File.                           (M)
    May Scan for File.                         (F)
* Create is necessary to salvage a file that has been deleted.


F:\USER\AMUNDSEN\DATA\DATA1>_
```

(1) The directory contents are displayed for control.
(2) The command to display the rights must be given along with the file name, otherwise the rights for the directory are displayed.
(3) The user has all rights for the file except S (Supervisor) and A (Access). The system states that the C (Create) right is necessary to recover a deleted file using the SALVAGE program.

It is possible to display, add and remove trustees (users and user groups) by means of the FILER utility program. Proceed as follows:

1. Activate the FILER program in the required directory.
2. Activate the *Directory Contents* menu option.
3. Activate the name of the required file (or several files using F5). The *File Options* menu appears.

4. Activate the *View/Set File Information* menu option. The file information window appears.
5. Activate the default setting behind the word *Trustees* (see list). A window appears containing the users or user groups and the rights.

If you have the A (Access Control) right, you can add other users or user groups:

6. Press the Ins key. Select a user or user group from the subsequent list and confirm this selection by pressing Enter.

Remove a user or user group as follows:

7. Mark the name of the user or user group and press Del.

Example 36:
The users or user groups which have been assigned to the X1.999 file are to be displayed.

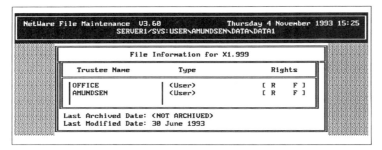

The users or user groups which have been assigned to a file as trustees can be displayed using the following command:

```
TLIST file_name
```

file_name   Specify the name of the file here.

Displaying and altering file attributes and access rights 93

Example 37:
The trustees who have been assigned to the X1.999 file are to be displayed.

```
F:\USER\AMUNDSEN\DATA\DATA1>tlist x1.999                    (1)

SERVER1/SYS:USER\AMUNDSEN\DATA\DATA1\X1.999                 (2)
User trustees:
   AMUNDSEN              [ R    F ] Roald Amundsen
   OFFICE                [ R    F ]
No group trustees.
F:\USER\AMUNDSEN\DATA\DATA1>_
```

(1) The command is given with the file name.
(2) The same users are displayed as in the previous example. The full names are also displayed, if present.

Using the first of the following two commands, you can assign rights to the file user; the second command removes these rights once more.

```
GRANT rights FOR file_name TO user/group
REVOKE rights FOR file_name FROM user/group
```

GRANT　　Grant, assign.
REVOKE　Revoke, remove. You cannot remove the user as a trustee from the file by means of this command.
rights　　Specify the abbreviations of the rights here; if several rights are specified, they should be separated from one another by spaces.
file_name　Specify the name of the file here.
user/group　Specify the name of a user or group of users here.

Example 38:
The AMUNDSEN trustee is to receive the M (Modify) and C (Create) rights for the file. The M right is subsequently revoked.

```
F:\USER\AMUNDSEN\DATA\DATA1>tlist x1.999                              (1)

SERVER1/SYS:USER\AMUNDSEN\DATA\DATA1\X1.999
User trustees:
  AMUNDSEN                  [ R    F ] Roald Amundsen
  OFFICE                    [ R    F ]
No group trustees.

F:\USER\AMUNDSEN\DATA\DATA1>grant m c for x1.999 to amundsen          (2)

SERVER1/SYS:USER\AMUNDSEN\DATA\DATA1\X1.999                           (3)
X1.999                         Rights set to [    C M ]

F:\USER\AMUNDSEN\DATA\DATA1>revoke m for x1.999 from amundsen         (4)
SERVER1/SYS:USER\AMUNDSEN\DATA\DATA1\X1.999
Trustee's access rights set to [   C    ]                             (5)

Rights for 1 files were changed for AMUNDSEN

F:\USER\AMUNDSEN\DATA\DATA1>_
```

(1) The trustees of the X1.999 file are displayed as a check.
(2) The M and C rights are added.
(3) These rights are indeed shown as a result of the command. At the same time, the current rights are removed. If these rights are to remain, they must be specified separately in the command.
(4) The M right is revoked from the user.
(5) The result is self-evident.

The following command enables you to remove a trustee (a user or user group) from a file, just as you would do using the FILER utility program:

```
REMOVE user/group FROM file_name
```

REMOVE This command can also be used to remove a trustee from a directory. In that case, replace the file name with the name of the relevant directory.

user/group Specify the name of a user or user group.
file_name Specify the file name here.

Example 39:
The AMUNDSEN trustee is to be removed from the X1.999 file.

Displaying and altering file attributes and access rights 95

```
F:\USER\AMUNDSEN\DATA\DATA1>remove amundsen from x1.999          (1)

SERVER1/SYS:USER\AMUNDSEN\DATA\DATA1\X1.999
User "AMUNDSEN" no longer a trustee to the specified file.

Trustee "AMUNDSEN" removed from 1 files.


F:\USER\AMUNDSEN\DATA\DATA1>tlist x1.999                         (2)

SERVER1/SYS:USER\AMUNDSEN\DATA\DATA1\X1.999
User trustees:
  OFFICE                              [ R    F ]
No group trustees.

F:\USER\AMUNDSEN\DATA\DATA1>_
```

(1) This command removes the AMUNDSEN trustee from the X1.999 file.
(2) The effect of the command is displayed.

The effective user rights for a file can be restricted by means of the inherited rights mask, the FILER utility program or the ALLOW command. Using the FILER utility program, proceed as follows:

1. Activate the FILER program in the required directory.
2. Activate the *Directory Contents* menu option.
3. Activate the name of the required file, or press F5 to activate several file names. The *File Options* menu appears.
4. Activate the *View/Set File Information* menu option. The file information window is shown.
5. Activate the *Inherited Rights Mask* option. A window appears displaying the allocated rights.
6. Select the right you wish to delete and press Del. This will produce the *Revoke Right* window. Confirm your choice.
7. Repeat step 6 for each right you wish to remove, although it is easier to mark the files in question using F5 and to delete them all at once.

The figure on the following page shows the window containing the available rights for the X1.999 file.

File management in the network

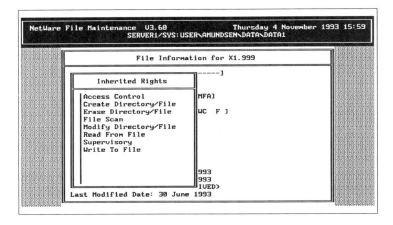

The ALLOW command has the following syntax:

```
ALLOW file_name rights
```

ALLOW   Allow, assign.
rights   Specify the abbreviations of the rights here; if you specify several rights, they should be separated from one another by spaces.
file_name   Specify the name of the file.

4 Supervisor tasks

4.1 Control of access by the supervisor

The programs and data which are stored on a central fileserver, available to several users, are organized in a directory structure just as on an independent personal computer. In the network, the access to this directory structure must be stringently controlled to ensure smooth operation. In chapter 3, we have seen that the supervisor in the Novell NetWare network regulates access control by means of the allocation of rights and attributes.

In the regulation of usage, the supervisor can primarily apply the SYSCON utility program. This abbreviation stands for SYStem CONfiguration. The supervisor ensures that the individual user can log in as a trustee on the network and may make use of the programs and files on the central fileserver of the network. Several examples of this were given in chapter 3.

In order to accept users quickly and easily into a large network, Novell NetWare has the facility to adopt one or more users with the same access profile by means of a previously edited batch file. For this, use is made of the MAKEUSER and USERDEF utility programs. In chapter 3, we discussed the ALLOW, GRANT, REVOKE and REMOVE NetWare commands which make it possible to assign access rights in a straightforward way. Within the same context, several examples were given to illustrate the facilities for rights management provided by the FILER utility program. A description was also given of how FILER can be used to modify or remove attributes for files and directories. The commands FLAG (for files) and FLAGDIR (for directories) also perform these functions.

4.2 User management

We shall now discuss the SYSCON utility program for user administration.

Activating SYSCON. We have already mentioned that, after logging in, it is possible to start up NetWare applications and utility programs by means of a user name.

■ Activate the SYSCON utility program using the command of the same name.

The main menu will then appear, as shown in the figure below.

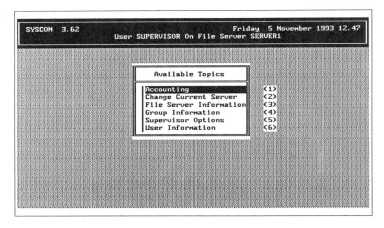

(1) Accounting: charging fileserver services to the user (management function).
(2) Change Current Server: switching to another server
(3) File Server Information: fileserver data (display function)
(4) Group Information: user group information (management function)
(5) Supervisor Options: (management function)
(6) User Information: (management function)

User management 99

More information concerning the various menu options is given below.

Exiting SYSCON. The SYSCON program is closed down in two stages:

- First press the Esc key. The *Exit SYSCON* window appears.
- Using Cursor Up or Cursor Down, mark the *Yes* menu option. If you really wish to quit SYSCON, press the Enter key.

The figure below illustrates this procedure.

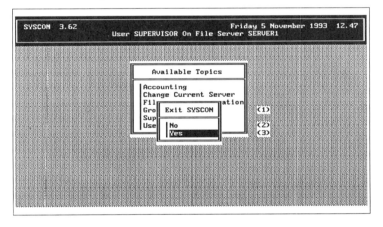

(1) The *Exit SYSCON* window is displayed by pressing the Esc key.
(2) If you highlight the *No* option and press Enter, you will remain in the SYSCON program and will return to the main menu of the program.
(3) If you highlight *Yes* and press Enter, you will exit the SYSCON utility program.

Working with SYSCON. Select the required function using the cursor keys and confirm the choice by pressing Enter. This procedure is identical in all Novell NetWare utility programs.

By pressing the F1 function key, you can activate a Help text for the currently active text boxes. The F3 function key activates the edit mode for a field or line. The F5 key marks an area. If you wish to quit a function window without saving the data, press the key combination Alt-F10. You can quit a submenu by pressing Esc. Any alterations to the text boxes will then be saved.

We shall assume that you are now familiar with these functions; they will not be described further in the rest of this book.

4.2.1 User group management

Before going on to deal with individual users, we shall first give an outline of user group management. The compilation of user groups makes it easier to allocate rights to individual users, since the rights of user groups can be passed on to individual users.

User groups. The network operating system makes the following demands on the hierarchical structure when defining the network users:

- Supervisor
- Supervisor Equivalent (File Server Console Operators)
- Workgroup Manager
- User Groups
- Users

The supervisor has unlimited access to all files and directories of the fileserver. The assignation of rights and attributes to the other user levels takes place in line with the hierarchical setup. The user who is logged in as the supervisor in the network must determine the access criteria for all users. Because a great many users are to receive the same rights, by compiling a user group Novell NetWare provides the possibility of assigning identical rights to the members of the user group in a quick and orderly fashion (see section 3.2).

User management

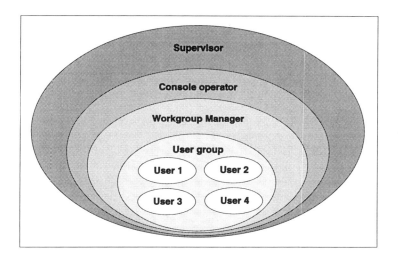

Access filter using rights:

Directory and file rights	**Directory attributes**	**File attributes**
- Supervisory - Read - Write - Create - Erase - Modify - File Scan - Access Control	- Delete Inhibit - Rename Inhibit - Copy Inhibit - System - Hidden - Purge - Normal	- Delete Inhibit - Rename Inhibit - Copy Inhibit - System - Hidden - Purge - Transactional - Execute only - Read only - Read/Write - Shareable - Archive Needed - Read Audit - Write Audit

Activating user groups. Proceed as follows:

- Activate the *Group Information* option in the *Available Topics* menu. The *Group Names* list containing the existing user groups is displayed. The figure below provides an example of existing user groups on the SERVER1 fileserver:

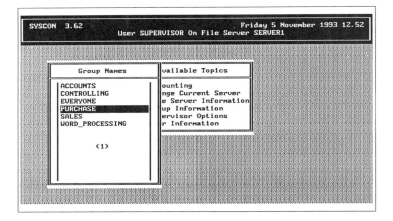

- In order to gain more extensive information about a user group, activate the group name. In the example, the PURCHASE group name has been activated. The *Group Information* submenu appears simultaneously on the screen. The figure on the following page illustrates this procedure:

(1) Full Name: Use this function to specify a full group name.
(2) Managed Users and Groups: This function indicates the users or user groups which are under the auspices of this workgroup manager.
(3) Managers: This function indicates the user who is the workgroup manager for this user.
(4) Member List: Displays a list of users who are members of the user group.
(5) Other Information: This function displays information about group identification etc.

User management

(6) Trustee Directory Assignments: This is used to display the group rights in the subdirectories of the fileserver.

(7) Trustee File Assignments: This function displays the rights for individual files on the fileserver.

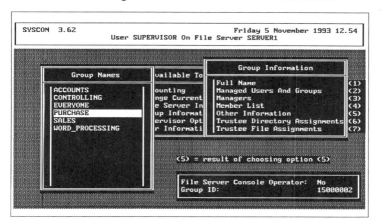

Displaying, adding and removing members of user groups. To perform one of these options, proceed as follows:

- Activate the *Member List* option in the *Group Information* menu. This displays the list of group members of the currently active user group. The figure on page 205 illustrates this. The users AMUNDSEN, POLO and TASMAN belong to the PURCHASE user group:

- Using the Ins key, you can add other users to the user group. The Del key enables you to remove existing members from the user group. The procedure is described extensively in section 4.2.2.

- The *Group Members* list can be cleared from the screen by pressing the Esc key.

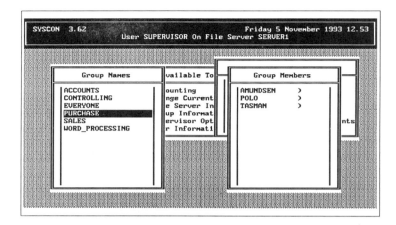

Displaying directory rights for user groups. You can now display existing rights for the selected user group for directories.

- Activate the *Trustee Directory Assignment* function in the *Group Information* menu. A window appears containing the directories for which the user group has rights. The effective rights are also shown. The figure below displays the directories for which the PURCHASE user group has rights.

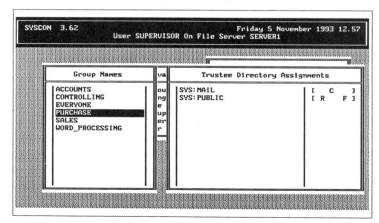

User management 105

Adding subdirectories to a user group. It is quite simple to make additional directories available to a user group. To do this, you must first add the subdirectory to the group.

Example 40:
The PURCHASE user group is to acquire rights for the \LOGIN subdirectory. Proceed as follows:

- Activate the *Trustee Directory Assignment* window, as in the previous example.
- Press Ins. This activates a text box for the subdirectory name.
- Specify the full name of the subdirectory along with volume name. Place a colon between the names. It is also possible to select the name of the subdirectory using the Ins key. Confirm by pressing Enter. The figure below gives an example of a text box which has been filled in:

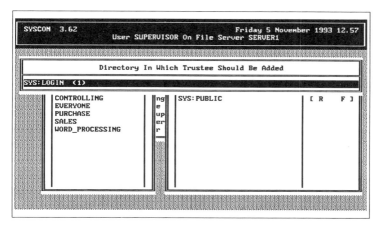

Adding rights to a subdirectory. As soon as a new subdirectory is added to a user group, the group receives initially the following standard access rights:

- File Scan (searching in the subdirectory)
- Read (reading in the subdirectory).

However, these rights can be altered quite easily, as the following example illustrates.

Example 41:

The rights for the \LOGIN subdirectory are to be extended with the C (Create) right.

Proceed as follows:

■ Mark the line with the directory in the *Trustee Directory Assignments* window, in this case SYS:LOGIN. Confirm by pressing Enter. The rights granted and not granted to this directory appear in two adjacent windows.

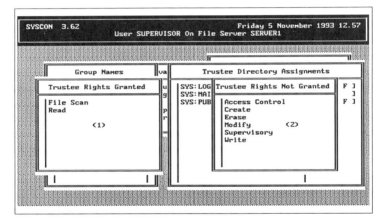

(1) Window displaying assigned rights.
(2) Window displaying rights not assigned.

■ Now mark the Create option and press the Ins key. The Create right is thus added to the list of granted rights and disappears simultaneously from the Not Granted list.

User management

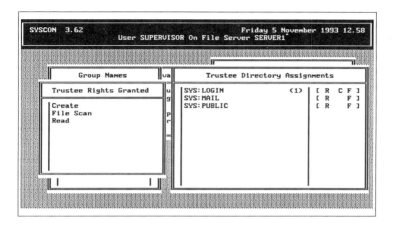

(1) As the above figure illustrates, the first letter of the assigned right appears on the same line as the corresponding directory. This produces a clear display of the available rights in the subdirectories of the user group.

- You can conclude the rights assignation process by pressing Esc.
- If an assigned right is to be cancelled, mark the right in the assigned rights list and then press the Del key.

Assigning user rights at file level. By means of the *Trustee File Assignments* function in the *Group Information* menu, the access rights can be assigned for individual files in subdirectories. The procedure corresponds to that for assigning rights to directories.

Adding or removing user groups. A new user group is created or an existing group removed in the same way as a subdirectory is created or removed.

- Press the Esc key until the list of user groups appears.
- Press Ins. In the subsequent window, you can create a new user group.

- In order to remove an existing user group, mark its name using the cursor keys and then press Del.
- As a safety measure you will be asked to confirm this action. Activate the *Yes* option by pressing Enter. All user rights are automatically removed along with the group name.

4.2.2 User management

Displaying a list of users. If users are already logged into your network, you can display a list of these. Proceed as follows:

- In the *Available Topics* main menu, activate the *User Information* option. A list of *User Names* appears, as shown in the figure below.

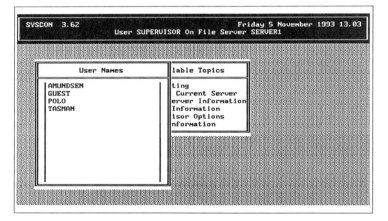

Adding users. A new user is added to the list in the following way:

- When the list of users is displayed on the screen, press the Ins key. You can now enter the new user name in a text box. The new user is actually added when the Enter key is pressed.

User management

Removing users. In order to remove a user from the user list, proceed as follows:

- Mark the user name in the list of users and then press Del. You will have to confirm this removal in the subsequent *Delete User* window by selecting *Yes*. The *No* option is the default setting.
- Select *Yes* and press Enter. The user name is then removed and the list adjusted.

Displaying user information. It is possible to display precise information about the user.

Example 42:
Extensive information is to be displayed about the status of the user POLO. Proceed as follows:

- First mark the name POLO in the list of *User Names* and then press Enter. The *User Information* submenu appears for the selected user. If required, extensive information can be displayed by activating each menu line.

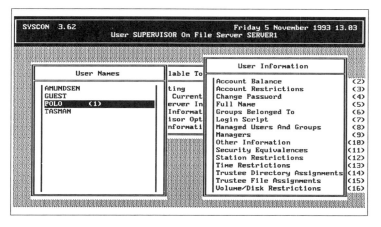

POLO is the selected user

Taking user POLO as reference, we shall examine the most important information and management functions.

Changing a user password. The user can create or alter a password by means of the function *Change Password* (see also section 2.3).

Specifying users using the full name. A user is often adopted into a network using an abbreviated name. In a large network with a large number of users it is practical to use full names to retain an orderly overview.

Example 43:

The POLO user is to be registered under his full name POLO, Marco.
Proceed as follows:

- Activate the *Full Name* option in the *User Information* menu.
- Enter the full name in the subsequent text box. The figure below illustrates this procedure.

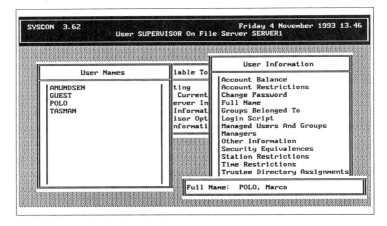

Displaying the members of user groups. Dividing users into user groups makes it very easy to assign user rights to certain users. The groups to which a user belongs should be known.

Example 44:
The group membership of the user POLO is to be displayed. Proceed as follows:

- Activate the *Groups Belonged To* option in the *User Information* menu. A window appears containing the names of the groups. In the example, the user POLO belongs to the PURCHASE and EVERYONE user groups.

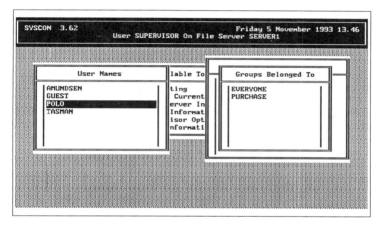

Adding membership of a user group. A user can be attached to other groups, providing him/her with the corresponding rights.

Example 45:
The user POLO is to be attached to other existing user groups. Proceed as follows:

- Activate the *Groups Belonged To* window.
- Press the Enter key. This displays the groups to which the user is not attached in the *Groups Not Belonged To* window.
- Select the user group to which the user is to be assigned and press Ins. This adds the user to the group. In the example shown below, the SALES group name has been selected in the *Groups Not Be-*

longed To list. This will now be transferred to the *Groups Belonged To* window.

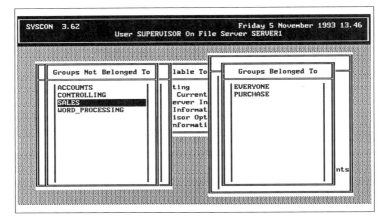

Revoking membership of a user group. User membership of a group is revoked in a similar way.

■ Mark the group name in the *Groups Belonged To* window and press the Del key. All rights which the user had by means of this group become invalid and are removed.

Displaying the individual login script of a user. A user can log in by means of a certain log in script. This is a normal text file which is executed during the start up procedure, just as the AUTOEXEC.BAT file under MS-DOS. These login scripts are not obligatory for each user. Generally, a collective login script for all users is sufficient. In the user login script, you can apply the same commands as in the system login script (see also sections 4.3, 9.1 and chapter 11).
Proceed as follows in order to display, and edit if required, a user login script:

■ Activate the *Login Script* option in the *User Information* window. If the previously selected user has his/her own login script, it is displayed in a window, otherwise a message indicating that no login script yet exists will appear as in the case of the POLO user in the example.

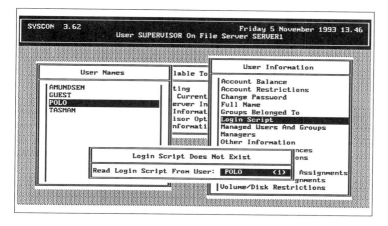

(1) The message that there is no special login script for POLO.

■ If you wish to compile a login script for the corresponding user, press Enter. An edit window appears for the creation or modification of the login script. In practice, a user login script is applied to activate a relevant menu for a certain user. In this example, the following command to start the Novell NetWare menu system could be placed in the login script (see section 9.1):

```
EXIT "MENU POLO.MNU"
```

The figure shown on the following page provides an example:

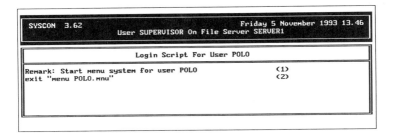

(1) Comment line in the login script.
(2) The command to start the MENU menu program with the POLO.MNU file. The menu file must be compiled according to the rules which apply to the creation of menu files in Novell NetWare (see section 9.2).

Assigning the status of workgroup manager to a user or user group. It has already been mentioned that it is possible to engage users as workgroup managers. In networks with many users, this is extremely practical. The workgroup managers execute co-ordinating tasks supporting the system manager. For instance, they can create and alter passwords, account restrictions, accounts, security regulations and user login scripts for the users or user groups assigned to them.

Example 46:
The user POLO is to be engaged as workgroup manager for other users or user groups. Proceed as follows:

- Activate the *User Information* option in the *Available Topics* main menu.
- In the subsequent *User Names* window, activate the name of the user to which you wish to allocate the function, POLO in this case.
- In the *User Information* menu, select the *Managed Users And Groups* option.

This function displays the current list of workgroup managers. In our example, only the EVERYONE user is shown initially. This status has not been assigned to any user as yet.

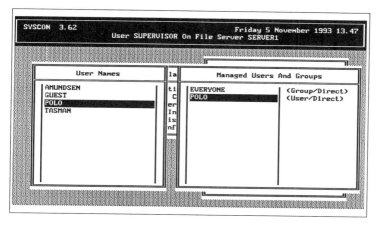

- Press the Ins key. The *Other Users And Groups* window appears (this is not shown in the figure).
- From this window, select users and user groups which you wish to adopt and confirm the choice by pressing Enter. The *Managed Groups and Users* list now shows the groups managed by the user POLO. He now has the status of workgroup manager.

Displaying the user workgroup manager. A user can request which workgroup manager he/she has been assigned. The procedure is as follows:

- Activate the *User Information* option in the *Available Topics* menu.
- In the subsequent *User Names* window, activate the name of the user whose workgroup manager you wish to discover. In our example, we shall choose the name AMUNDSEN.
- Activate the *Managers* option in the *User Information* menu.

The example on page 116 illustrates that the user AMUNDSEN has POLO as his workgroup manager.

Supervisor tasks

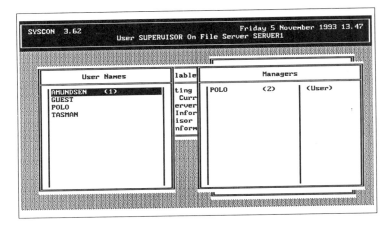

(1) The user AMUNDSEN was activated in the *User Information* menu.
(2) Using the *Managers* menu option, the name of the workgroup manager (POLO) assigned to the user AMUNDSEN was requested.
- Using the Del and Ins keys in this screen, you can also add or remove workgroup managers. Proceed according to the steps outlined above.

Displaying additional information about the user. It is also possible to display extra information about the user, such as the time of previous login, whether he/she has the status of console operator, the disk capacity currently occupied and user identification. Proceed as follows:

- Activate the *Other Information* option in the *User Information* menu (see next page):

(1) The previous user login time.
(2) Status as console operator.
(3) Disk capacity currently occupied.
(4) User Identification.

User management

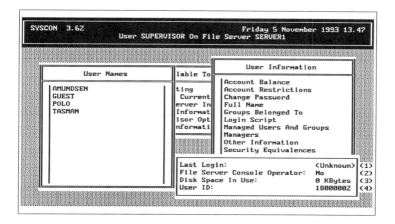

Equal allocation of rights. It is possible to assign all existing access rights in a network to another user, in one go.

Example 47:

The user POLO is to receive the same rights as the users in the PURCHASE group. Proceed as follows:

- Activate the *User Information* option in the *Available Topics* main menu.
- In the subsequent *User Names* window, activate the name of the user you wish to bring into line with the other users. In our example, that is POLO.
- In the *User Information* menu, activate the *Security Equivalences* option.
- Press the Ins key. The *Other Users And Groups* window appears, containing the users or user group with which you wish to put the user on a par.
- Select the user or user group with which the user in question is to be brought on to par (here PURCHASE), and press Enter.

The figure illustrated shows the procedure:

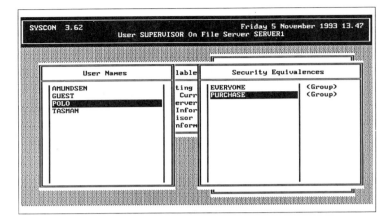

Restricting users to certain network addresses. In large networks, it may be important, for security reasons, to allow users to log in only on certain workstations. To ensure, for instance, that Personnel Office staff can only log in on workstaions in the Personnel Department, a unique link must be made between the user name and the workstations present in the relevant department. In this way, a security measure has been introduced by means of a localised setting. In order to apply this restriction, proceed as follows:

- Activate the *User Information* option in the *Available Topics* menu.
- In the subsequent *User Names* window, activate the name of the user for whom you wish to restrict the login possibilities. In our example, we choose the name POLO.
- In *User Information* menu, activate the *Stations Restrictions* option. The *Allowed Login Addresses* window (shown in the figure below) appears. Since no data are displayed in the window, this means that the user POLO has no restrictions regarding login possibilities. He may log in on all workstations in the network.
- Press the Ins key to apply the restrictions. In the *Network Address* text box, you must specify the network

User management 119

address of the fileserver. In our example, SERVER1 has the network address 00002000, and SERVER2 has the address 00000001. Network addresses can be displayed using the SLIST command (see section 2.7).
- In the subsequent *Allow Login From All Nodes* window, select the *Yes* option. A text box appears once again.
- Type the station address at which the user may log into the network. It is possible to specify several workstation addresses. These addresses can be requested using the FCONSOLE utility program, if required.

The figure below shows the screen containing the *Allowed Login Addresses* window prior to the entry of the data for POLO.

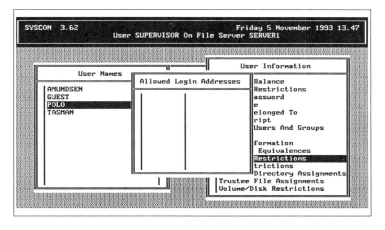

When you have specified station restrictions for a user and the user attempts to log in on another workstation, the login is refused and the following message appears:

```
Attempting to login from an unapproved
station.
The Supervisor has limited the stations
that you are allowed to login on. Access to
```

server denied and you have been logged out.
You are attached to server SERVER1.

Restricting user login time. It may be necessary to restrict the user login time for company reasons. Proceed as follows:

- Activate the *User Information* option in the *Available Topics* main menu.
- In the subsequent *User Names* window, activate the name of the user whose login time you wish to restrict. In our example, we shall choose POLO. The *User Information* menu appears.
- Activate the *Time Restrictions* option. The *Allowed Login Times For User* window appears, showing a timetable consisting of asterisks.
- If you wish to apply restrictions, select the appropriate time periods using the cursor keys. You can remove the selected period by pressing the spacebar.

The figure below displays unrestricted usage of the network for the POLO user. All the days of the week have asterisks for 24 hours of the day.

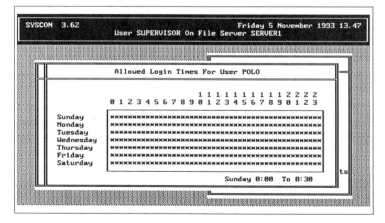

Managing directory and file rights for individual users. Analogous to the management of user rights for user groups (see section 4.2.1), user rights at directory and file level can also be assigned to individual users. The functions for displaying, inserting and removing directories and their access rights are executed in the same way as described in section 4.2.

■ In the *User Information* menu, activate the *Trustee Directory Assignments* (for directories) and *Trustee Files Assignments* (for files) options.

The figure below shows the specific directory rights for the POLO user:

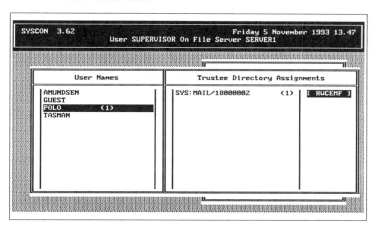

(1) The user, POLO, has all rights in the MAIL directory except S (Supervisor) and A (Access Control).

Restricting usage of server harddisk capacity. If you wish to limit the amount of server harddisk capacity a particular user may use, proceed as follows:

■ In the *Available Topics* main menu, activate the *User Information* option.
■ In the subsequent *User Names* window, activate the name of the user for whom you wish to limit usage of

the server harddisk. In our example, that is POLO. The *User Information* menu appears.

■ Activate the *Volume/Disk Restrictions* option in this menu. A list of available volumes is shown in the *Select A Volume* window.

■ Select the required volume. The *User Volumes/Disk Restrictions* information window appears containing all possible restrictions. The figure below illustrates our example. There are no restrictions for the POLO user for the selected fileserver.

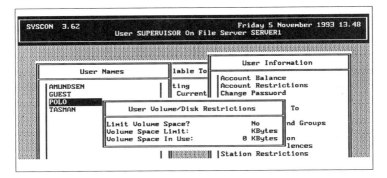

4.2.3 User accounts

Creating user accounts. Under Novell NetWare, it is possible to open accounts for users. Use of network facilities by certain or by all users can be checked, charged and settled in this way.

To create a user account, proceed as follows:

1. In the *Available Topics* main menu, activate the *Accounting* option.
2. Confirm the selection in the *Install Accounting* window by selecting *Yes* and pressing Enter.

User management 123

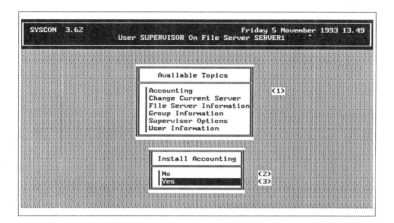

(1) The *Accounting* menu option is activated.
(2) By activating the *No* option, you will cancel the procedure and return to the main menu.
(3) The *Yes* option confirms your intention of creating an account.

The installation menu for creating a user account appears, as shown in the figure below:

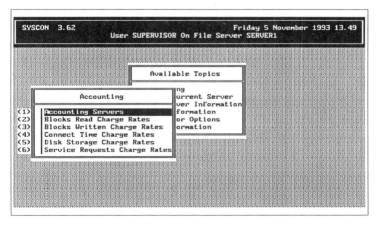

(1) Accounting Servers: By means of this menu option, the Accounting default setting is applied to the SERVER1 server. If there is only one server in the network, the default setting is automatically correct.

The figure below displays the default setting:

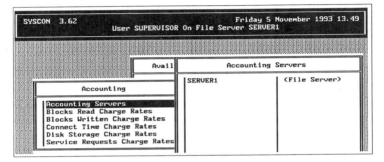

(2) Blocks Read Charge Rates: Charges based on the data blocks read by the fileserver.
(3) Blocks Written Charge Rates: Charges based on the data blocks written by the fileserver.
(4) Connect Time Charge Rates: Charges based on the period between the user login and logout.
(5) Disk Storage Charge Rates: Charges based on the data stored on the fileserver by the user.
(6) Service Requests Charge Rates: Charges based on usage of the central utility programs on the fileserver.

Example 48:

In the *Service Requests Charge Rates* method, we have changed the charge factor by a factor of 3 for the period Sunday 9.00 to 9.29 am. The factor 1 is the default setting.

The figure on the following page shows the alteration in the charge factor for the user account:

User management

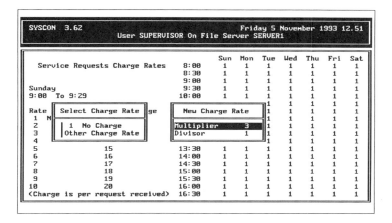

However, this does not actually activate the user account. Only the default settings of all possible charge units (factors) are determined. The account still has to be activated for the individual users. This process is described in section 4.3 (*Restricting user accounts*).

4.2.4 Activating a different server

In section 2.2, we mentioned that it is possible to activate a different fileserver by means of one of the options in the main menu.

■ In the *Available Topics* main menu, activate the *Change Current Server* option. The available fileservers are displayed in a window (see next page):

(1) The SERVER1 server: the supervisor is registered as the user.
(2) The SERVER2 server: POLO is registered as the user.

126 *Supervisor tasks*

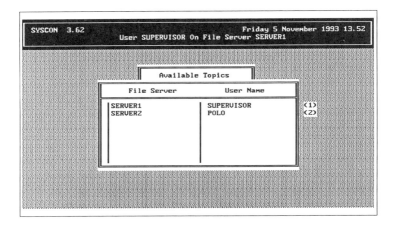

4.2.5 File Server Information

In addition to the information described in section 2.7, it is possible to display information concerning all the servers available in the network.

- In the *Available Topics* main menu, activate the *File Server Information* option. The figure below shows a window containing the names of two registered fileservers.

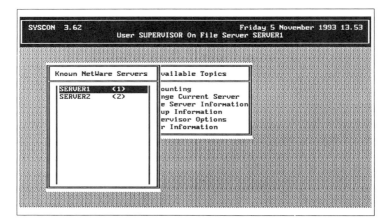

User management

(1) The first fileserver, SERVER1.
(2) The second fileserver, SERVER2.

■ Now activate one of the fileservers displayed. Another window appears containing important information concerning the fileserver, such as the logical name of the fileserver, the Novell NetWare version, the revision status, the node address, the Novell NetWare serial number etc. The figure below displays the screen containing the information requested.

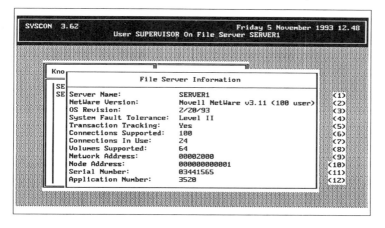

(1) Name of the server.
(2) Version of the Novell NetWare operating system.
(3) Version date.
(4) Security level.
(5) Transaction tracking has been activated.
(6) Maximum number of network connections.
(7) Connections in use.
(8)-(10)
   Specified network addresses; consult the Novell NetWare manual for more details.
(11) Operating system serial number.
(12) Operating system application number.

The data for SERVER2 are shown below. Both servers are logically and physically included in the network.

Logging in to two servers at the same time is possible by means of the ATTACH command (see also chapters 2 and 11).

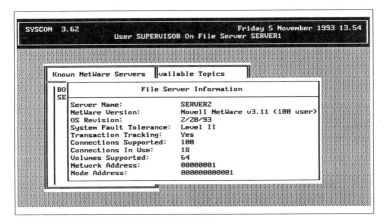

4.3 Specifying the user work environment

By means of the *Supervisor Options* functions, the system manager is able to specify the parameters which apply to all fileserver users. When a new user is registered, these options are initially set to the default access rights.

The function is activated as follows:

- Start up the SYSCON program.
- In the *Available Topics* main menu, activate the *Supervisor Options* option. A menu subsequently appears showing the available functions. The figure on the following page gives an example:

Specifying the user work environment 129

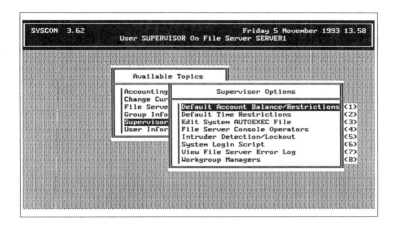

(1) Default restrictions on the user account.
(2) Default restrictions on time access.
(3) Edit program for the AUTOEXEC.BAT system file.
(4) Specification of users as console operators for the fileserver.
(5) Restriction of login attempts.
(6) Definition of the system login script.
(7) Display the error log.
(8) Define the workgroup managers.

The menu functions are illustrated below in the light of an example.

Default Account Balance/Restrictions. It is possible to restrict a user account by specifying a number of parameters. Proceed as follows:

- In the *Supervisor Options* menu, activate the *Default Account Balance/Restrictions* option.
- You can select different function parameters using the cursor keys. These are then activated by pressing Enter.

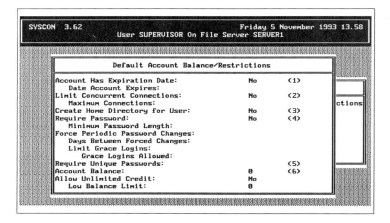

(1) Account Has Expiration Date: This blocks the user account at a certain date. If you wish to ensure that users cannot log in on a certain date - because the supervisor wishes to make thorough system alterations, for instance - set this function to *Yes* and specify the relevant date on the *Date Account Expires* line.

(2) Limit Concurrent Connections: This option enables you to limit the possibility of a user logging in on different servers in the network at one time. If this function is set to *Yes*, the number of permitted connections must be specified on the *Maximum Connections* line.

(3) Create Home Directory for User: This defines the user home directory.

(4) Require Password: This setting defines whether a user is required to use a password or not. If this is set to *Yes*, the minimum number of positions for the password has to be specified on the *Minimum Password Length* line. On the following line, the period within which the password must be changed can be specified. The *Grace Logins Allowed* parameter defines a period in which it is still allowed to log in after the expiry of the specified period.

(5) Require Unique Passwords: By setting this parameter to *Yes*, a different password must be

chosen to replace the previous one after expiry of the password validity time.
(6) Account Balance: The state of the user account can be determined by this setting (see section 4.2). As soon as the specified limit is reached, access to the fileserver is blocked for the user in question. The limit may be exceeded, however, by means of the *Low Balnce Limit*. The *Allow Unlimited Credit* setting is self-evident.

Caution: The restrictions described here enable the system manager to accurately control the activities of the users in the network. The registration of the data used provides the possibility of calculating the relevant charges. In practice however, the system may come into conflict with legislation concerning confidential personal information and the labour representation laws. When activating this component of the system, the labour representative council may have to be consulted.

Time restrictions. If you wish to limit use of the network to a certain amount of time each week, proceed as follows:

- In the *Supervisor Options* menu, activate the *Default Time Restrictions* option. The window containing the timetable appears (see the figure below). An asterisk indicates that it is possible to work using the fileserver at the specified time on the specified day of the week. The usage timetable is divided into half-hour periods. When the table is activated for the very first time, all 24 hours of all days of the week are provided with asterisks, which means that the user may use the fileserver the whole day long, every day.
- If restrictions have to be applied, use the cursor keys to select the required periods and press the spacebar to remove the asterisk.
- If you wish to revoke the restrictions, type asterisks at the appropriate empty positions.

The figure following gives an example of applied restrictions:

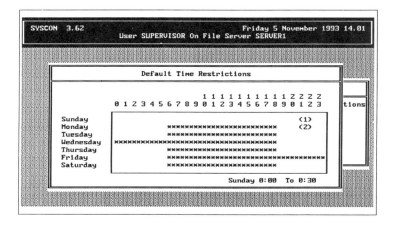

(1) The user may not work in the network on Sunday.
(2) The user may work using the fileserver on Monday, Tuesday, Thursday and Saturday between 6.00 and 18.00 hours, on Wednesday between 0.00 and 18.00 hours and on Friday between 6.00 to 23.30.

If a user logs in on the fileserver outside of the specified periods, the following message appears:

```
F:\LOGIN>login POLO
SERVER1/OFFICE: Attempting to login during an unauthorized time period.
The supervisor has limited the times that you can login to this server.
```

Editing the AUTOEXEC system file. The *Edit System AUTOEXEC File* menu function enables you to determine or edit the parameters for the system login procedure in the AUTOEXEC system file. Proceed as follows:

- In the *Supervisor Options* menu, activate the *Edit System AUTOEXEC File* option. The edit window for the AUTOEXEC file appears.
- You can type modifications directly in the window. Normally however, this file remains unchanged once Novell NetWare has been installed.

Specifying the user work environment 133

The figure below displays the edit window of the AUTO-EXEC system file, with several commands serving as examples:

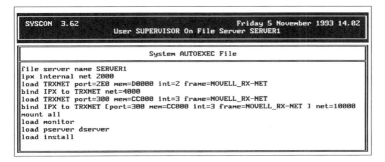

Specifying console operators. The supervisor of a large network containing various user levels can specify users as console operators to help lighten the work load. These users have more rights than workgroup managers. For instance, they can implement important functions of the FCONSOLE utility program. Proceed as follows:

■ In the *Supervisor Options* menu, activate the *File Server Console Operators* option. The specified console operators are shown in the right-hand window. A window containing all users and user groups is opened by pressing the Ins key.
■ By marking the required users or user groups and pressing Enter, these are added to the list of console operators (see next page):

(1) No console operators have been specified as yet.
(2) The user TASMAN has been marked. He can be added to the list of console operators by pressing Enter.

Supervisor tasks

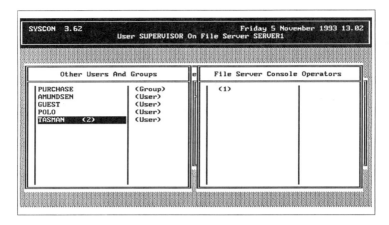

Restricting login attempts. Normally, a user may make any number of attempts to log in on the network. This also allows an unauthorized person the chance to try out various password combinations in order to gain access to the system. If you wish to prevent this, you can check and restrict the number of login attempts. Proceed as follows:

- In the *Supervisor Options* menu, activate the *Intruder Detection/Logout* option. A dialog window appears, as shown in the figure below.
- Make the required modifications as indicated by the instructions below.

The figure on page 135 displays the default settings. No special measures have been taken to control unauthorized login attempts.

(1) The *No* parameter means that no special control occurs if a wrong password is specified. This is the default setting. If you switch this setting to *Yes* by pressing the Enter key, the system will check the logins.
(2) The following setting specifies the number of attempts allowed. When this point has been reached, the intruder's attempts will be blocked.

Specifying the user work environment 135

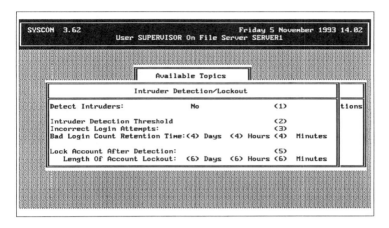

(3) In order to make it difficult for *hackers*, the number of attempts can be restricted using the *Incorrect Login Attempts* function. Specify the required number of attempts here. The default setting is seven.
(4) Specify here the number of days, hours and minutes for the duration of the network access blockage when an unsuccessful login procedure has taken place.
(5) If you specify *Yes* here, the account of the user whose name has been used in the login attempt is subsequently blocked.
(6) If (5) has been set to *Yes*, specify here the number of days, hours and minutes for the duration of the blockage of the user account.

Displaying and editing the system login script. Prior to a login script being created for a certain user, the supervisor normally compiles a general system login script, or has a minimum login automatically generated in the installation process. All commands in a login script are processed one by one during the user login procedure, in the same way as the boot procedure and the AUTOEXEC.BAT file are processed on a PC running under MS-DOS. When the user has logged in correctly on the network, the system login script is first executed and then, if available, the login script of the user.

You can retrieve and edit, if necessary, the system login script in the following way:

- In the *Supervisor Options* menu, activate the *System Login Script* option. The text window of the same name appears:

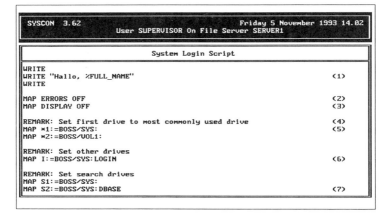

(1) Greetings line on the user screen with display of the full user name (script variable %Full_Name).
(2) Error messages switched off during login procedure.
(3) Display of the script command is switched off.
(4) Comment line in the login script file.
(5) Set to the most commonly used fileserver drives.
(6) Place the drive letter I: in front of the \LOGIN directory.
(7) Specify the search drives S1 and S2. Often, a menu specially compiled for the user is started up using the last command in the login script (see section 9.2).

Working with the login script editor. Commands may not be longer than one line and a line may not be longer than 150 characters. The most important functions when editing the text are:

key	function
Enter (Return)	conclude a line
Cursor Up, Down, Left, Right	move the cursor
PgDn	move one screenpage downwards
PgUp	move one screenpage upwards
Ins	insert a character
Del	remove a character
Esc	save text and quit the editor

A survey of the available script commands is given in chapter 11, along with the variables which can be used in Novell NetWare.

Displaying and removing the error logbook. All errors which occur using the server, particularly in the user login procedure, are registered in a logbook along with the date and time of origin, priority number and explanation. You can display the contents of this logbook. Proceed as follows:

- In the menu *Supervisor Options*, activate the *View File Server Error Log* option. A window appears displaying any errors which may have occurred.
- You can quit the logbook display by pressing the Esc key. Prior to actually quitting the logbook, you must decide whether you wish to delete the contents of the logbook or not. If you confirm the *Yes* default setting in the *Clear Error Log* window, the registrations in the logbook are deleted. This is useful in order to prevent storage space being occupied unnecessarily.

The figure on page 138 provides an example of a system logbook with an option window for the deletion of data.

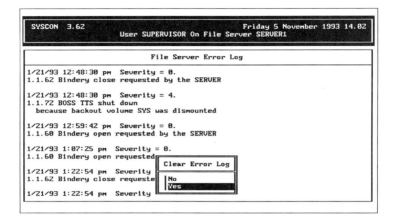

Specifying workgroup managers. It has already been mentioned that the supervisor in a large network can delegate some of the system tasks to the users under his/her auspices. In the Novell NetWare system hierarchy, console operators can, in turn, assign tasks to workgroup managers. These have much fewer rights and can only perform management tasks to a limited extent. By means of the *User Information* menu option, in conjunction with the *Managed Users And Groups* and *Managers*, management tasks can be allocated to users at a lower level.

To specify workgroup managers, proceed as follows:

- In the *Supervisor Options* menu, activate the *Workgroup Managers* option. A window appears, displaying current workgroup managers, if any.
- Press the Ins key. The *Other Users And Groups* window appears, displaying the names of users and user groups. In our example, the user POLO is to be engaged as workgroup manager.
- Mark this user and press Enter. This user will now be included in the table of *Workgroup Managers*.
- Repeat the procedure for each workgroup manager to be engaged.

Specifying the user work environment 139

The figure below displays the example before POLO is engaged as the workgroup manager:

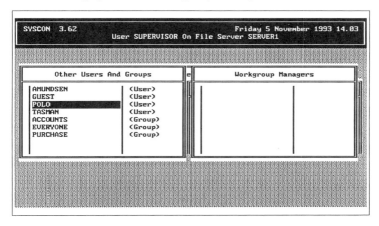

Proceed as follows to remove workgroup managers:

- In the list of *Workgroup Managers*, mark the name of the user you wish to remove and press Del.
- In the *Delete Workgroup Manager* window, confirm the *Yes* default setting by pressing Enter.

The figure below shows the procedure at the moment confirmation of the deletion is requested:

Supervisor tasks

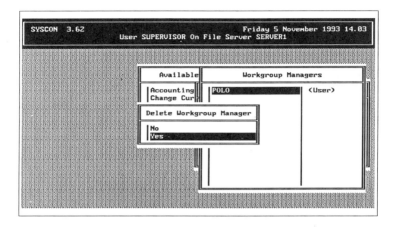

5 Installing applications in the network

The previous chapters have shown that working with programs in the network differs substantially from working with a stand-alone personal computer. On a normal personal computer, one user works with one program and the relevant data. In a network, several users can work with the same program and the same data, like an article file, for instance. The main advantage is that all network users have continual access to the most recent data.

However, the procedure of addressing data in a network does not always take place smooothly. As long as the data are only addressed for reading purposes, there is scarcely any difference with a normal personal computer. However, in the case of simultaneous addressing for writing purposes by several users, the situation is somewhat different. In that case, the program, in combination with the network operation system, ensures that the processes are dealt with coherently, otherwise conflicts may arise between the various user data. Moreover, working with peripheral devices, as with the output of data to printers and data exchange with external storage media, is not entirely free of problems. Uncontrolled output from several users to one printer is relatively harmless. The irreversible damage of a file due to uncontrolled output to a harddisk is much more serious. In the worst scenario, the file integrity of the harddisk is affected or a complete directory may be damaged, leading to definitive loss of data.

Accordingly, the applications and the network operating system must be exactly geared to one another to produce a flawlessly functioning network environment.

5.1 Applications and their suitability for a network

With the increase in use of local networks, more and more programs, during their development stages, are being made suitable for use in a network. In this development, the co-ordination of addressing (for writing purposes) of files and devices which are available to several users must be formulated. Two security measures in particular are applied: file locking and record locking.

File locking means that a file can only be opened by one user at one time. If, for instance, a user is working on a file with article source data, another user can only address this file at the moment this process has ended and the file has been closed.

Record locking means that different users can address a file simultaneously, but only one user can alter a record in the file at any given moment. For instance, all staff in the PURCHASE department can address the same article file, but only one user can modify the data concerning an article, as in the case of a settlement or transfer for example.

Applications are thus only really suitable for networks if at least one of these two security mechanisms has been put into operation. If, in addition, applications must be suitable for several workstations or users, the requirements of record locking must be satisfied. This is the only way to allow various users to work with file data in a safe fashion. Commercial applications such as order processing, storage management, financial administration and all database applications must, without exception, be suitable for use by several people, since several users work simultaneously with the same files in these programs.

This requirement is less important for applications which do not exclusively address common-use files, such as word processors, spreadsheets and graphical applications. Most spreadsheets which are currently available are not suitable for use by several people at the same time. This also applies to situations in which database functions are present. In the application of such programs in the network, you must take the following into account. If two users are working on the same worksheet in a spreadsheet program and wish to save it when the work is completed, only the worksheet which is saved ultimately is actually retained. All the previous worksheets of the same name are replaced by the version last saved.

Summarizing:

- **Suitable for a network**: all programs which are installed on the fileserver and which can be activated from the workstations. This applies to most programs which are currently available under MS-DOS.
- **Suitable for use by several users**: all programs which enable several users to work simultaneously with one file, and thus possess the special file locking or record locking security mechanisms.

5.2 Examples of applications for several workstations

5.2.1 The dBASE IV database program

A well-known database program for personal computers is dBASE. The program is suitable for use by several users from version III onwards. The dBASE IV database program can be installed in a network from version 1.1 onwards.

To do this, proceed as follows:

1. Activating the installation program
dBASE IV is supplied on 3.5 inch diskettes. Diskette 1 is the installation diskette which should be placed in the drive from which the installation is to be carried out. In our example, we shall refer to this as drive A:.

- Place the installation diskette in drive A: and type the command INSTALL behind the prompt A:.
- Confirm the command by pressing Enter.

In the opening window, you may choose one of the three installation methods: *Quick*, *Full* or *Menu-driven*.

- Select the *Full* option and confirm this choice by pressing Enter.

This is the most straightforward way to install dBASE for use by several users.

- In the subsequent menu, select the *Multi-user* installation option and confirm the choice by pressing Enter.

The most recent version of dBASE IV, 2.0, has a slightly different introduction menu. You must choose between the options *Stand Alone Installation*, *Network Installation* and *Optional Software Installation*. The *Network Installation* option is the correct one in our case. Highlight it using the cursor keys and press Enter. You will then have to specify the User name, Company name and Serial number. Select the first by pressing Enter, specify the data and press Enter to confirm. Then move to Company name using the cursor keys. Press Enter and specify the data. Press Enter to confirm. Move to the serial number. This is the license number supplied along with the package. Press Enter, specify the number and press Enter again to confirm. When all the data have been specified, press F2 to continue, as indicated at the bottom of the screen. Follow the instructions on the screen closely.

2. Specifying destination directories

The destination directories for the dBASE files and the SQL system files must now be specified. Keep in mind the DOS requirements for file names when entering path names.

- Type the following directory names: F:\PROGRAM\DBASE and press Enter.
- Press Enter to confirm the default directory for the installation of the SQL system files.

3. Entering registration information

Subsequently, a number of files are copied from the installation diskette to the destination directory. The registration of the program then takes place. (If you have dBASE IV version 2.0, this will have already taken place.)

- Enter the registration information. This consists of the name of the user, the name of the company and the registration number. This number can be found on the original documentation belonging to the dBASE package. Confirm the data entered by pressing the key combination Ctrl-End.

The rest of the installation depends on the data entered and can only continue if the appropriate registration number is specified.

4. Copying dBASE files

The installation program now ensures that all necessary files are copied to the specified directories. Insert the diskettes in the drive when requested. The diskette containing the examples may be omitted if you consider it unnecessary.

5. Specifying other users

dBASE IV can make the fullest use of the possibilities provided by Novell NetWare. For instance, dBASE registers how many users are currently working with the program at any given moment. Accordingly, it is obvious that more users than the licence permits will not be allowed access. The installation program automatically creates the \DBNETCTL.300 directory on the server harddisk for user management. The files needed for this task are stored here, such as those dealing with the registration and the number of users installed.

If several users wish to work with dBASE at the same time, the other users must be added to the file containing the licence data. This can take place either at the initial installation or at a later time. A precondition of this is that a licence for several users must be valid. This licence is assigned under the name LAN-Pack and consists exclusively of a file with the number of licences.

If, during the initial installation, you activate the *Add User* option, the ADDUSER4 program in the installation program is activated. This program places a menu on the screen which enables you to examine and alter the number of users.

If you select number 1, the program will ask you to insert the diskette with the required data in the chosen drive. Normally, this will be the network diskette from the LAN-Pack. When you have entered the name of the drive, the program reads the data stored there and alters the number of users in the DBNETCTL.300 directory. Pressing number 3 will display information about the number of installed licences.

This largely completes the installation of dBASE IV in the multi-user version. Only the settings which depend on Novell NetWare still have to be specified.

6. Specifying access rights in Novell NetWare

In order to work in the multi-user mode in dBASE IV, you must allocate the users certain access rights in the directories created during the installation. The SYSCON utility program is used to do this (see section 3.2).

The following access rights are necessary for the complete functionality of dBASE:

Directory SYS:DBNETCTL.300	Read Write File Scan
Directory SYS:DBASE	Read Write

	File Scan
	Create
	Erase
	Access Control
Directory SYS:DBASE\SQLHOME	Read
	Write
	File Scan
	Create
	Erase
	Access Control
Directory SYS:DBASE\EXAMPLE	Read
	Write
	File Scan
	Create
	Erase

These rights can be assigned more easily by placing all dBASE users in one group. Then you only need to assign the above rights to the group (see chapter 4).

7. Specifying search paths in Novell NetWare

Working with dDASE becomes more straightforward when you create a search path and logical drives. This can be done using the login scripts, for instance. In any case, it is advisable to create a search path to the dBASE directory.

Example 49:
The search path with the number 5 is to be included as a command in the system login script.

- Type the command MAP SEARCH5:=SERVER1/SYS:DBASE in the system login script (see also chapter 4).

In addition, you can make it easier by assigning logical drives to the most important directories. To do this, you can include, for instance, the following commands in the system login script:

```
MAP G:=SERVER1/SYS:DBASE
MAP H:=SERVER1/SYS:DB-DATA
MAP I:=SERVER1/SYS:DBASE\EXAMPLE
MAP J:=SERVER1/SYS:DBASE\SQLHOME
```

8. Using Novell NetWare attributes

In principle, all files which are accessible to several users must have the **Shareable** attribute. In addition, you can protect the program files against unintentional removal by allocating the Read Only attribute to them (see section 3.4).

Example 50:
dBASE programs and overlay files (extension OVL) are to receive the Read Only attribute.

- Activate succcessively the DBASE and DBNETCTL.300 directories and type the following commands there:

```
FLAG *.* S
FLAG *.COM RO
FLAG *.EXE RO
FLAG *.OVL RO
```

5.2.2 The Word 5.5 word processor

The most recent version of the word processor Word 5.5, is one of the most well-known programs in the area of word processing. This program is also suitable for application in a network and can be installed in Novell NetWare reasonably easily. Word has a graphic user interface, which means that the program must be configured to the hardware (particularly the graphic card) of the workstation upon which it is to be active. However, since quite a number of differently configured workstations exist in a network, the installation takes place in two stages. Firstly, Word is installed completely on the fileserver and subsequently the program must be installed separately for each user on each workstation where it is to be run. For this, all Word files can be stored on the fileserver. In this way, each user can install a correct version on his/her workstation, appropriately adjusted to the hardware. It is also possible to install Word on the fileserver for immediate common use. Each user then has certain files for personal use on his/her own workstation or in his/her own directory, such as drivers to operate the screen or the printer.

Storing the Word files on the fileserver.
Word is supplied on 3.5 or 5.25 inch diskettes. The first diskette contains the Setup program. Proceed as follows to store the files on the server harddisk:

1. Log in, preferably as Supervisor, on the network.
2. Activate a diskdrive and insert diskette number 1.
3. Start the installation on the fileserver by means of the command SETUP NETWORK.
4. The Setup program is then started. After indicating that Word is to be installed on a server, select the drive and the directory in which you wish to store Word.
5. The Setup program will automatically determine which drives are available on the harddisk. These appear in a window in which you can make a selection using the cursor keys and Enter. In Novell NetWare this will normally be drive F:.
6. Now specify the destination directory. The Setup program suggests reserving the selected drive and the \Word directory for the program. However, you can alter this if you wish by typing a different directory name. Setup creates the specified directory if it does not yet exist.
7. Then the program asks you to insert the diskettes in the drive, one by one. The contents of the diskette are copied to the specified directory of the selected drive. When the last diskette has been copied, the installation procedure is concluded with a message to this effect.

The figure on the following page shows the structure which has been created by copying the files to the \PROGRAM\WORD55 directory on drive F:.

```
F:\PROGRAM\WORD55>dir

 Volume in drive F is SYS
 Volume Serial Number is 18D2-B111
 Directory of F:\PROGRAM\WORD55

.              <DIR>       18-06-93    23:26
..             <DIR>       18-06-93    23:26
SETUP          <DIR>       18-06-93    23:26
PROG1          <DIR>       18-06-93    23:27
PROG2          <DIR>       18-06-93    23:28
UTIL1          <DIR>       18-06-93    23:31
THES1          <DIR>       18-06-93    23:32
PRINT1         <DIR>       18-06-93    23:34
PRINT2         <DIR>       18-06-93    23:36
LEARN1         <DIR>       18-06-93    23:39
SPELL1         <DIR>       18-06-93    23:40
OPT            <DIR>       18-06-93    23:42
SETUP    EXE      138712  12-03-93    12:00
WORD55   INF      126617  12-03-93    12:00
       12 file(s)         265329 bytes
                       84147264 bytes free

F:\PROGRAM\WORD55>_
```

Caution: No properly-functioning version has been installed as yet. The directories created here contain all files which are necessary to install properly-functioning versions of Word 5.5. on the connected workstations. To execute this, each user must activate the Setup program and install Word on his/her own workstation. Apart from the fact that Setup is started up on the fileserver, this procedure is identical to the installation of Word on a normal personal computer. The installation also resembles the installation of Word on the fileserver.

Installing Word on the fileserver for common use. Proceed as follows:

1. Start up the Setup program from the diskdrive using the SETUP command:

The process is menu-driven further; the Setup program requests information concerning the size of the installation. The following options are available for dealing with this:

2. Select option 3 from the subsequent menu: installation in a network.
3. Then select option 1: install a new version of Word.

Examples of applications for several workstations

4. Select option 1 as destination drive for the installation: the F harddisk.
5. Specify the destination directory and confirm it by pressing Enter. The Setup program suggests the following:

`F:\WORD`

This default suggestion can be altered by typing a different directory if required, for instance:

`F:\PROGRAM\WORD55`

6. Then select the country setting: UK.
7. In the subsequent menu, select the required option for the driver installation, for instance, option 2 if you wish to install all drivers. If you know which printer you are going to use, you only need to choose the corresponding driver along with option 1.
8. Now you must specify whether you wish to install the spelling program.
9. The thesaurus (book of synonyms) is installed by selecting option 1 in the following menu.
10. If you wish to install the tutorial, select option 1 in the next menu.
11. Setup will then begin to install the Word files in the specified directory. You will be asked to insert the required diskettes, one by one. During the first installation, you will be asked to specify the name of the licensee (maximum of 30 characters). This name is saved and displayed each time the program is activated. When you have specified the name and have pressed Enter, you will have to confirm the name once again. The rest of the files will then be copied, creating a well-functioning version of Word.

Adjusting Word to the user requirements. Word contains a speller, a thesaurus and a tutorial. These program components are almost always included in the installation on a stand-alone personal computer. However, the installation on a network takes place separately, since the files are stored on the diskettes in compressed form and have to be unpacked.

■ To do this, activate the Setup program without parameters.

Adjusting Word to the workstation hardware. Subsequently, Word has to be installed separately for each user. Proceed as follows:

1. Give the command SETUP USER. The Setup program now adapts Word to the hardware in use (monitor, keyboard, mouse, printer).
2. You probably wish to install Word on a harddisk. Place the cursor on the first option and confirm this selection by pressing Enter.
3. The Setup program provides a list of all harddisks available in the system. It is possible to select a local disk (C or D), but you can also select a server harddisk.
4. Then specify the directory in which Word is to be installed. Normally, Setup specifies the WORD directory on the drive which you have registered. If you selected drive F: on the server harddisk, you must install Word in your home directory, for instance F:\USER\VESPUCCI\WORD. The name of the directory should be specified in the same way as in the installation on the server, and confirmed by pressing Enter.
5. If you start up Setup from the corresponding workstation, Setup recognizes the configuration used. You still have to select the country and keyboard settings by means of the cursor keys and Enter.
6. An important element of the installation is the selection of the proper printer drivers; these are responsible for the correct output of data on the printer. In general, drivers are installed for the printers which are accessible to the workstation (local and network printers). In the installation of the printer drivers, you may choose from an extensive list of drivers for a large number of different printer models.

Examples of applications for several workstations

By typing the first letter of the name of your printer, you can speed up the printer driver selection process considerably. For instance, if you press the letter H, the cursor jumps to the first printer whose name begins with an H. At the beginning of the printer driver list, there is the option *Continue Setup*. Press Home to switch to this option.

7. The following steps in the installation process are:

   ➤ adapting the mouse driver
   ➤ modifying the Word settings
   ➤ adapting the system files.

The last step is very important. If you install Word on a local harddisk, you can have Setup make the adjustments. However, if your version is located in your home directory on the server harddisk, or if you start up the program in the network via your workstation, these adjustments must be included in the login script.

When the installation has been completed correctly, a user directory will look something like this:

```
F:\USER\VESPUCCI\WORD>dir

 Volume in drive F is SYS
 Volume Serial Number is 18D2-B111
 Directory of F:\USER\VESPUCCI\WORD

EPLQ     DBS     17589 12-03-93   12:00                    (1)
MW       INI       257 18-06-93   23:48                    (2)
SCREEN   UID     16081 18-06-93   23:47                    (3)
UPDAT-UK CMP         9 21-06-93   22:16                    (4)
STANDARD TBS      4096 21-06-93   22:16                    (5)
NETINFO  MOI         2 21-06-93   21:54                    (6)
NORMAL   OPM      1024 21-06-93   22:16                    (7)
SPECIALS CMP        13 21-06-93   21:58                    (8)
        8 file(s)       18436 bytes
                     84769792 bytes free

F:\USER\VESPUCCI\WORD>_
```

(1) Printer driver for an Epson printer in the LQ series.
(2) Initialisation file with data concerning the Word settings; this is rewritten after each correct shutdown of Word.
(3) Screen driver.
(4) Special dictionary for this user.
(5) Special file with text fragments for this user.
(6) Initialization file created by Setup.
(7) Special layout profiles for this user.
(8) Special dictionary for this user.

Adapting the system environment to Word. In order to enable the program to run properly in the network, adjustments have to be made in the AUTOEXEC.BAT file. A directory is first added to the search path in order to enable the addressing of the directory containing the Word files on the file server. In addition, a DOS environment variable is specified which indicates the directory from which the user activates Word.

In our example, the commands appear as follows:

```
PATH F:\PROGRAM\WORD55
```

and

```
SET MWSNET55=F:\USER\VESPUCCI\WORD
```

These data can now be easily adopted in the login script (see chapter 4). If all users in the network are working with Word, it is advisable to alter the system login script. Otherwise the login script of the relevant user should be modified.

Example 51:
The commands should be entered in the system login script (the number for the search path is randomly chosen):

```
MAP S8:=SERVER1/SYS:\PROGRAM\WORD55
DOS SET MWSNET55="F:\USER\%LOGIN_NAME\WORD"
```

By means of the %LOGIN_NAME variable (capitals must be used) the MWSNET55 environment variable is always assigned the correct value for each user.

Note: In the login script, the part behind the equals sign in the DOS SET line must be placed between inverted commas, in contrast to the DOS command SET!

You can also include the same data in the user login script. However, it is better to use the MAP INSERT command instead of MAP, in order to prevent other search paths being replaced unintentionally.

Example 52:
The commands are to be included in the user login script as follows (Search 16 is chosen because there is a maximum of 16 search directories):

```
MAP INS S16:=SERVER1/SYS:\PROGRAM\WORD55
DOS SET MWSNET55="F:\USER\%LOGIN_NAME\WORD"
```

Specifying file attributes. In order to make the files meant for common usage accessible to several users they must be equipped with the Shareable attribute.

- To do this, switch to the directory containing the files for common usage and specify the attribute (in the most simple case) using the command:

```
FLAG * S
```

Confirm this command using Enter.

The attribute will now be placed at all files in this directory. It is also possible to place the attribute for only a certain group of files by specifying the common extension of these files along with the command (see section 3.4).

If the files have to be protected against accidental removal, place the Read Only attribute:

```
FLAG * RO
```

Caution: This attribute should only be allocated to files to which nothing may be written. All Word files in the common directory on the server harddisk which are not meant for one particular user should be equipped with the Shareable and Read Only attributes.

Assigning access rights to users. Only a user with the appropriate access rights is permitted to work with a program. If access rights have been assigned for the SERVER1/SYS:\PROGRAM directory, users with access rights to this program are also entitled to access to the WORD55 subdirectory. These users are therefore able to work with the Word program.

If that is not the case, users or user groups must obtain access rights from the system manager using the SYSCON or FILER utility programs (see chapters 3 and 4). In the common directories, the users must receive the F (File Scan) and RW (Read Write) rights in any case. In the home directories containing specific files and work data for the user, more extensive rights must be assigned, such as C(reate), E(rase) and M(odify) (see section 3.2).

5.2.3 The Windows graphical user interface

The installation of Windows 3.1 takes place in a way similar to that of Word. Firstly, all Windows files must be copied to the server harddisk and then configuration files must be created to fit the requirements of the particular users.

Copying Windows files to the fileserver. The Windows files are stored on the diskettes in compressed form. In order to be able to use Windows on all required workstations, all files should be decompressed and copied to the fileserver. Proceed as follows:

1. Log in as the Supervisor on the network.

Examples of applications for several workstations 157

2. Switch to the diskdrive from which you wish to start up the installation, and insert the first diskette. Activate the Setup program using the SETUP /A command.
3. This starts the installation for network management. Setup asks you to specify a user or user group name and a company name. You can display this later, for instance, by clicking on the Info button. Subsequently, you only have to specify a destination directory. In our example, that would be F:\PROGRAM\WINDOWS. Then insert the appropriate diskettes in the drive when requested. Setup allocates the RO attribute to the diskettes which have been copied and decompressed so that it is impossible to delete the files unintentionally, and simultaneous addressing of the files by several users presents no problems.

Creating Windows files for certain users. All files necessary to fulfil the particular requirements of the work environment of the individual user should be created. To do this, the required files are copied to the user working directory from where he/she will activate Windows. This can be either the user home directory (in workstations without a harddisk or diskdrive, for instance) or a directory on the harddisk of the user workstation.

1. Before beginning the installation, you must create a search drive using the command:

MAP INS S16:=SERVER1/SYS:\PROGRAM\WINDOWS

2. Now switch to the directory which is to contain the special user files for Windows and specify there the command SETUP/N.

This activates the Setup program to install Windows for a certain user. You may choose between a full and a custom installation. Generally, the former is chosen.

Setup then checks the hardware configuration. If you are using an older version of the Novell NetWare utility program IPX, Setup will ask you to re-create IPX using the IPX.OBJ file and the WSGEN utility program which are supplied along with the package. This is strongly recommended otherwise problems may arise in the 386 enhanced mode.

The directory containing the specific user files for Windows could look something like this:

```
Directory of F:\USER\UESPUCCI\WIN3

WIN       INI         3497 30-06-93   10:12                  (1)
WIN       COM        45664 30-06-93   10:07
SYSTEM    INI         1622 30-06-93   10:12
MOUSE     INI           24 30-06-93   10:07
CONTROL   INI         3602 30-06-93   10:10
WINVER    EXE         4256 10-03-93    3:10
_DEFAULT  PIF          545 30-06-93   10:08                  (2)
DOSPRMPT  PIF          545 30-06-93   10:08
PROGMAN   INI          294 30-06-93   10:12
MAIN      GRP         5844 30-06-93   10:12                  (3)
REG       DAT         2588 30-06-93   10:08
ACCESSOR  GRP         9439 30-06-93   10:12
GAMES     GRP         1479 30-06-93   10:12
STARTUP   GRP           46 30-06-93   10:12
QBASIC    PIF          545 30-06-93   10:12
MP        PIF          545 30-06-93   10:12
WORD      PIF          545 30-06-93   10:12
XTG       PIF          545 30-06-93   10:12
DBASE     PIF          545 30-06-93   10:12
DBASE00   PIF          545 30-06-93   10:12
TEMP      <DIR>             14-02-93   15:27                 (4)
       24 file(s)          98553 bytes
                        83317760 bytes free
```

(1) All files with the INI extension are initialization files which are required by Windows for its own configuration. The two most important configuration files are WIN.INI and SYSTEM.INI. You can gain more information about a network installation in the NETWORK.WRI file which is located in the Windows directory after Windows has been installed.

(2) All files with the PIF extension are files containing specific information about a program (*Program Information File*). These ensure that programs can be activated in Windows under optimum conditions. In addition to the actual program file name, they contain information about how the program should use system facilities such as working memory, monitor, printer port and startup directory.

(3) All files with the GRP extension contain data concerning program groups which have been made by Setup or the user.

(4) The TEMP directory is very important, especially in the case of workstations without diskdrives. The Windows Print Manager stores the print commands in a print queue which is stored in the TEMP directory, an environment variable. If TEMP has not been installed, the root directory of drive C: is used for this function. This means that it is not possible to print in the case of workstations without a harddisk. Therefore a TEMP directory should be created for each Windows user and the TEMP environment variable must be adapted accordingly.

Adapting the system environment to Windows. In order to ensure optimum working of the program, alterations should be made in the AUTOEXEC.BAT and CONFIG.SYS files.

Note: Modifications to the CONFIG.SYS file should cause no problems. However, if you are using Windows 3.1 in conjunction with MS-DOS 5.0 on a workstation with a 386 processor, problems may arise when you address the Upper Memory Area if the workstation has no diskdrive of its own and is active in the 386 enhanced mode. In that case, you must use the EMM386.EXE driver and ensure that this can be loaded again if required. This is possible from any random directory if you include the following command in the CONFIG.SYS file (assuming that EMM386.EXE is located in the F:\PUBLIC directory):

```
DEVICEHIGH=EMM386.EXE/Y=F:\PUB-
LIC\EMM386.EXE NOEMS
```

The directory in which EMM386.EXE is stored should be accessible to all users. The PUBLIC directory or a subdirectory of this, containing the DOS version programs, could be used.

In the AUTOEXEC.BAT file, a search path is defined making accessible the directory on the fileserver containing the complete Windows version. In addition, a DOS environment variable is defined indicating the directory in which the Print Manager places the print queue. The corresponding commands look something like this:

```
PATH F:\PROGRAM\WINDOWS
```
and
```
SET TEMP=F:\USER\VESPUCCI\WIN3\TEMP
```

It is possible to include these data in the login script just as with Word. If all users in the network are working with Windows, it is advisable to alter the system login script. Otherwise the login script of the relevant user should be altered.

The commands should be adopted into the system login script as follows (the number for the search path has been chosen at random):

```
MAP S9:=SERVER1/SYS:\PROGRAM\WINDOWS
DOS SET TEMP="F:\USER\%LOGIN_NAME\WIN3\TEMP"
```

By means of the %LOGIN_NAME variable (capitals must be used) the TEMP environment variable is always assigned the proper value for each user.

The same data can also be adopted into the user login script. It is then preferable to use the MAP INSERT command instead of MAP, to prevent other search paths being replaced unintentionally.

The commands can be adopted into the user login scripts as follows (Search 16 is chosen since there are a maximum of 16 search directories possible):

```
MAP INS S16:=SERVER1/SYS:\PROGRAM\WINDOWS
DOS SET TEMP="F:\USER\%LOGIN_NAME\WIN3\TEMP"
```

Specifying file attributes. In order to make files accessible for common usage, they must be assigned the Shareable attribute.

- To do this, switch to the directory containing the files for common usage and place the attribute (in the most straightforward case) using the command:

```
FLAG * S
```

Confirm this command using Enter. Then all files in this directory are assigned the Shareable attribute.

Assigning access right to users. A program may only be used by a user possessing the appropriate rights. If rights have been assigned for the SERVER/SYS:\PROGRAM directory, the WINDOWS subdirectory is also accessible to users with access rights to this directory. These users are thus able to work with the Windows program.

If that is not the case, the users or user groups must obtain access rights by means of one of the SYSCON or FILER utility programs (see chapters 3 and 4). In the common directories, the users must receive at least the F (File Scan) and RW (Read Write) rights. In the home directories containing user-specific files and work data, more extensive rights should be allocated, such as C(reate), E(rase) and M(odify) (see section 3.2).

5.3 Multiplan as an example of a network application

Multiplan (version 4.02) is a widely-used spreadsheet program. It is characterized by easy operation and it can produce very attractive results on paper if the proper printer drivers are installed. Multiplan is installed by means of the Setup program just as other Microsoft products.

Installing Multiplan on the server harddisk. Proceed as follows:

1. Log in on the network as the Supervisor.
2. Insert the installation diskette in the diskdrive and activate the installation program using the SETUP command.
3. The screen displays some information at first and then the option of installing Multiplan on a harddisk, a diskette system or a network is presented. Select the network installation and confirm that this refers to a new installation.
4. The Setup program first checks how many harddisks are present in the system. Select the F: harddisk which appears in the list.
5. Then specify the directory in which Multiplan is to be installed. Setup proposes F:\MP. Alter this if required. In our example the directory is altered to F:\PROGRAM\MP.
6. Now determine whether you wish to install all or only the selected printer drivers. Since these drivers do not occupy a disproportionally large amount of space, we shall opt for the installation of all printer drivers.
7. Then the Setup program will ask you to insert certain diskettes in the drive. The contents of these diskettes are copied to the specified directory. Setup indicates which file is currently in the process of being copied.
8. When everything has been copied, Setup states that the program has been installed on the fileserver. However, there have been no special adjustments as yet to meet the requirements of a particular workstation.

Installing Multiplan on a workstation. Proceed as follows:

1. Switch to the directory in which Multiplan has been installed. In our example, that is the F:\PROGRAM\MP directory. Switch using the command:

Multiplan as an example of a network application 163

```
CD\PROGRAM\MP
```

Activate Setup along with the directory in which your user directories are located. In our example, the command is as follows:

```
SETUP USER
```

3. Setup is now activated to install Multiplan on a workstation. During this process, alterations are made in relation to the graphic card, the printer and the mouse to be used. Select the option for installation on a harddisk from the installation menu. A list of available harddisks will subsequently appear. Select the harddisk where the workstation-oriented version of Multiplan is to be installed. If you are working with a local harddisk, this will probably be drive C:. If your workstation has no harddisk, select the server harddisk F:.
4. Then select the option to install a new version of Multiplan and specify the directory in which Multiplan is to be installed. In our example, that is the directory F:\USER\SCOTT\MP.
5. Now select the card which is used on your workstation from the list of graphic cards.
6. Now select the appropriate driver for the connected printer. Setup displays all available drivers in a list. You may select one or more drivers from this list. If you copied all the printer drivers to the fileserver during the basic installation, you will not require the Multiplan diskettes further. Select the relevant drivers using the cursor keys and confirm the selection by pressing Enter.
7. The Setup program now suggests modifying the mouse driver, the CONFIG.SYS configuration file and the AUTOEXEC.BAT starting up file. In this process, Setup regulates the activation of the mouse driver, specifies the maximum number of opened files (FILES=n), defines a search path (PATH=...) and sets the MPVID environment variable (SET MPVID=*screen driver*) if special graphic cards are being used. If you have installed Multi-

plan on a local harddisk, you can allow Setup to perform these alterations. The old files are written to files of the same name with the extension OLD. Otherwise you must supplement the login script with the corresponding commands.

Adapting the system environment for Multiplan. In the case of Multiplan, it is necessary to supplement the login script with the relevant search path and, if required, the definition of the DOS environment variable for the graphic card (see also chapter 4). For instance, the following commands may be specified (the number of the search path has been chosen at random):

```
MAP INS S9:=SERVER1/SYS:\PROGRAM\MP
DOS SET MPVIDM="F:\USER\%LOGIN_NAME\PM\ATT.VID"
```

Setting file attributes. In order to make files which are meant for common-usage actually accessible to several users, the Shareable attribute should be set.

■ Switch to the directory containing the shareable files and place the attribute using the command:

```
FLAG * S
```

Confirm this command by pressing Enter.

This assigns the attribute to all the files in the directory. It is also possible to assign the attribute to only a selected group of files by specifying the common extension of these files along with the command (see section 3.4).

If the files are to be protected against unintentional deletion, you can also place the Read Only attribute:

```
FLAG * RO
```

Note: This attribute should only be assigned to files which may not be altered. All Multiplan files in the common directory on the server harddisk which are not meant for a particular user, should be equipped with the Shareable and Read Only attributes.

Assigning access rights to users. These rights correspond to those allocated in the Word and Windows programs. Refer to these descriptions for the appropriate information (sections 5.2.2 and 5.2.3).

6 Printing

6.1 Printers in the network

All common printers and plotters can be used in a Novell network if they can be linked to a personal computer by means of a serial or parallel port.

Printers with a parallel port are faster than printers with a serial port because they process data one character at a time (in the case of 8 bit transmission). Printers with a serial port process the data one bit at a time. A disadvantage of printers with a parallel port is that they can only be connected by means of relatively short cables (a few metres long), while printers with a serial port also work excellently using longer cables.

In addition to these differences, the quality and the capacity of the printers in a network also play a large role. If several or all users in the network have to print their data on the printer, severe demands are placed on the speed and quality of the printer. A local printer, upon which only one user is working, need not be so powerful. The following aspects play a part in determining the printer capacities:

- in the case of matrix printers, the printing speed in characters per second and the number of pins in the printhead,
- in the case of laser printers, the printing speed in pages per minute, the resolution in dpi (*dots per inch*) and the PostScript quality.

A printer which is connected to your workstation can be used in the same way as if it were connected to a stand-alone personal computer. However, this can only be done with printers which are connected to the appropriate ports on your computer. We refer to these printers as *local printers*.

A printer is accessible to several users by means of the network operating system. A network user can direct print commands from his/her workstation to a network printer. Novell NetWare ensures that no *print job* is lost. The print command is submitted to the fileserver or to a special print server and placed in a *print queue* before the server sends the command to the network printer. This print queue is actually a subdirectory of the fileserver in the SYS:SYSTEM directory. The print command is stored there as a file until the required network printer is ready to execute the command.

In Novell NetWare, a print command contains the information as to which file via which server is to be directed to which printer. Additional information may consist of the number of printout copies required and the desired form. This information can be specified using the SYSCON utility program.

Network printers can be connected to the following devices:

- the fileserver,
- personal computers with a local harddisk which are exclusively used as print servers and are therefore not active as workstations (so-called *dedicated print servers*),
- selected workstations from which the printer operation must take place by means of a special utility program.

Printers connected to a fileserver or a print server are called *local network printers*. Printers which are connected to workstations in a network are called *remote network printers*.

6.2 Printing from applications on a network printer

When working with most applications on your workstation such as word processors, spreadsheets, database programs, graphic applications, administration packages etc., it does not make much difference whether you print the data on a local printer or on a network printer. You just activate the print function as normal and the network operating system ensures that the data are sent to the required (network) printer.

Activating the print direction (CAPTURE). If you are working with applications which support the print queues directly, the system manager will have specified, during the installation, that your print commands will be placed in the proper print queue and then directed to the correct printer. If the program does not support this facility, the data to be printed are directed to the printer via the port which was specified during installation (normally LPT1). Since this is generally a local printer, a process must ensure that the data to be printed are directed to a network printer. Novell NetWare has the following command to bring this about:

```
CAPTURE [parameters ...]
```

CAPTURE   All local parallel ports of a workstation can be directed to a network printer. This is not possible with serial ports unless you acquire special hard- and software to do this. Novell NetWare indicates the redirection by means of the message *Device LPT1: set to local mode*.

ENDCAP   This command terminates the redirection. Each user possessing the relevant rights can redirect the print data from his/her computer to a chosen print queue, at the same time determining several features of the printout. The following parameters enable you to do this; you must specify at least the capitals indicated.

SHow

The current status of the local parallel printer ports is displayed. The following information is shown:

- which ports are redirected,

- whether data are being directed to a network printer or written to a file,
- which CAPTURE options are active.

SHow only gives information about the CAPTURE status. It cannot be used to make modifications and cannot be used with other parameters.

NOTIfy
This parameter enables you to determine whether a message is to be displayed when the data have been printed. Normally, NOTIfy is not active. If this parameter is active, a message is shown at the bottom of the screen when the print procedure has been completed. It looks something like this:

```
>> LPT1 CATCH printed on PRINTER008/1      (CTRL-ENTER to clear).
```

In the example above, printing has taken place from an application (a word processor for instance); CATCH was the name of the print instruction.

Note: If you have specified the command CASTOFF so that no messages are to be shown on the screen, no messages will be displayed even if NOTIfy is active.

NoNOTIfy
NoNOTIfy switches off the message option activated by either NOTIfy or by the specifications in the printer configuration (see PRINTCON).

TImeout=*n*
This parameter enables you to determine how many seconds should elapse between the time Novell NetWare receives a print command and the time it should begin printing. The *n* represents a value between 1 and 1000. The TImeout parameter works when NoAutoendcap is activated. This directs all print commands to the same network file which is only printed *n* seconds after the last output via the printer port has taken place. If the

value specified by TImeout is too small, problems may occur in printing: files may be only partially printed out, or even not at all. If that case, you will have to increase the value. Normally the TImeout option is inactive; the value is then set to 0.

Autoendcap

By means of this parameter, each print command received from a workstation is placed in a separate queue file so that each command is actually treated and processed as a separate print command. Autoendcap does not terminate the redirection produced by CAPTURE, although the name seems to indicate this. The effect of Autoendcap is that a new CAPTURE file is automatically created when you activate a program. When you quit the program, the CAPTURE file is automatically closed and printed. Normally, Autoendcap is activated.

NoAutoendcap

This parameter ensures that various print commands are stored in one queue file and are therefore printed together. This file is only closed and directed to the network printer if no other print commands are sent within the time limit specified by TImeout. If the value of TImeout is smaller than one second, Novell NetWare will wait constantly for print commands being included in a queue file. In that case, printing must be started by means of the ENDCAP command when the application has been closed.

Local=*n*

This determines which local parallel port is to be redirected. 1, 2 or 3 should be entered for *n*. The default setting is 1.

Server=*fileserver*

This parameter determines to which fileserver (specify the name) the print command should be redirected. If you do not specify this parameter, the fileserver where you are logged in is taken to be the destination.

Queue=
This parameter determines the queue in which your print command is placed. Accordingly, it is possible to implement the print command on a certain printer.

CReate-*server\path\file*
Using this parameter, you can redirect the print commands to a file, but only on a network drive. A file created in this way can be printed later, for instance, using the NPRINT or PCONSOLE commands.

Job=*print configuration*
This determines which print configuration, defined using the PRINTCON utility program, is to be used for printing. If you do not specify anything here, the default print configuration or the configuration first defined using PRINTCON will be used.

Form=*form* or *n*
This determines upon which form the print command should be printed. Forms are defined by the system manager using the PRINTDEF utility program. You should specify either the name or the number of the form. The form number 0 is the default setting in Novell NetWare.

Copies=*n*
If you wish to print several copies, specify the required number using this parameter. The valid range is between 1 and 999. The default setting is C=1.

NoTabs
Using this parameter, all tabs are directed to the printer unchanged. This option is applied when a file which has been created using, for instance, a word processor should be printed exactly as it has been laid out. In addition, this setting should be used if graphic problems occur during printing. NoTabs is the most well-used default setting (see PRINTCON), since all control characters are directed to the printer unchanged.

NoBanner
Use this parameter to prevent Novell NetWare printing an introductory page (*banner*) with the print command. A banner displays information about the user, the file name, the directory, the print queue, the print server, the date and time.

NAMe=*name*
Novell NetWare places the name of the user on the first seven lines of the banner. By applying the NAMe parameter, you can ensure that a text of maximum twelve characters is displayed instead of the user name. This text may not include any spaces.

Banner=*name*
Novell NetWare can display an additional text on the bottom seven lines of the banner. The Banner parameter ensures that a text of maximum twelve characters is printed. This text may contain no spaces.

FormFeed
This parameter ensures that the paper is moved on at the conclusion of the print procedure. The following print command can then begin on a new page. This is the default setting.

NoFormFeed
If this option is activated, the paper is not moved on at the end of a print procedure. This may be useful when using applications which perform paper moving functions themselves. This prevents blank pages being produced.

Keep
This parameter prints data which is not yet complete or directs it to a file. This may occur, for instance, if the workstation is disabled during printing or the link to the fileserver is severed owing to a power failure.

Example 53:
The data to be printed are to be directed from the workstation to the network printer. This is possible by giving the following command:

Printing from applications on a network printer

CAPTURE

A message appears on the screen, like that shown below:

```
Device LPT1: re-routed to queue PQ_R008 on server SERVER1
```

This message indicates that all print output is directed from this moment onwards from port LPT1 to the queue PQ_R008 on the SERVER1 fileserver. In this case, PQ_R008 is the queue which was first defined using PCONSOLE.

Example 54:
Information is to be displayed about the current CAPTURE status. Give the following command along with the SHow parameter:

CAPTURE SH

Note: A parameter added to the CAPTURE command must be separated from the command by a space. A new CAPTURE command deletes the previous one, with the exception of the command CAPTURE S.

If CAPTURE is not active, the following message appears:

```
LPT1:   Capturing Is Not Currently Active.
LPT2:   Capturing Is Not Currently Active.
LPT3:   Capturing Is Not Currently Active.
```

If CAPTURE is active, the message may appear as follows:

```
LPT1:   Capturing data to server SERVER1 queue PQ_R008.
        User will not be notified after the files are printed.
        Capture Defaults:Enabled    Automatic Endcap:Disabled
        Banner   :<None>            Form Feed      :Yes
        Copies   :1                 Tabs           :No conversion
        Form     :0                 Timeout Count  :30 seconds
LPT2:   Capturing Is Not Currently Active.
LPT3:   Capturing Is Not Currently Active.
```

Example 55:
All three local parallel ports of a workstation are to be redirected to different queues: LPT1 to the DRAFT queue, LPT2 to the HLPJET queue and LPT3 to the PSTSCRPT queue. This enables you, depending on the application in use, to print on different printers by selecting the printer port.

To do this, you must execute the CAPTURE command three times, specifying the port to be redirected and the required queue as parameters. Novell NetWare accepts these commands as:

```
CAPTURE LPT1 TO QUEUE DRAFT
CAPTURE LPT2 TO QUEUE HPLJET
CAPTURE LPT3 TO QUEUE PSTSCRPT
```

or:

```
CAPTURE L=1 Q=DRAFT
CAPTURE L=2 Q=HPLJET
CAPTURE L=3 Q=PSTSCRPT
```

The CAPTURE SHow command then confirms that all three ports are redirected.

Example 56:
The current contents of the screen are to be printed on the network printer (a *screendump* is to be made). Proceed as follows:

- Give the CAPTURE command.
- Ensure that the screen displays that which you wish to have printed.
- Press the PrintScreen key or the Shift-PrintScreen key combination.
- Give the ENDCAP command to start the printing procedure.

Note: If your computer freezes during this procedure because of a missing printer installation, you must include the command LOCAL PRINTERS = 0 in the

Printing from applications on a network printer 175

SHELL.CFG file. The file must be located on the start up diskette. If you start up the workstation via the network, the network manager must make the alterations to the start up file.

Example 57:
In order to edit a file later, various screen dumps are to be made. Proceed as follows:

- Give the CAPTURE command along with the parameters CReate and NoAutoendcap. The directory of the destination file must be added to the CReate parameter.

```
F:\USER\DV\SCREEN01.TXT:
CAPTURE CR=F:\USER\DV\SCREEN01.TXT NA
```

- Ensure that the screen displays that which you wish to save and start up the saving procedure in the SCREEN01.TXT file by pressing the PrintScreen key or the Shift-PrintScreen key combination.
- Give the ENDCAP command to terminate the redirection to the SCREEN01.TXT file. The saved screen contents are now available for further editing.

Proceed in the same way when, for instance, you are using various applications and you wish to save data from these applications in one file.

Example 58:
Five copies of a document are to be printed on form 3 from a word processor via the HPLJET queue. In addition, a banner displaying the large heading: REGULATIONS is to be created. Since the network printers are in intensive use, Novell NetWare should send a message when the print procedure has been completed.

Proceed as follows:

- Give the CAPTURE command with the parameters Q, F, B, TI, C, NOTI and NA:

```
CAPTURE Q=HPLJET B=REGULATIONS F=3 TI=20
COPIES=3 NOTI NA
```

- Activate the word processor, create the text and start the print procedure.

All the print jobs are placed in a file in the HPLJET queue. The file is closed and allowed to be printed if no new print command is given within the TImeout limit of 20 seconds. Novell NetWare indicates when the print command has been sent to the printer. However, the specification of a TImeout does not mean that your print command will be printed immediately after the specified time has expired. The time of printing depends on the position of your command in the print queue. When the document has been printed, the following (or similar) message will appear on the bottom line of the screen.

```
>> LPT1 CATCH printed on LASERJET    (CTRL-ENTER to clear)
```

Example 59:
Various texts are to be placed in a queue and printed from there.

- To do this, you must alter the command shown in the previous example as follows:

```
CAPTURE Q=HPLJET B=REGULATIONS F=3 TI=0
COPIES=3 NOTI NA
```

Since TImeout is now set to 0 and Autoendcap is inactive, Novell NetWare waits indefinitely before closing the queue file and starting the print procedure. This means that you must give the ENDCAP command to start printing.

Example 60:
The CAPTURE default setting is to be automatically activated each time you log in on the network. Accordingly, it is advisable to adopt the CAPTURE command in your loginscript. Proceed as follows:

Printing from applications on a network printer 177

- Start the SYSCON utility program using the SYSCON command.
- Select the *User Information* option from the *Available Topics* main menu. A list of *User Names* appears at the left-hand side of the screen.
- Select your user ID. Type the first letters of the ID; in general you only have to press Enter to then continue.
- Select the *Login Script* option from the *User Information* menu.
- Supplement your personal login script with the required CAPTURE command, such as:

    ```
    CAPTURE Q=HPLJET NB NOTI
    ```

    This command intializes the redirection from the first parallel port to the HPLJET print queue, suppresses the printing of the banner (NB) and informs you when the command has been executed.
- Conclude the alteration by pressing the Esc key and select the *Yes* option in the *Save Changes* window. The alterations are now saved.
- Press Alt-F10 and confirm the *Yes* default setting in the *Exit* window by pressing Enter.
- Log out and then in again in order to activate the CAPTURE command immediately.

The CAPTURE command which you have defined will be activated each time you log in on the network, regardless of the workstation at which this takes place. The CAPTURE command is connected to you via your personal login script.

If however, this command should not be connected to the user in person but to the workstation (due to a certain hardware configuration for instance), the command should be included in the AUTOEXEC.BAT start-up file on the start-up diskette of the relevant workstation. The command is thus always activated when the workstation is started up in the network, regardless of the user.

Ending the print redirection. The print redirection is always ended when you log out of the network or when you sever the connection to the network in another way. However, if you remain in the network and you wish to discontinue the print redirection or direct the data to a network printer, you should give the following command:

```
ENDCAP [parameters...]
```

ENDCAP   Give the command without parameters when you wish to end the redirection from the LPT1 local parallel port.

parameter   However, if you wish to end the redirection from LPT2 or prevent all data in the print queue being printed, you must make use of the parameters listed below. You must specify at least the letters shown in capitals.

Local=*n*

Replace *n* with the number of the parallel port from which the redirection is to be ended. You may also specify the name of the port instead of the equals sign and a number. The commands ENDCAP L=2 and ENDCAP LPT2 have an identical effect. Both end the redirection from the second local parallel port.

ALL

The redirection from all local parallel ports is ended.

Cancel

The redirection from the first local parallel port is ended. If there are still data in the print queue, these will be removed; nothing will be printed.

CancelLocal=*n*

The redirection of a specified port is ended; the corresponding data are removed.

CancelAll

The redirection of all local parallel ports is ended. If

there are still data in the print queue, these will be removed; nothing will be printed.

Example 61:
The redirection from parallel port 3 is to be ended and all data in the print queue are to be removed. Proceed as follows:

```
ENDCAP CL=3
```

Novell NetWare reacts as follows:

```
Device LPT3: set to local mode.
Spooled data has been discarded.
```

Port LPT3 is reset to the local mode. Data in the print queue are removed.

Sending print commands without activating an application. If you wish to print data which are already available in file form, you can use the Novell NetWare utility program NPRINT. No output redirection need be specified for this program.

Example 62:
The PASORD.DOC file in the \USER\DV\TXT directory is to be printed. Give the following command:

```
NPRINT \USER\DV\TXT\PASORD.DOC
```

After a few moments, confirmation of the print command is given in the form of the following (or a similar) message:

```
Queuing data to Server SERVER1, Queue PQ_R008
SERVER1/SYS: USER\DV\TXT
     Queuing file PASORD.DOC
```

This message indicates that the PASORD.DOC file has been directed to the PQ_R008 print queue on the SERVER1 fileserver.

This simple command should be sufficient in the majority of cases. However, if this command alone is not sufficient, it is possible to add parameters for a more extensive configuration. The list below displays all parameters which, in conjunction with the NPRINT command, produce an effect similar to that when applied along with the CAPTURE command.

- NOTIfy
- NoNOTIfy
- Queue=
- Job=
- Form=
- Copies=*n*
- Tabs=*n*
- NoTabs
- NoBanner
- NAMe=*name*
- Banner=*name*
- FormFeed
- NoFormFeed

In addition, the following parameters may be applied:

PrintServer=
Specify the name of the required print server in order to direct your print command to the appropriate print server.

Server=
Normally, the data of a print command are directed to the fileserver on which the user is logged in. If printing has to take place via a different fileserver, the name of the fileserver must be specified along with the Server parameter.

Delete
If this parameter is applied, the file is deleted after printing. Therefore apply this parameter with care.

Printing from applications on a network printer 181

Example 63:
Two documents have been created using the Word word processor. Instead of being directed to the printer, they were redirected to the DOC_PRT1.TXT and DOC_PRT2.TXT files in order to be printed via the HPLJET print queue. When printed, the banner should contain a heading with the text 'PERSONAL'. A search path has been created to the directory in which the file is located by means of the MAP command. The task is executed as follows using the command:

```
NPRINT DOC_PRT1.TXT,DOC_PRT2.TXT B=PERSONAL
Q=HPLJET NT
```

A message similar to the following appears on the screen:

```
Queuing data to Server SERVER1, Queue HPLJET
SERVER1/SYS:USER\DV\TXT
     Queuing file DOC_PRT1.TXT
     Queuing file DOC_PRT2.TXT
```

The NT (NoTabs) option is applied because the files have been created using a program which has its own printer driver with specific printer codes. Just to be sure, it is advisable to display this kind of file by means of the DOS command TYPE. The files are directed to the SERVER1 fileserver where they are included in the HPLJET print queue. The files in question were located in the SERVER1/SYS:USER\DV\TXT directory.

Checking and modifying parameters in print commands. Sometimes network printers are being used intensively, which means that your print commands cannot be executed straight away. It is therefore convenient to be aware of the current printing situation so that you can take this into account when working.

- To do this, activate the PCONSOLE utility program. The opening screen displays the *Available Options* main menu.
- Select the *Print Queue Information* option. A window

appears at the left-hand side of the screen showing all print queues in alphabetical order.
- Select the queue containing the data you sent by highlighting it using the cursor keys. Novell NetWare opens a window containing the *Print Queue Information* menu on the right-hand side of the screen.
- Select the first option, *Current Print Job Entries*. The required overview of the print queue is then displayed.

The figure below shows an example of this kind of overview:

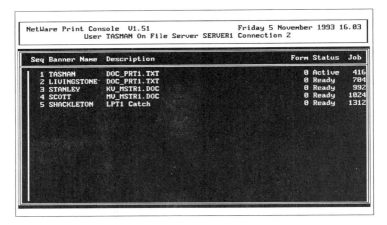

This display indicates that the queue currently contains five print jobs. The first four are to be printed using the NPRINT utility program or an application which supports print queues. This is indicated by the fact that the file names are shown. The fifth print job is the result of a redirection using the CAPTURE command.

In the *Banner* column, the text specified using the NAME parameter is shown. If nothing has been specified here, the name is shown under which the user logged in.

In the *Form* column, the number of the form is shown upon which the printout is to take place. The *Status* column displays the word *Active* if the print server is currently dealing with that job, the word *Ready* if the command has been passed on for processing, *Waiting* if the job has not yet been passed on and is to be be dealt with later and *Held* if the print process has been discontinued by the user or the operator. The *Job* column shows a number assigned by Novell NetWare.

If you wish to gain more extensive information concerning a certain print job, place the cursor on that job and press Enter. In the *Print Queue Entry Information* window which then appears, all information about the print job is shown which is needed by Novell NetWare to print the document. An example is given below:

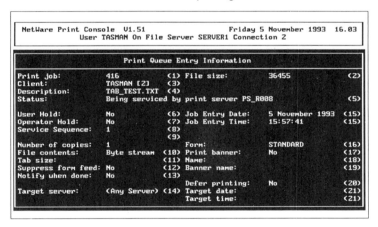

(1) The print job number.
(2) Size in bytes of the file to be printed.
(3) Name (user ID) of the person giving the command; the number of the logical connection to the fileserver is shown between brackets.
(4) The file name (in the case of NPRINT or an application supporting print queues) or the source of the print command (redirection of a printer port - CAPTURE).
(5) The current status of the command: *Being serviced, Ready to be serviced, Waiting for Target Ex-*

ecution Date and Time, User/Operator Held on Job.

(6) The default setting is *No;* but the user who has given the command can specify Y (*Yes*) and thus activate the *User Hold* status. The print command will not be implemented until the user resets this option to *No.*

(7) This has the same effect as *User Hold* but can only be altered by the network manager (or the supervisor equivalent) or by the *Queue Operator.*

(8) Shows the position of the print command in the print queue and thus, simultaneously, the priority of the print command. The lower the number, the higher the priority. You may alter the priority by simply altering the number. However, only the network manager, the queue operator and the supervisor equivalent are allowed to do so.

(9) The number of copies of this print job which are to be made.

(10) A description of the contents of the file to be printed. This may be *Byte stream* or *Text.* The default setting is the result of the *Print Job Configuration* which was created using the PRINTCON utility program. Select *Byte stream* if you are printing from an application which has created the the file with layout codes for printing. If you select *Text* here, the control characters included in the text will be interpreted. For instance, tabs will then be replaced by the number of spaces specified in *Tab size.* This may produce problems if control characters are directed to the printer in a form which the printer may wrongly interpret.

(11) If you have selected the *Text* option at the *File contents* line, specify the number of spaces to replace the tabs.

(12) If *Yes:* is specified, Novell NetWare will not move the paper on after printing.

(13) If this option is set to *Yes*, you will receive a message when the print job has been carried out.

(14) Specify here which print server is to carry out the print job. The default setting is *Any Server.* Retain this if it is not important which server is to execute

the print job. If you wish to select a certain print server, a list of available print servers will appear if you press the Enter key (*Valid Target Servers*). Select the required server from the list.
(15) Date and time when the print command was placed in the list.
(16) Displays which form, defined by PRINTDEF, is to be used for printing. If you press the Enter key, a list of defined forms will appear from which you can select the required form.
(17) *Yes:* The banner will be printed. *No:* The banner will not be printed.
(18) The user ID is the default setting here. This is replaced by the text specified in the NAME parameter if given along with CAPTURE or NPRINT.
(19) The default setting is the name of the file to be printed. If the source is not LPT1 CATCH, nothing will be entered here unless a NAME parameter has been specified along with NPRINT or CAPTURE.
(20) Normally this setting is *No*; this means that the print procedure corresponds to the position of the print job in the queue and the status of other determining parameters (*User/Operator Hold*) is activated immediately. If you switch this option to *Yes*, you can determine the date and time of printing using *Target date/Target time*.
(21) Date and time can be specified in the common notation. A precondition is that the current CONFIG.SYS configuration file contains the command COUNTRY=044.

Example 64:
For very important reasons, a print job is to executed as quickly as possible. You wish to know when the printout will be completed. You decide to place the print job at the top of the list in the print queue. Proceed as follows:

- Give the PCONSOLE command.
- Select the *Print Queue* option from the *Available Options* menu by highlighting it using the cursor keys or by pressing P. Confirm the choice by pressing Enter.
- In the *Print Queues* window at the left-hand side of

the screen, select the print queue in which your print command is located.
- In the *Print Queue Information* window at the right-hand side of the screen, select the *Current Print Job Entries* option and confirm the choice by pressing Enter.
- A list will appear, similar to that shown earlier in this section. This displays the position of your print job in the queue.
- Select your print job by highlighting it using the cursor keys or by pressing the first letter of the print job name in the *Description* column. Confirm this by pressing Enter. The *Print Queue Information* window appears on the screen.
- Change the priority of the print job by altering the number shown under *Service Sequence* to 1. Your print command is now placed at the top of the list and thus executed first. However, remember that you can only alter this value if you are the network manager or queue operator.
- When the position has been altered, press Alt-F10 in order to end PCONSOLE. Confirm your choice by choosing *Yes* in the *Exit* window.

Example 65:

A voluminous print command is given at 10 am. on the 5th of November 1993. However, this may only be implemented after 5 o'clock so that the print jobs of the other network users will not be delayed. Proceed as follows:

- Activate the PCONSOLE program and, in the same way as described in the previous example, execute all the steps until the *Print Queue Information* window appears.
- Move the cursor to the *Defer printing* option and active this by specifying Y. *Yes* is shown on the screen.
- Move the cursor to the *Target date* option. Set the date to 05-11-93.
- Move the cursor to the *Target time* option and set the time to 17.00.
- Press Alt-F10 in order to end PCONSOLE. Confirm your choice by selecting *Yes* in the *Exit* window.

Printing from applications on a network printer 187

Inserting print commands in the print queue. If you wish to print a file, you can insert a print command in the queue directly by means of the PCONSOLE program. This may be important if the file has been laid out for printing by a word processor for instance. Proceed as follows:

1. Give the PCONSOLE command.
2. Select the *Print Queue Information* option from the *Available Options* menu.
3. Select the print queue in which you wish to place your print job by highlighting it using the cursor or by pressing the first letter. Confirm this by pressing Enter.
4. In the *Print Queue Information* submenu, select the *Current Print Job Entries* option. A list of the print jobs currently in the queue is displayed.

The figure below shows the list and the selection window:

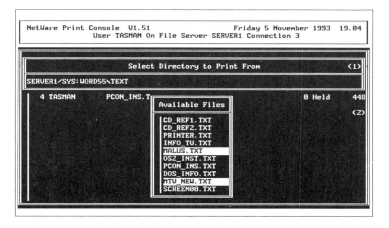

(1) Press the Ins key to insert your print job. The current directory is shown in a text box. If the file is not located in this directory, press the Ins key once more. A window containing a list of the *Network Directories* appears. Select the required directory

and adopt this into the text box by pressing the Enter key. Confirm one more by pressing Esc.
(2) Press Enter in order to activate a list of the files in the directory (*Available Files*). Select the file to be printed using the cursor keys, Enter and Esc.

5. If you wish to include several files in the queue, you can mark these by pressing F5. A group of files can be marked using F6 after which you should specify the group file pattern, such as *.TXT. When the Enter key is pressed, Novell NetWare automatically marks all files which conform to this pattern. Marked files are, depending on the graphic card and monitor, displayed in a different colour, with a different intensity or blinking.
6. Then select the *Print Job Configuration* for the print job. In cases of doubt or if you have not yet determined a configuration, select the standard configuration (*PConsole Defaults*). Confirm your choice by pressing Enter.
7. You must then allocate the print parameters to the program. You can specify all parameters of your choice, except the position of the print job in the print queue (*Service Sequence*) and the date and time of insertion (*Job Entry Date/Job Entry Time*). These data are assigned automatically by Novell NetWare itself. Any modifications in the priority of the print job can be made at the conclusion of the definition.
8. The print job is actually placed in the print queue by pressing Esc and confirming the *Save Changes* question.
9. Then the list of print jobs is shown on the screen. Your print job should be among these.

The figure on the following page displays the print parameters for a print job added to the print queue:

Printing from applications on a network printer

Removing print jobs. If print jobs no longer need to be printed out, they can be removed from the print queue. Proceed as follows:

1. Activate the PCONSOLE program.
2. Select the *Print Queue Information* option from the *Available Options* main menu.
3. Select the print queue containing your print job by moving the cursor or by pressing the first letter. Confirm by pressing Enter.
4. From the *Print Queue Information* submenu, select the *Current Print Job Entries* option.
5. Highlight the print job you wish to delete by moving the cursor keys or by pressing the first letter.
6. If you wish to remove several files from the queue, you can mark these using the F5 key. A group of files is marked using F6, after which you must specify the file pattern, such as *.TXT. When the Enter key is pressed, Novell NetWare automatically marks all files which fulfil this criterion. Marked files are, depending on the graphic card and monitor being used, shown in a different colour, with a different intensity or blinking.
7. The procedure of removing print jobs is activated by pressing the Del key. Confirm the subsequent

question *Delete Queue Entry* or *Delete All Marked Queue Entries* by pressing Enter.

The figure below displays the procedure for removing print jobs:

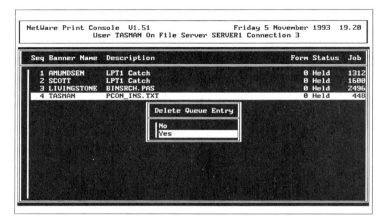

Defining the queue users. When a new queue is created, Novell NetWare allocates the EVERYONE group as a user of this queue. Since Novell NetWare always places a new user in the EVERYONE group during installation, every user is initially entitled to use every queue. If you wish to restrict this, you must remove the EVERYONE group as a user from the queue and determine which users or user groups are entitled to make use of the queue. However, only the network manager, the supervisor equivalent or a queue operator is authorized to take these measures. To remove users or user groups, proceed as follows:

1. Activate the PCONSOLE program.
2. Select the *Print Queue Information* option in the *Available Options* main menu.
3. Select using the cursor keys or press the first letter of the queue where you wish to alter the user rights. Confirm this by pressing Enter.
4. Select the *Queue Users* option from the *Print*

Queue Information submenu. A list appears of the current users assigned to the queue, including the *EVERYONE (Group)*.
5. Press the Ins key to determine new users. A list, in alphabetical order, of *Queue User Candidates* appears at the left-hand side of the screen. All installed users and user groups are shown here. If you only wish to define one queue user or group, make the appropriate selection using the cursor keys or press the first letter of the name and confirm it by pressing Enter. If you wish to define several users, mark the other users using F5. All defined users and groups are actually established by pressing the Enter key.

The figure below shows a list of Queue User Candidates:

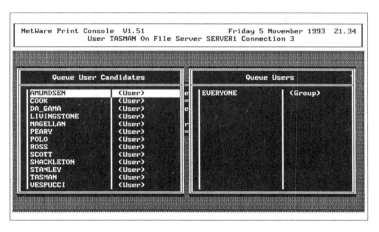

6. It is advisable to remove the EVERYONE group as a queue user, otherwise you will not be able to limit the user group to the selected users. Accordingly, place the cursor on the EVERYONE group and press Del.

The figure on the following page shows the procedure:

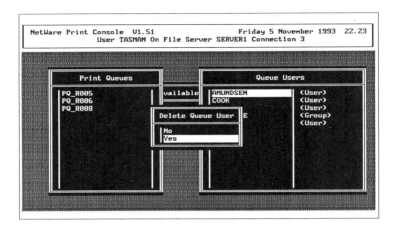

7. If you wish to remove several users, mark these using F5.
8. The procedure to remove the users is activated by pressing the Del key. Then press Enter to confirm the subsequent question *Delete Queue Entry* or *Delete All Marked Queue Entries*.

Defining the queue operators. When defining a queue, Novell NetWare automatically assigns the task of queue operator to the network manager. The network manager can delegate this task to other network users. A queue operator assumes all tasks involving the queue, such as:

- Altering the parameters of the print jobs of all other users (such as the allocation of a different print server).
- Removing print jobs from the queue, even if they are in the process of being printed.
- Altering the status of the queue by changing the *Operator Flag*.
- Altering the priority of the print jobs in the queue.

The assignment of new queue operators takes place as follows:

1. Activate the PCONSOLE program.

Printing from applications on a network printer 193

2. Select the *Print Queue Information* option from the *Available Options* main menu.
3. Use the cursor keys or press the first letter to select the queue to which you wish to assign a new queue operator. Confirm this by pressing Enter.
4. Select the *Queue Operators* option from the *Print Queue Information* submenu. A list of the currently assigned operators, including SUPERVISOR (User) appears. It is also possible to define a group as the queue operator.
5. Press the Ins key to add new operators. A window containing an alphabetical list of *Queue Operator Candidates* appears. All users and user groups are displayed here. If you only wish to define one queue operator or group, select this by highlighting it using the cursor keys or by pressing the first letter of the name and then confirm by pressing Enter. If you wish to define several operators, mark the other operators using F5. All defined operators or groups are actually established by pressing Enter.
6. If you wish to remove one or more queue operators, place the cursor on the required name or use F5 to mark all the operators to be removed. Press Del and confirm the subsequent question with *Yes* in order to implement the removal.

Examining and altering the queue status. A quick overview of the queue status can be gained by means of the so-called *Operator Flags*. If you are the queue operator these also enable you to alter the general parameters of a queue.

Example 66:
The network printer is due to receive a maintenance overhaul. The technician may arrive any minute. You wish to get an idea of the number of jobs in the queue for this printer. If necessary, new commands will have to be refused for the time being. Proceed as follows:

1. Activate the PCONSOLE program.
2. Select the *Print Queue Information* option from the *Available Options* main menu.

3. Select the queue whose status you wish to display using the cursor keys or by pressing the first letter of the name. Confirm the selection by pressing Enter.

The figure below shows the queue status:

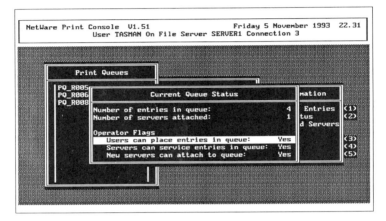

Steps 1 to 3 are included in the description below:

4. In the *Print Queue Information* submenu, select the *Current Queue Status* option. A window appears showing the number of print jobs in the queue (1), the number of assigned print servers (2) and the status of the *Operator Flags*.
5. If you are the queue operator, you may alter the operator flags. Mark the flag to be altered using the cursor keys. We have marked the *Users can place entries in queue* option in our example. You can switch this option to *No* by pressing N, so that no additional print jobs can be placed in the queue (3). At *Servers can service entries in the queue*, the flag should remain on *Yes* so that the current print jobs in the queue can be processed (4). The third flag, *New servers can attach to queue* can also remain on *Yes* since the allocation of new servers can expedite the processing of the remaining jobs (5).

6.3 Installing print routines in the network

The previous section illustrated that print jobs in the Novell network are dealt with in such a way that the print jobs specified by the user are placed as files in a print queue. This is necessary because in a network, in contrast to a stand-alone personal computer, several users direct data to a network printer at the same time. The print jobs (files) in the queue are processed one by one. This means that they are directed to a network printer to be printed. The network printer must be allocated to the queue (*printer mapping*) which contains the print jobs awaiting the printer. This also means that several queues may be allocated to one printer, or that several (similar) printers may be allocated to one queue.

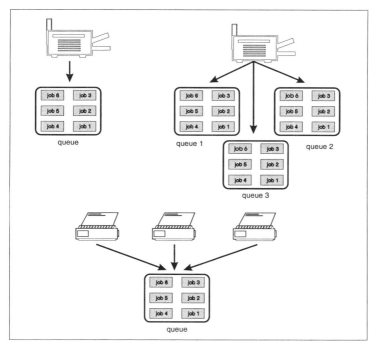

Under Novell NetWare, the term **print server** represents programs which are either active on a fileserver or on a workstation in the network. Only one print server can run on each fileserver. The workstation upon which a print server is active cannot be used for other tasks.

In order to enable printing to take place in the Novell NetWare network, the following allocations are necessary after the print queues and print servers have been installed:

- Printer to Print Server. This deals with the physical features of a printer, particularly the type of printer (local or remote network printer) and the way in which data transmission to the printer takes place (parallel or serial).
- Print Queue to Printer. This deals with the internal capacity of the printer. This may differ considerably from printer to printer according to type and manufacturer. Therefore, a specific printer, for instance IBM ProPrinter or HP LaserJet, must be allocated.
- Print Queue to Print Server. One or more print servers are assigned to a print queue in order to implement the transport of print jobs to the required network printer. One print server can serve a maximum of 16 network printers.

This leads to the following procedure in the installation of print routines. The optional procedures are shown in italics.

1. installing hardware
   ➤ ports
   ➤ printers
2. installing print queues
   ➤ specifying the print queue
   ➤ defining the queue operators
   ➤ *defining the queue users*
3. installing the print server
   ➤ specifying the print server
   ➤ *assigning a password*
   ➤ assigning a full name

Installing print routines in the network

- ➤ specifying the print server operators
- ➤ *defining the print server users*
4. configuring the print server
   - ➤ *assigning the fileserver*
   - ➤ printer configuration
   - ➤ *installing the message list*
   - ➤ assigning the queue
5. activating the print server
   - ➤ on a workstation acting as a dedicated fileserver: activating PSERVER
   - ➤ on a fileserver: loading PSERVER.NLM
6. *activating a remote network printer*
   - ➤ *on a workstation: activating RPRINTER*
7. *configuring print modes*
   - ➤ *configuring printer driving*
   - ➤ *configuring print jobs*

Installing print queues. The print queues have a central role in all print procedures in the network. Accordingly, the installation of the print routines in the network begins with the installation of the print queue. Note here that Novell NetWare automatically assigns an ID number to this print queue during the definition of the print queue and creates a subdirectory in the SYS:SYSTEM directory with this ID number. The print jobs in the queue are placed in this subdirectory. The effective result of this is that only the network manager is able to install print queues since only he/she possesses the appropriate rights for the SYS:SYSTEM directory.

Proceed as follows to install a queue:

1. Log in on the network as the Supervisor or as the supervisor equivalent.
2. Activate the PCONSOLE program.

The figure on the following page displays the PCONSOLE main menu.

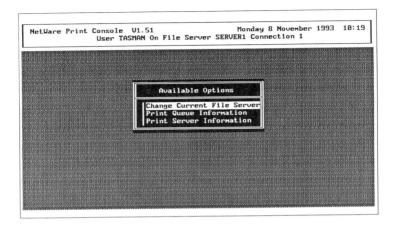

3. Activate the *Print Queue Information* option in the *Available Options* main menu. A list of the current print queues is displayed.
4. Start the installation of a new print queue by pressing the Ins key. Specify the name of the queue in the subsequent text box (*New Print Queue Name*). This may be, for instance HPLJET to represent the HPL LaserJet printer. Confirm this by pressing Enter. The name of the print queue may not be longer than 18 characters. This name is then shown in the (alphabetical) list of print queues.

The on the following page shows the installation of a new print queue:

Steps 1 to 3 are described in the text below.

5. The new print queue is now installed. You can still define the queue users (3) and the queue operators (1). It is also possible to first adopt the Novell NetWare default settings. In that case EVERYONE is specified as the queue user and the SUPERVISOR user is specified as the queue operator.
6. In order to be able to work with the print queue, the print servers (2) must now be defined. If print servers have already been defined, these can be as-

Installing print routines in the network

signed. If that is not the case or if a new print server is to be installed, that should take place now. This also occurs using the PCONSOLE program, so you should not yet quit the program. Press Esc twice to return to the main menu.

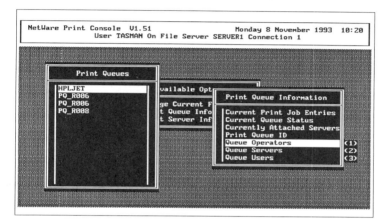

Specifying the default queues for NPRINT and CAPTURE If you do not define a default queue, Novell NetWare will use the queue which is assigned to printer 0 of the relevant print server for the print jobs created using CAPTURE and NPRINT. This definition occurs by means of the *Print Server Configuration Menu*.

A different queue can be specified using the SPOOL command. SPOOL is a console command and therefore can only be given on the server itself (or on a workstation being used as a remote console).

Example 67:
The PQ_HPLJET queue is to be installed as the default queue. Give the following command on the fileserver console:

```
SPOOL 0 TO QUEUE PQ_HPLJET
```

In this, the 0 is the assigned number which is regarded

as the default. The following message appears as confirmation:

```
Spooler 0 directed into queue PQ_HPLJET.
```

Example 68:
A list of spooler allocations is to be displayed. To do this give the following command on the console:

SPOOL

A list of allocations may look something like this:

```
Spooler 0 directed into queue PQ_HPLJET.
Spooler 1 directed into queue PQ_R008.
Spooler 2 directed into queue PQ_R006.
```

If no allocations have been made, the message is as follows:

```
No spoolers are active.
```

If you have allocated the print queues from several fileservers to one print server, you must also specify the spooler allocations on the other fileservers.

Installing print servers. It is possible to assign a name to a print server. Proceed as follows:

1. Activate the PCONSOLE program.
2. Select the *Print Server Information* option from the *Available Options* menu. A list of the currently installed print servers is displayed.
3. Press the Ins key in order to define a new print server. You must specify a name for the print server in the subsequent text box (*New Print Server Name*). In our example, shown below, that is the

name PS_001. The name of the new print server may consist of a maximum of 18 characters and this name is then included in the alphabetical list of print servers.

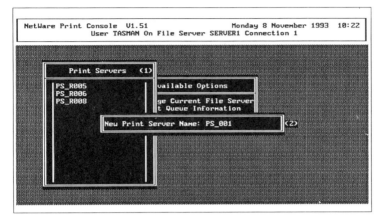

(1) List of the currently installed print servers.
(2) Text box for the name of the print server.

Defining the range of application of the print server.
In the *Print Server Information* menu, all possible options are shown for defining the nature of the fileserver. Only the *Print Server ID* menu option has a purely informative character since only the ID number allocated by Novell NetWare and the name of the allocated fileserver are shown there. All other menu options can be used to define the features of the print server. The figure on the following page gives an overview of the *Print Server Information* menu. The workings of the various menu options are described on the following pages.

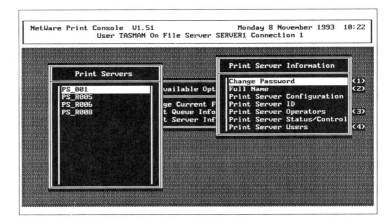

(1) Assign password. This is not absolutuely essential but it is advisable if you wish to safeguard your data. If you define a password, this will have to be entered each time you start up the computer. Proceed as follows:
➤ Select the *Change Password* option from the *Print Server Information* menu.
➤ Type the password twice in the text box which subsequently appears.
Note: If the print server is active for print queues on various fileservers, the password must be defined on each fileserver.

(2) Assign a full name to the print server. In order to designate a print server more specifically, it is possible to assign another name than that specified during the installation. This name may consist of a maximum of 62 characters. Proceed as follows:
➤ Select the *Full Name* option from the *Print Server Information* menu.
➤ Specify the required name in the subsequent text box.
Note: If the print server is active for print queues on various fileservers, this procedure must be repeated on each fileserver.

(3) Specifying print server operators. During the instal-

Installing print routines in the network 203

lation of print servers, Novell NetWare normally defines the SUPERVISOR user as the print server operator. The network manager can engage other users as print server operators by delegating management tasks in order to increase the efficiency in the network. Proceed as follows:
- ➤ Select the *Print Server Operators* option from the *Print Server Information* menu.
- ➤ A list of print server operators is shown on the screen. In the case of a newly installed print server, that is only the Supervisor.
- ➤ Press the Ins key. You can now select the user or user group who is to acquire the status of print server operator, from the *Print Server Operator Candidates* window
- ➤ If you wish to define several users/groups, mark them using F5.
- ➤ When Enter is pressed, the selected user/groups are established as print server operator(s).

4. Defining print server users. The EVERYONE group is always initially specified as a user (*Server Users*). This means that all network users may use the print server. If the group of users has to be restricted, the network manager will have to remove the EVERYONE group from the list of print server users and include other users or groups instead. Proceed as follows:
- ➤ Select the *Print Server Users* option from the *Print Server Information* menu.
- ➤ The list of print server users appears on the screen. This contains only the EVERYONE group at the first installation of the print server.
- ➤ Mark the EVERYONE group by placing the cursor on it. Press Del in order to remove the group. Confirm the question *Delete Print Server User* with *Yes*.
- ➤ Press the Ins key. You can now select, from the *Print Server User Candidates* window, the user or group who is entitled to use the print server.
- ➤ If you wish to define several users or groups, mark them using F5.

➤ When Enter is pressed, the selected users/ groups are adopted as print server users.

Determining the features of the print server. In order to determine the features which are absolutely necessary to work with the print server, activate the *Print Server Configuration* option from the *Print Server Information* menu. A submenu appears. The following options from this menu must be implemented in any case:

- *File Servers To Be Serviced*
- *Printer Configuration*
- *Queues Serviced by Printer*

The figure below illustrates the *Print Server Configuration* menu.

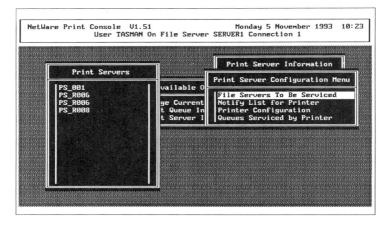

Allocation of fileservers. Proceed as follows:

- Select *File Servers To Be Serviced*. A window appears displaying a list of allocated fileservers. Normally the fileserver on which the print server was defined is shown.
- Press the Ins key to activate a list of *Available File Servers*.

Installing print routines in the network

- Mark one or more fileservers by placing the cursor key on it or by using the F5 key.
- Adopt the marked fileserver(s) in the list of fileservers by pressing Enter.

Note: This allocation is only in force when the print server is restarted. If you wish to make immediate use of it, you must switch the print server off and then on again.

The network printer configuration. A print server can serve a maximum of 16 printers having the numbers 0 to 15. In order to ensure that the printers function properly, the print server should be familiar with their features. This involves the way in which the data transmission to the printer takes place (serial or parallel) and the position of the printer (fileserver or workstation). Proceed as follows:

- Select *Printer Configuration*. A window appears showing 16 possible printers. Printers for which a configuration has been defined are shown here with their name. Otherwise *Not Installed* is stated along with the number.
- Mark the printer which you wish to configure and confirm this using Enter.
- An input screen appears (*Printer* n *Configuration*) in which the configuration values must be entered.
- Close the screen containing the configuration values by pressing Esc and confirm the subsequent question *Save Changes* with *Yes*.

The figure on page 206 shows the input screen for the configuration values:

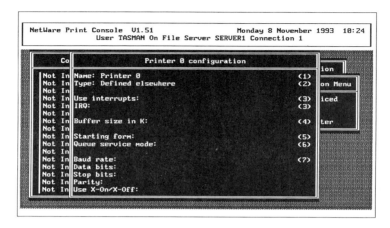

(1) Normally the name shown in the list appears here. In the case of printers which have not yet been installed that is *Printer 0*. Specify here a conspicuous name in order to be able to find it easily later.

(2) Normally *Defined elsewhere* appears here. You can retain this if you define printers on several fileservers. In this case, the exact definition only needs to take place on the fileserver on which you originally defined the print server. For all other fileservers, the statement *Defined elsewhere* will suffice. Otherwise adopt the corresponding type of printer from the *Printer Types* window which opens at the moment you wish to specify something next to *Type*. Other possible printer types are (*n* represents the number of the printer port):

➤ Parallel, LPT*n*
➤ Serial, COM*n*
➤ Remote Parallel, LPT*n*
➤ Remote Serial, COM*n*
➤ Remote Other/Unknown.

Select *Parallel/Serial* if a local network printer is connected to the print server. This may be a fileserver or a dedicated print server on a workstation.

Select *Remote Parallel/Serial* if a remote network printer is connected to a workstation. In that case, the RPRINTER program must be loaded on the

Installing print routines in the network 207

workstation to which the network printer is connected.

Select *Remote Other/Unknown* if you wish to define the printer at the moment you start up the RPRINTER program. If you select this option, you can react flexibly to changing printer and port configurations at workstations.

(3) *Interrupts* are signals which ensure that the processor discontinues the operation of a program to deal with another command. If the printer port is operated via interrupts, which is normally the case with ATs, you must activate this parameter by pressing Y. The execution then takes place more quickly than when using the *polling* method which does not use interrupts. When defining a remote network printer, the printer operation must take place via an interrupt. If you have activated the interrupt option, you must specify the number of the interrupt used. This number lies between 3 and 7; the values 5 and 7 are normally used. Consult the computer manual or the interface card to find out the appropriate number, or request it using a special utility program (CheckIt, for instance). You must, of course, pay attention to possibility of the interrupts which you configure causing conflict with other computer elements, such as network cards.

(4) Specify the size of the printer buffer here (1 to 20 Kb). In Novell NetWare a size of 3 Kb is recommended.

(5) The print jobs can be printed on certain forms, such as invoices and other letter-headed paper. The forms are defined using the PRINTDEF program, in which they receive a number between 0 and 255. Enter the number of the form which is normally used.

(6) Determine here what Novell NetWare should do when printing various forms. You can select the following options from the list:

Change forms as needed
Minimize form changes across queues
Minimize form changes within queues
Service only currently mounted form.

The default setting is *Change forms as needed*. This means that all print jobs are to be printed in the order they arrive, regardless of the type of form to be used.

If you select *Minimize form changes across queues*, the print jobs requiring the currently active form from all assigned print queues will be processed first, keeping in mind the allocated priorities.

Minimize form changes within queues means that the print jobs requiring the currently active form from one print queue will be processed first.

If you select the *Service only currently mounted form* option, the print jobs requiring the currently active form will be processed, keeping in mind the priorities allocated to the print queues. Commands requiring other forms will not be implemented.

(7) The remaining parameters - *Baud rate, Data bits, Stop bits, Parity* and *Use X-ON/X-OFF* - specify the data transmission to a printer connected via a serial port. Consult a manual to find out the correct values. With the exception of the *Data Bits* and *Use X-ON/X-OFF* parameters, selection takes place in a list of default values, so that erroneously specified values are reduced to a minimum.

Removing the allocation of a printer to a print server. If you no longer wish to have a printer served by a print server, it can be removed from the *Configured Printers* list. Proceed as follows:

- Activate the PCONSOLE program and select the *Print Server Information* option from the *Available Options* main menu.
- Select the required print server.
- Select *Print Server Configuration* from the *Print Server Information* list.
- Select a printer from the *Configured Printers* list and press the Del key. Confirm the following question *Delete Printer* with *Yes*. This removes the allocation of the printer to the print server.

Installing print routines in the network 209

Altering the printer configuration. The printer configuration determines which features of the printer are accessible to the print server. If modifications are necessary, due to the installation of another printer for instance, you can also apply these by means of the PCONSOLE program.

- Activate the PCONSOLE program and select the *Print Server Information* option from the *Available Options* main menu.
- Select the required print server.
- Select *Print Server Configuration* from the *Print Server Information* list.
- Select a printer from the *Configured Printers* list and press the Enter key.
- Change the relevant parameters in the *Printer n Configuration* screen.
- Conclude the configuration alterations by pressing Esc and confirm the subsequent *Save Changes* question with *Yes*.

Creating a list of users to be notified in the case of printer problems. Printers possess the trait of not being able to function for very long without the help of humans. For instance, a new ribbon or new toner has to be applied or a different kind of paper has to be inserted. Novell NetWare provides the possibility of making a list of all those who have to be notified if printer problems arise.

The figure on the following page displays this type of *Notify List*.

To make the list, proceed as follows:

- Activate the PCONSOLE program and select the *Printer Server Information* option from the *Available Options* main menu.
- Select the required print server.
- Select *Print Server Configuration* from the *Print Server Information* list.
- Select *Notify List for Printer* from the *Print Server Configuration* menu and press Enter.

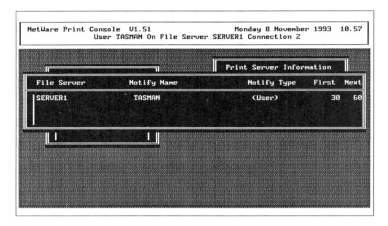

- In the *Defined Printers* list shown, select the printer for which you wish to create the list. Confirm this by pressing Enter.
- Press the Ins key and select from the subsequent *Notify Candidates* list the user or group to be notified if printer problems arise. Confirm this by pressing Enter.
- In the subsequent *Notify Intervals* text box, specify the time in seconds between the messages which are given by Novell NetWare until the problem is solved.
- When you have specified all values, quit the window by pressing Esc and confirm the subsequent *Save Changes* question with *Yes*.

In the case of printer problems, such as the paper having to be replenished, the following (or similar) message will appear on the bottom line of the screen:

Note: If you have activated CASTOFF, no message will appear.

Defining printer features and forms (PRINTDEF). By means of the PRINTDEF program, it is possible to determine which features of the printer and which forms Novell NetWare will use in the print procedures.

The data determined by PRINTDEF are used by the PRINTCON, NPRINT, CAPTURE and PCONSOLE (via PRINTCON) programs in order to implement print jobs correctly.

Whether or not it is really necessary to define the printer features using PRINTDEF depends on the programs used. When applications are used which supply the files tailor-made for printing, you can probably omit the definition of printer drivers by means of PRINTDEF. However, if you are working with programs which do not have their own printer drivers, it is very worthwhile and effective to generate printer drivers for the application in question. On the other hand, you should *always* define forms if you wish to use different sorts of forms when printing by means of the CAPTURE and NPRINT commands. This is because this is the only way to make use of the facilities these programs provide when working with forms.

Novell NetWare 386 has 34 standard printer drivers in version 3.11, from the A of Apple ImageWriter II to the T of Toshiba P321d. They are located in the SYS:PUBLIC directory and are equipped with the extension PDF (*Print Device Definition File*). These drivers are only accessible to the Novell NetWare programs when they are copied to the PRINTDEF database (NET$PRN.DAT in the SYS:PUBLIC directory). Only the network manager is authorized to work with this PRINTDEF database.

The figure on page 212 displays an overview of the functions available to the network manager in the PRINTDEF program:

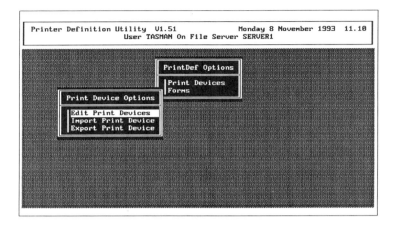

Including printer drivers in the printer database. To do this, proceed as follows:

- Log in as the Supervisor or as the supervisor equivalent.
- Activate the PRINTDEF program.
- Select the *Print Devices* option from the *PrintDef Options* window.
- Select the *Import Print Devices* option from the *Print Device Options* menu.
- If you have not activated PRINTDEF from the SYS:PUBLIC directory, you must now use the Backspace key to delete the directory name shown and then type PUBLIC instead.
- From the *Available PDFs* list showing the available printer drivers, select the required file by placing the cursor on it. It is not possible to select several files using the F5 key. If you attempt to import a definition having the same name as a file which is already present in the database, an error message appears. You can then change the name. Press Enter to include the new driver in the printer database.
- Press Esc once and confirm the *Exit PrintDef* question with *Yes*. In the *Exit Options* window, select the *Save Database, then EXIT* option in order to establish the alterations.

Installing print routines in the network 213

Defining the printer functions. You can also make use of the PRINTDEF program if you wish to use a printer without a standard driver. Consult the printer manual to create the necessary escape sequences for the printer driver.

Example 69:
A driver has to be created for the Panasonic KX-P1124 printer. The following printer functions must be available (the escape sequences are shown between brackets; ESC represents the control character with the ASCII code 27):

- Reset (ESC+@)
- Boldface (ESC+E)
- NLQ mode (ESC+x+1)
- Draft mode (ESC+x+0)
- Sans Serif font (ESC+k+1).

The printer functions are created as follows:

- Log in as the Supervisor or as the supervisor equivalent.
- Activate the PRINTDEF program.
- Select the *Print Devices* option from the *PrintDef Options* window.
- Select *Edit Print Devices* from the *Print Device Options* menu.
- A list of *Defined Print Devices* appears. Press the Ins key in order to add a new driver.
- In the *New Device Name* text box, enter Panasonic KX-P1124 (maximum of 32 characters). Press Enter to confirm.
- Press Enter once more to activate the *Edit Device Options* menu. Select the *Device Functions* option.
- The *Panasonic KX-P1124 Functions* window, which is still empty, now appears on the screen. Press the Ins key to specify the first function definition.
- In the *Function Definitions* window, enter the name *Reset*. Press Enter and specify in the *Escape Sequences* field the corresponding value. Since the ASCII value of ESC is under 33, this has to be speci-

fied as a special character: <ESC> or <27> (decimal value) or <0X1b> (hexadecimal value). (Note that the greater-than and smaller-than signs must be specified here, see figure below.) <ESC>@ is the escape sequence for the Reset function. Then press the Esc key and confirm the *Save Changes* question with *Yes*.

An extensive description of the specification of escape sequences can be obtained by pressing F1 (the Help function) when in the *Function Definition* window.

■ Repeat this procedure for the remaining functions.

The figure below displays the specification of printer functions.

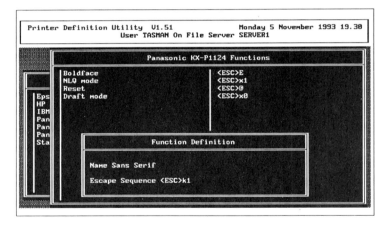

Defining print modes. When the printer functions have been defined, it is possible in the following stage to combine several of these printer functions in one print mode.

Example 70:
In order to obtain a workable print mode for the Panasonic printer, the NLQ (Near Letter Quality) and Sans Serif functions are to be combined. To do this, proceed as follows:

Installing print routines in the network 215

- Select the *Device Modes* option from the *Edit Device Options* menu. The subsequent window, *Panasonic KX-P1124 Modes* contains one piece of data: *Reinitialize*. The function for the printer reset must be allocated to this field, so that the printer can return to the original state at the end of the print job. Activate the Reinitialize mode by pressing Enter.
- Press the Ins key in order to activate a list of all functions which have been defined for the current printer. Select *Reset* by placing the cursor on this function and press Enter. In this way, the escape sequence for the printer reset will be adopted.
- Press the Esc key in order to switch to the *Panasonic KX-P1124 Modes* window.
- The NLQ mode can now be defined. Press the Ins key and type the name of the new *New Mode Name:* NLQ Mode.
- Press Enter to activate the *NLQ Mode Functions* window. Press Ins in order to activate a list containing all the defined functions for the Panasonic printer.
- Mark the *NLQ Mode* and *Sans Serif* functions using F5.
- Exit PRINTDEF by pressing Esc several times and answer the *Exit PrintDef* question with *Yes*. From the *Exit Options* select *Save DataBase, then EXIT* in order to establish the alterations. Do not quit the program using Alt-F10 as this will lead to your data being lost.

The figure on the following page shows the definition of the new print modes using the PRINTDEF program.

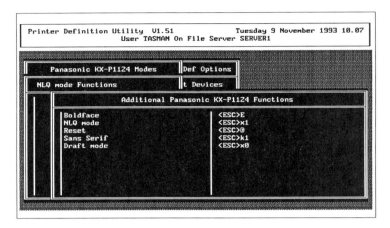

Exporting printer definitions. The printer definitions newly made using PRINT DEF are then part of the NET$PRN.DAT printer database. In order to be able to use this printer definition in the definition of other, comparable printers, it is possible to export the definition to a PDF file.

Example 71:
The printer definition for the Panasonic printer is to be exported from the printer database and be adopted in the SYS:PUBLIC directory as a file under the name PAN1124.PDF. Proceed as follows:

- Log in as the Supervisor or as the supervisor equivalent.
- Activate the PRINTDEF program.
- Select the *Print Devices* option from the *PrintDef Options* window.
- Select *Edit Print Devices* from the *Print Device Options* menu.
- A list of the currently defined printer drivers (*Defined Print Devices*) appears. Mark the *Panasonic KX-1124* item using the cursor keys.
- Press Enter and specify the destination directory in the *Destination Directory* input screen. If you have not activated PRINTDEF from SYS:PUBLIC, you will first have to remove the default value.

Installing print routines in the network 217

- In the *Export File Name* text box, specify the name of the printer definition file to be created, without extension: PAN1124. (This name must conform to the MS-DOS conventions.) Press Enter to confirm this and the file will be created.

Defining print forms. Print forms provide a description of the paper on which printing takes place. In the definition, each form is assigned a name and number which enables the print server to distinguish between the forms. If a certain form is specified in the submission of print jobs, the print server only processes the print job when the required form has been placed in the printer. Only the network manager may apply the required settings.

Proceed as follows to define a new form:

- Log in as the Supervisor or as the supervisor equivalent.
- Activate the PRINTDEF program.
- Select the *Forms* option in the *PrintDef Options* window.
- The list of currently defined forms appears. Press the Ins key in order to create a new form.
- In the *Form Definition* window, specify the data which are displayed in the figure below.

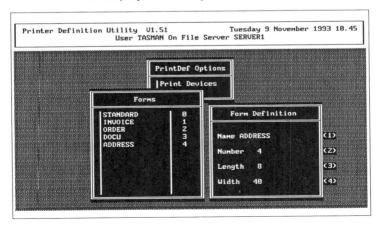

- Press Esc and confirm the *Save changes* question with *Yes* in order to save the definition of the form.

(1) The form name which you allocate yourself. The name may consist of a maximum of 12 characters. The first character must be a letter.
(2) Number of the form. Specify a number between 0 and 255, where the form having the number 0 must be the standard form. Form numbers may not be used more than once.
(3) Length of the form. Specify here the length of the form in lines per page. The possible values range from 1 to 255.
(4) Width of the form. Specify here the width of the form in characters per line. The possible values range from 1 to 999.

Determining the default options for print jobs (PRINTCON) Using the menu-driven PRINTCON utility program (PRINTjob CONfiguration), it is possible to define print options and to establish them as the default options. The configurations defined by PRINTCON form the basis for the printouts made using CAPTURE, NPRINT and PCONSOLE. If you do not use these instructions, there is no point using PRINTCON to make definitions. PRINTCON is only necessary if you are working with programs which cannot make direct use of the network print routines.

The PRINTCON *Available Options* main menu provides the following options:

- *Edit Print Job Configurations.*
- *Select Default Print Job Configuration.*
- *Copy Print Job Configurations.*

In the MAIL directory of the user who has activated the program, PRINTCON creates a file with the name PRINTCON.DAT in which the options for this user's print jobs are located. This means that the required configurations for print jobs much be specified for each user individually. Since most users have writing rights for

Installing print routines in the network

their MAIL directories, the configuration can be compiled by each user.

The possibility of copying configurations for print jobs is the exclusive right of the network manager. In this, he/she can copy print job configurations to the directories of the various users in order to facilitate their work with the network print routines.

Print job configuration parameters. Prior to beginning work with PRINTCON, you must have made printer definitions using PRINTDEF. PRINTDEF determines which printers and which forms are available on the fileserver.

The print job configuration takes place in the *Edit Print Job Configuration* input screen (see figure below).

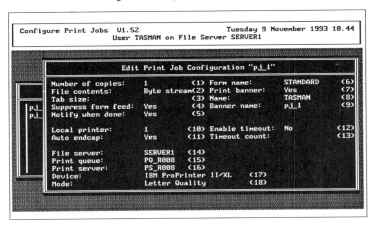

In order to configure a print job, modify the parameters. These are outlined below:

(1) The number of copies: this may range from 1 to 65,000. The default value is 1.
(2) File contents: Press Enter to select either *Text* or *Byte stream* in a window. Select *Text* if you wish to print an ASCII text in which tabs have to be converted into spaces. The *Byte stream* option en-

ables you to print from an application which already provides the layout for the printer. Use this option if you also wish to load softfonts in a laser printer. The latter option is the default value.

(3) Tab size: If you have chosen *Text* at the *File contents* option, you must specify here the number of spaces to replace the tab in a text. The default setting is 8, the possibilities range from 1 to 18.

(4) Suppress form feed: The options are *Yes* or *No*. These are specified by pressing Y or N. If you select *Yes*, the last sheet of paper will be moved on after a print job has been implemented. If you are printing from an application which regulates this form feed automatically, *Yes* here will produce a blank sheet of paper at the conclusion of the print job. In this case, you should select *No* which is the default setting.

(5) Notify when done: If you set this parameter to *Yes*, you will receive a message on the screen at the conclusion of the print job. The default setting is *No*, thus no message.

(6) Form name: If you have defined forms using the PRINTDEF program, the name of the form which you defined as the standard (ie. with the number 0) will appear here. If you wish to specify a different form, use the Enter key to activate a list of the currently defined forms, from which you can make a selection.

If you have not defined any forms, an error message will appear at the beginning of the new configuration to indicate this. In that case *None defined* is the default value and no alterations are possible. Since form definitions are linked to the fileserver on which they were made, an alteration of the *File server* option may effect the alteration of the defined form.

(7) Print banner: The default setting here is *Yes*, which means that a banner (an introductory page) will be printed with each print job. If you wish to prevent this, change the setting to *No*.

(8) Name: If the previous option is set to *Yes*, you may specify a text here consisting of a maximum of 12

Installing print routines in the network 221

characters which will be printed large at the top of the banner. The default setting is your user name.
(9) Banner name: If the parameter for printing a banner is set to *Yes*, you can enter a text here, with a maximum of 12 characters, which will printed large at the bottom of the banner. The default setting is the name of the file which is being printed (thus using CAPTURE, nothing here will be printed).
(10) Local printer: This parameter is necessary for the print jobs which are submitted via CAPTURE. The number of the local parallel port which is to be redirected to the network printer must be specified here. The default setting is 1 (thus LPT1), the possible values are 1, 2 and 3.
(11) Auto endcap: Automatic closure of the print queue file. This parameter is used in combination with the CAPTURE command. The *Yes* default setting means that the printing of a print job will begin automatically at the moment of closure of the application from which the printing is to be done, or when this application closes the printer channel at the conclusion of the print instruction. If you select *No* here, printing will only begin when you activate the *Timeout* option or when the ENDCAP program is activated.
(12) Enable timeout: This parameter is also required in combination with the CAPTURE command. The *No* default setting means that a print job is only submitted when ENDCAP is activated (see also *Autoendcap*). *Yes* means that the submitted data have been included in the print queue and they will be printed if no other data are submitted within the number of seconds specified at *Timeout count*.
(13) Timeout count: If Timeout has been activated, you can specify the length of the timeout in seconds. The possible values range from 1 to 1000, the default setting is 5 seconds.
(14) File server: Specify here the fileserver from which printing should take place. The default setting is the fileserver on which you logged in. If you wish to specify a different fileserver, press Enter to activate a list.

Caution: When switching to another fileserver, it may be necessary to alter all the parameters which are linked to the fileserver in various ways: *Print queue, Form name, Device modes.*

(15) Printqueue: This parameter determines the print queue to which the print job will be directed. The default setting is the alphabetical first print queue defined on the fileserver. When you press Enter, an alphabetical list of all print queues installed on this fileserver appears. Select the required queue from the list.

(16) Print server: The default setting is *Any*. If you press Enter, a list of all print servers which may serve the selected print queue will appear. Select the print server you require. CAPTURE does not support names of print servers.

(17) Device: Specify here the type of printer on which printing is to take place. When you press Enter, a list of all printers which have been defined using PRINTDEF will appear. Select the required printer from this list. Ensure that the selected type conforms to the selected queue. The default setting is *None*.

The figure below displays the print job configuration with the list of printer modes:

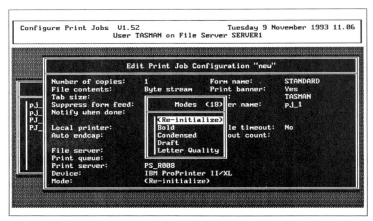

(18) Mode: When you have pressed Enter, a list of all modes appropriate to the selected printer, such as *NLQ, Bold, Condensed*, wiil be shown. The default setting is *None* if no printer has been selected, otherwise it is the first mode belonging to the printer.

Example 72:
A standard configuration has to be defined for print jobs. The standard printer is a HP LaserJet II with the 12-point Courier Bold font. The configuration is to be adopted under the name PJ_STANDARD. Proceed as follows:

- Activate the PRINTCON program.
- Activate the *Edit Print Job Configuration* options in the *Available Options* main menu.
- A list of all available *Print Job Configurations* appears.
- Press the Ins key and specify the name PJ_STANDARD in the *Enter new name* window.
- You must subsequently specify the required parameters in the edit window. Specify the following values which deviate from the default settings:

    Suppress form feed: Yes.
    Print queue: PQ_HPLJET.
    Device: Pres Enter and select HP LaserJet II/IID from the list.
    Mode: Press Enter and select Courier Bold 12pt from the list.

- Press Esc and confirm the *Save changes* question with *Yes*.
- Press Esc in order to return to the main menu and now select *Select Default Print Job Configuration* in order to determine the default configuration.
- Place the cursor on PJ_STANDARD and confirm the choice using Enter. This defines the selected item as the default setting.
- Press Alt-F10. Confirm the *Exit Printcon* question and the following *Save Print Job Configuration* question with *Yes* in order to establish the alterations.

Example 73:
The print job configuration has to be renamed PJ_IBM-PROP. Proceed as follows:

- Activate the PRINTCON program.
- Activate the *Edit Print Job Configuration* option in the *Available Options* main menu. A list of all available print job configurations appears.
- Place the cursor on pj_2.
- Press the F3 key and specify the new name in the following *Change name to:* window. Confirm this using Enter.
- Press Alt-F10 and confirm the *Exit Printcon* question and the following *Save Print Job Configuration* question with *Yes* in order to establish the alterations.

Removing print job configurations. Superfluous print job configurations can be removed individually or collectively.

Example 74:
The superfluous print job configurations, pj_3 and pj_4, are to be removed. Proceed as follows:

- Activate the PRINTCON program.
- Activate the *Edit Print Job Configuration* option in the *Available Options* main menu. A list of all available *Print Job Configurations* will appear.
- Mark the items pj_3 and pj_4 by placing the cursor on them and pressing F5.
- Press the Del key and confirm the *Delete Marked Print Job Configuration* question with *Yes*.
- Press Alt-F10 and confirm the *Exit Printcon* and the following *Save Print Job Configuration* questions with *Yes* in order to establish the changes.

Copying the print job configurations. If you are the network or workgroup manager, you can copy the print job configurations from one user to the other. In this, the entire PRINTCON.DAT file (containing all defined configurations) is copied to the MAIL directory of the relevant user. Any configuration which is already present will be recognized, leading to the question *Delete Existing File*.

If you wish to copy a configuration file which you have altered during the current session, you must exit PRINTCON first because the alterations are only then made permanent.

Example 75:
The SUPERVISOR print job configurations are to be copied to the User COOK. Proceed as follows:

- Activate the PRINTCON program.
- Activate the *Edit Print Job Configuration* option in the *Available Options* main menu.
- In the *Source User* window, specify the name of the user from whom you wish to copy the configuration file (in our case, SUPERVISOR). Confirm this using Enter.
- In the subsequent *Target User* window, specify the name of the user who is to receive the configuration file (in our case, COOK). Confirm this using Enter.

The User COOK, can now make use of all the SUPERVISOR configurations. Unfortunately, PRINTCON does not allow you to adopt the receiver from a list of all available users. The name must be typed.

6.4 Control and operation of network print routines

Operation possibilities for print servers. Print servers can be activated on a fileserver and on a dedicated workstation. As soon as a print server is active, in the *Print Server Information* menu of the PCONSOLE program the *Printer Server Status and Control* option appears. If you activate this option, you will see a number of possibilities for examining and controlling the features of an activated print server. You can only make use of these operating possibilities if you are the network manager or have the status of a *Print Server Operator*. All other users may only request information. Alterations which you may make by means of the *Print Server Status and Control* menu are lost when you switch off the print server.

The following facilities for requesting information and operating the print server are provided:

- Adding or removing fileservers which are served by the print server.
- Altering the *Notify List* in the case of printer problems.
- Altering the status of the active printer.
- Assigning new print queues to the print server or removing existing assignments; altering print queue priorities.
- Examining the print server status or switching off the print server.

The figure below displays the operating possibilities for an active print server:

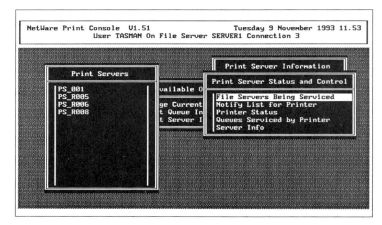

Examining and altering the print status. It is possible to alter some features of active network printers, which come into effect immediately without the print server having to undergo a restart. If you wish to examine the

Control and operation of network print routines 227

status of a print server and perhaps alter it, proceed as follows:

- Activate the PCONSOLE program and select the *Print Server Information* option from the *Available Options* main menu.
- Select the required print server.
- Select the *Print Server Status and Control* option from the *Print Server Information* list.
- Select *Printer Status* from the *Print Server Status and Control* menu and press Enter.
- Select the printer whose status you wish to examine or alter, from the subsequent *Active Printers* list. Confirm this using Enter.
- If you are the print server manager, you can now immediately operate the printer *(Printer Control)*, alter the printer working mode *(Service mode)* or select a different print form *(Mounted form)*.
- Mark the *Printer Control* option and press Enter. Select the required course of action from the subsequent list:

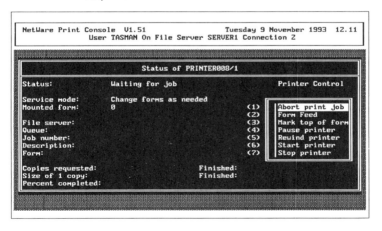

(1) The print job which is currently being processed is closed and removed from the print queue.
(2) A form feed is specified for the selected printer.

(3) A line of asterisks is displayed on the printer. This function is useful for inserting the paper correctly at the beginning of the sheet.
(4) The execution of the current print job which is interrupted. This will be continued when the *Start printer* command in the *Printer Control* list is given.
(5) Using this option, parts of the current print job can be printed again. A window is opened in which the sections to be printed can be specified. This is done in terms of the *Text* or *Byte stream* settings. Enter the number of pages or bytes (or specify from which page or which byte) of which copy the printout is to be made. This is useful if, during printing, problems have arisen which can be remedied by printing a part of the text anew.
(6) Activates the printer again if this has been interrupted using the *Pause printer* or *Stop printer* commands.
(7) Printing stopped: the command remains in the queue and may be executed once more from the beginning.

The rest of the *Status or Printer* screen shows information concerning the print job being currently processed. This cannot be altered.

Switching off a print server. Novell NetWare provides only one way of switching off a print server which is active on a dedicated workstation. This is done via the *Server Control* option in the *Print Server Status and Control* menu. If you select this menu option, a window will appear displaying the following data:

- the print server version number,
- the print server type (*Dedicated DOS* if it is active on a workstation, *386 Loadable Module* if it is active on a fileserver),
- the number of printers assigned to the print server,
- the *Queue service mode*,
- the *Current server status*.

If you are the network manager or print server manager,

the *Current printer status* is displayed in inverse video. Press any key; Novell NetWare provides three means of influencing the status of the print server:

- Down
- Going down after current jobs
- Running.

If you select *Down*, the print server is switched off immediately. If there are still print jobs in the print queue, these will not be carried out. However, they are not removed. On the screen of the computer on which the print server was active, the message *Print server <name> is down* appears.

If you select *Going down after current jobs*, all the print jobs in the queue will be carried out, then the print server is switched off.

The *Running* option does not alter the status of the print server. It remains active as before.

The figure below displays the status of the print server:

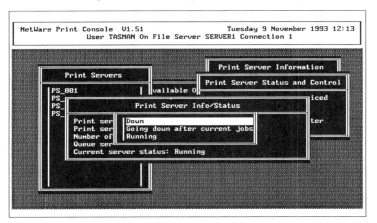

The console also provides the possibility of closing down a print server which is running on a fileserver.

Here you must give the following command on the console at system level (*System Console*):

:UNLOAD PSERVER

Novell NetWare switches off the print server and displays the following (or similar) message on the screen:

```
Print server PS_R008 is down.
<Press any key to close the screen>
```

The following message is shown on the system console:

```
Module PSERVER.NLM unloaded.
```

Examining and altering the allocation of queues to printers. If you wish to check which printers and which queues are linked to the print server, proceed as follows:

1. Activate the PCONSOLE program and select the *Print Server Information* option from the *Available Options* main menu.
2. Select the required print server.
3. Select the *Print Server Status and Control* option from the *Print Server Information* list.
4. Select *Queues Serviced by Printer* from the *Print Server Status and Control* menu and press Enter.
5. Select from the subsequent *Active Printer* list the printer whose allocated queues you wish to examine. Confirm this by pressing Enter.
6. If queues are allocated, these are shown in a window along with the fileserver, your name and the allocated priority. The figure following illustrates this window:

Control and operation of network print routines

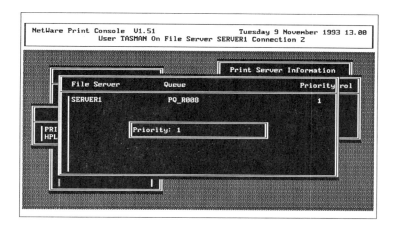

7. If you are the network manager or print server manager, you can change the priority here which has been assigned to a queue. Mark the required queue, Press Enter, specify the required priority and press Enter once more.

It is also possible to temporarily alter the allocation of print queues to network printers by removing existing allocations and defining new ones.

Note: This deals with temporary alterations which are only effective until the print server is switched off.

Example 76:
The print queues PQ_PHLJET, PQ_R005 and PQ_R006 are to be temporarily allocated to the PRINTER000/1 network printer.

■ Select the *Queues Serviced by Printer* option from the *Print Server Status and Control* menu.
■ Select the required printer in the subsequent *Active Printers* list, in this case *PRINTER008/1*. Confirm this using Enter.
■ A list of queues which have been allocated to this printer appears. Press the Ins key to activate the *Available Queues* list.

- If you only wish to assign one queue, you only need to mark the required queue using the cursor. Several queues can be selected using the F5 key. Pressing Enter confirms your choice and the allocation to the network printer.
- Subsequently, you determine the priority of the queue(s) by specifying a priority number between 1 and 10. You have now specified temporary new allocations

The figure below displays the allocated queues:

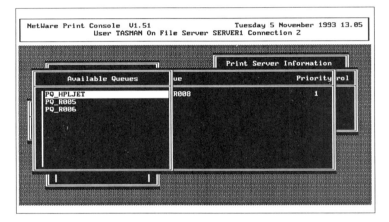

Example 77:
The PQ_PHLJET, PQ_R005 and PQ_R006 queues which have been allocated to PRINTER008/1 are to be removed. Proceed as follows:

- Select the *Queues Serviced by Printer* option from the *Print Server Status and Control* menu.
- Select the required printer from the *Active Printers* list, in this case *PRINTER008/1* and confirm this using Enter.
- A list of print queues allocated to this printer is shown.
- Mark the required queues using F5 and confirm the choice with Enter.
- Answer *Yes* to the following question *Delete Marked*

Control and operation of network print routines 233

Queues From Service List in order to effect the removal.

The figure below shows how the temporary queues are removed:

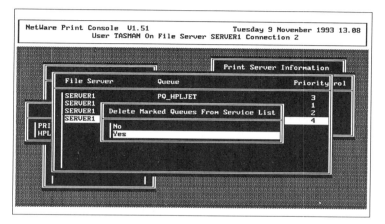

Examining and altering Notify Lists. It is possible to make a temporary alteration to the Notify List by means of the *Print Server Status and Control* menu.

- Select the *Notify List for Printer* menu option.
- Select the required printer from the list of active printers. A list of users/user groups who are notified in the event of something going wrong (if specified) will then appear.
- Press the Ins key in order to activate a list of users who can be notified in the event of printer problems.
- Select the user to be notified by moving the cursor to the name or by pressing the first letter. Confirm this using Enter. Several users can be selected by pressing F5.
- Then determine, in the *Notify Intervals* window, the number of seconds between the first notification and the repeated notifications. You may also accept the default value (30/60) by pressing Enter.

If you wish to remove users or user groups from the list, proceed in the same way, but press the Del key instead of the Ins key.

Note: If a user has suppressed the display of system messages by means of the CASTOFF program, no message will be given in the case of printer problems.

Using PSC to check the print server and network printer. PSC (Print Server Command) is a utility program which the network manager or print server manager can use instead of the PCONSOLE utility program in order to control and operate print servers and network printers. The program is not menu-driven; it works using a command line.

Network managers can use PSC to display information about the status of the print servers and network printers. All required data should be requested by applying parameters when activating the program. The command should be specified as follows:

```
PSC PS=print_server_name P=printer_number
flag
```

There must be no spaces in the print server name or in the printer number.

print server name   Specify the name of the print server to be checked.
printer number   Specify the number which was assigned to the printer at the configuration of the print server in the PCONSOLE program.
flag   The following parameters are valid. You must specify at least the letters shown here as capitals.

STATus
This parameter enables you to display the current status of one or all of the printers served by the specified print server. If a printer number is specified, the

status of the corresponding printer is shown; if no number is specified, a list showing the status of all printers will be displayed.

Example 78:
The status of the HPLJET printer, with the number 1, which has been assigned to the PS_R008 print server is to be displayed. To do this, give the following command:

```
PSC PS=PS_R008 P=1 STAT
```

In addition to the response message, *Printer 1: HPLJET*, the following status messages are possible:

Waiting for job:	The printer is ready.
Mount form n	Insert form *n*.
Printing job	The job is being processed.
Paused	Printing has been interrupted.
Ready to go down	The print server is ready to be switched off.
Stopped	The print job has been discontinued.
Mark/Form feed	Marking or the form feed is being executed.
Not connected	The remote network printer has not yet been activated: RPRINTER still has to be implemented.
Not installed	The printer with the specified number has not been installed.
In private mode	The remote network printer is not available because it is locally in use.
Off line/Out of paper	The printer is off line or lacks paper. These messages are only possible in combination with *Printing Job* or *Mark/Form feed*.

If you wish to check the status of all network printers, specify *all* instead of the printer number. If the specified print server is not active, the following message will appear: *Print server <print_server_name> is not up and running.*

PAUse
This parameter interrupts the printer temporarily.

Example 79:

    PSC PS=PS_R008 P=0 PAU

The system gives the following response:

```
The PAUSE command to printer 0 was successful.
```

ABort
The current print job is discontinued and removed from the print queue. The following print job is then executed.

Example 80:

    PSC PS=PS_R008 P=0 AB

The system gives the following response:

```
The current job on printer 0 was aborted successfully.
```

STOp/Keep
Printing is stopped. If the current print job is to be retained, use the *Keep* parameter. The print job is then placed at the end of the print queue. If *Keep* is not specified, the current print job is removed from the queue.

Example 81:
A current print job is to be discontinued and placed at the end of the print queue allowing another emergency job

Control and operation of network print routines 237

to be carried out. Printer 0 on the PS_R008 print server is to be used. To do this, give the following command:

```
PSC PS=PS_R008 P=0 STO K
```

The system gives the following response:

```
The STOP command to printer 0 was successful.
```

Do not forget to activate the printer again using STARt.

STARt
The printer is re-activated after being interrupted using *PAUse* or *STOp*.

Example 82:
A printer which has been stopped using the STOp command is to be activated once more. Give the following command:

```
PSC PS=PS_R008 P=0 STAR
```

The system gives the following response:

```
The current job on printer 0 was started successfully.
```

MArk [character]
A line is marked using asterisks in order to display the current position of the paper in the printer. If a print job has just been executed, marking is not possible. The *Mark* parameter can also be used with a character other than an asterisk.

Example 83:
A line of Ts is to be printed on printer 0, which has been assigned to the PS_R008 print server, in order to check the paper alignment. To do this, give the following command:

```
PSC PS=PS_R008 P=0 MA T
```

The system gives the following response:

```
Printer 0 was marked successfully.
```

FormFeed
This forces a form feed on the printer when it is not currently processing a job (or when a job has been interrupted using *PAUse* or *STOp*).

Example 84:

```
PSC PS=PS_R008 P=0 FF
```

The system gives the following response:

```
A form on printer 0 was successfully ejected.
```

MOuntForm=*n*
This parameter enables you to inform the system that a new form is being inserted. Printing can then be continued after a pause has been made to change paper for instance.

Example 85:

```
PSC PS=PS_R008 P=0 MOF=1
```

The system gives the following response:

```
Form 1 was mounted on printer 0 successfully.
```

PRIvate
This parameter enables you to remove a remote network printer from the list of network printers served by

the print server, so that it can only be used locally. This may lead to problems in the processing of the print queues.

Example 86:

```
PSC PS=PS_R008 P=0 PRI
```

The system gives the following response:

```
Remote printer 0 has become private.
```

SHared
The *PRIvate* parameter which has been previously specified is revoked, so that the printer can be served again as a remote network printer by the print server.

Example 87:

```
PSC PS=PS_R008 P=0 SH
```

The system gives the following response:

```
Remote printer 0 has become shared.
```

CancelDown
The *Going down after current jobs* option, which was specified by the print server manager using PCONSOLE, is revoked. The print server is not switched off. It is not necessary to specify a number for the printer.

Example 88:

```
PSC PS=PS_R008 P=0 CD
```

The system gives the following response:

```
The DOWN command to the print server was cancelled successfully.
```

By setting the DOS environment variable PSC, you can simplify working with the PSC command. For instance, if you only check the PS_R008 print server and the corresponding printer 0, give the following command behind the DOS prompt:

```
SET PSC=PSPS_R008 P0
```

SET enables you to check whether the environment variable has been set. You may need to reserve additional memory for the environment variable by altering CONFIG.SYS.

The syntax of the PSC command is now as follows:

```
PSC flag
```

You can check the status using the following command:

```
PSC STAT
```

If you wish to display the status of printer 1, the command is as follows:

```
PSC P1 STAT
```

It is possible to implement the definition of the environment variable each time the system is started up by including the SET command in the AUTOEXEC.BAT start-up file on your workstation. If that is not possible because you are working at a workstation without drives for instance, you can place the command in the login script instead. The command line is then as follows:

```
DOS SET PSC="PSPS_R008 P0"
```

Note: In the login script, the part behind the equals sign must be placed between inverted commas.

6.5 Activating a print server

Under NetWare 386, a print server, a fileserver or a dedicated workstation can be activated to fulfil the function of a print server.

Activating a print server on a dedicated workstation
The NetWare print server is located in the form of the executable file PSERVER.EXE in the SYS:PUBLIC directory and may be loaded from any workstation which is logged in on the network. The IBM$RUN.OVL, SYS$ERR.DAT, SYS$HELP.DAT and SYS$MSG.DAT files which are located in the same directory must, however, be accessible to the system.

The following specification must be located in the NetWare configuration file:

```
SPX CONNECTIONS = 60
```

SPX represents *Sequenced Packet Protocol Exchange* and contains functions for the data transmission. This specification ensures that there are sufficient system facilities available for the print server to enable it to function correctly.

A print server can serve a maximum of 16 printers and print queues on a maximum of 8 fileservers.

Example 89:
The PS_R008 print server is to be activated in order to serve the print queues on the active fileserver. Proceed as follows:

- Start up the workstation and make the connection to the network.
- Log in on the network. If a search path has been defined for the SYS:PUBLIC directory, you do not need to switch over to this directory. Start the print server using the following command:

```
PSERVER PS_R008
```

The print server is loaded and a list of connected printers appears on the screen along with their status. The screen consists of two halves; you can switch between these windows by pressing a random key. Each window shows information about eight printers.

The figure below illustrates this screen:

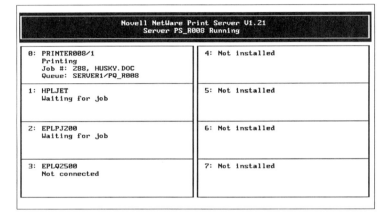

In the figure, four printers have been assigned to the print server *(PCONSOLE -> Print Server Configuration: Printer Configuration)*. Printers 0, 1 and 2 have been activated. Printer 0 is busy processing print job number 288 which is the HUSKY.DOC document. This print job comes from the PQ_R008 queue on the FILESERVER1 fileserver (allocation to the print server via *PCONSOLE, -> Print Server Configuration: Queues Serviced*). Printer 3 is apparently a remote printer with the *Not connected* status, since no allocation has taken place at the workstation to which this printer is connected (RPRINTER).

Example 90:
The print server is to be activated automatically on a workstation.

This can be realized in various ways. If you are using the print server on, for instance, a workstation which is

Activating a print server

started up via the network, you can use the specific workstation start-up files to ensure that the login procedure takes place automatically when the workstation is started up. In that case, the workstation can be used exclusively as a dedicated print server when it is started up via the network. By including commands in the AUTOEXEC.BAT start-up file, you can ensure that a similar procedure takes place on other workstations.

To do this, proceed as follows:

- Log in on the network as the Supervisor or as the supervisor equivalent.
- Activate the SYSCON program and select *User Information*.
- Press the Ins key to install a new user. Specify a unique *User Name*.
- It is not necessary to create a home directory. A password may not be assigned because otherwise input from the keyboard will be requested during the login. The absence of a password is acceptable in this situation because membership of the EVERYONE group provides sufficient rights for working with the print server. A print server which has been activated in this way can only be switched off using PCONSOLE (from another workstation). Switching off the print server (or another 'invalid' shutdown such as using Ctrl-Break) leads automatically to the workstation being logged out.
- You must create a login script. In this, the following command to activate the print server must be specified:

```
#PSERVER PS_R008
```

Save the login script and quit SYSCON. When you log in using the user ID for the print server, this will be activated automatically.
- If you also wish to automize the login procedure, the following command must be placed in the last line of the AUTOEXEC.BAT file:

```
LOGIN user_name
```

Since no password has been specified for the user ID, the login procedure and, at the same time, the loading of the print server can take place automatically.

Starting the print server on the fileserver

During the installation of NetWare, the PSERVER.NLM *loadable module* was copied to the SYS:SYSTEM directory, in addition to PSERVER.EXE. Loadable modules (NLM) have the property that they - as one of several tasks (applications) - may be directly active on the fileserver and thus can be started up via the NetWare console.

In order to activate the print server on the fileserver, proceed as follows:

- Give the following command on the *System Console:*

```
LOAD PSERVER PS_R008
```

  If an application other than the system console screen is to be placed in the foreground (the application monitor for instance), you can switch to the console by pressing the Alt-Esc key combination. The print server will then be loaded, appearing on the screen just like a print server on a workstation.

- If you wish the print server to be automatically loaded on the fileserver, include the *LOAD PSERVER print_server_name* command in the AUTOEXEC.NCF file. To do this, activate NLM INSTALL on the fileserver console (*LOAD INSTALL*) or press Alt-Esc to switch to INSTALL (you may have to press several times). Select *System Options* and then *Edit AUTOEXEC.NCF file*. Specify the command. Close the edit mode by pressing Esc and respond *Yes* to the question *Save AUTOEXEC.NCF file*. The print server will now be activated automatically when the fileserver is started up.

Switching the print server off

In principle, an active print server can be switched off by the print server manager by means of the PCONSOLE program. A print server which is active on a fileserver can be switched off using the following console command:

UNLOAD PSERVER

Since only one print server may be active on a fileserver, it is sufficient to specify the print server name when switching off.

Activating remote network printers

Under NetWare 386, it is possible for a print server to serve printers which are connected to a random workstation. These are the *remote printers*. The RPRINTER utility program (in SYS:PUBLIC) is required to do this. This makes the link between the print server and the remote network printer which is connected to the workstation. RPRINTER is a TSR program (Terminate and Stay Resident), which remains active in the background in computer working memory until it is removed or until the computer is reset.

RPRINTER must be loaded separately for each remote network printer to be connected to the workstation. Therefore, if you wish to operate two printers, you must load RPRINTER twice. In order to enable RPRINTER to function smoothly on a workstation, the following conditions should be fulfilled:

- There must be a search path to the SYS:PUBLIC directory.
- The RPRINTER.EXE, RPRINTER.HLP, IBM$RUN.OVL, SYS$ERR.DAT, SYS$HELP.DAT and SYS$MSG.DAT files must be accessible via the search path.
- At least one network printer must be defined using PCONSOLE. In this, the printer port by which the printer is operated can be defined by either in PCONSOLE or by RPRINTER (in the latter case, you must

specify *Remote Other/Unknown* as the type in PCONSOLE).
■ A print queue must be also be allocated to this printer by means of the PCONSOLE program.

Activating remote network printers via a menu

If you have activated a print server and you now wish to activate a workstation printer as a network printer and make this available to other network users, proceed as follows:

■ Activate the RPRINTER program.
■ From the subsequent list, select the required print server by placing the cursor on the name. Press Enter to confirm the selection.
■ Select the required printer from the list which then appears on the screen and confirm this using Enter.

The figure below shows a list in the RPRINTER program of the remote network printers available:

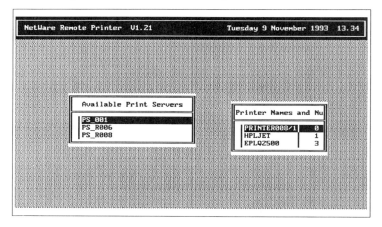

■ If the printer has been defined as *Remote Other/Unknown*, the *Printer n configuration* window is opened in which you must specify the data necessary to enable the printer to function (port, interrupt, baudrate, data and stop bits, parity and protocol for serial print-

Activating a print server 247

ers). Confirm these data and link the printer to the print server by pressing Esc.
- The following (or similar) message will appear to confirm a successful installation:

```
*** Remote Printer "PRINTER008/1" (printer 0) installed ***
```

Activating remote network printers via the command line. When you have specified the necessary data as parameters when activating the RPRINTER program, the printer is initialized as a remote network printer without you having to specify additional information.

The command line is as follows:

RPRINTER [print_server_name] [printer_number]

Print server name   Specify the name of the print server here.
printer number   Specify the printer number here.

Example 91:
A printer connected to port LPT1 is to be used as a remote printer. The printer is to be operated via the print server PS-001. During the installation of the print server, the network printer has been assigned the name EPLQ2500 and the number 3.

Proceed as follows:

- Log in on the network.
- Specify the following command behind the operating system prompt at the required workstation:

    RPRINTER PS_001 3

- The following system message appears on the screen:

```
*** Remote printer "EPLQ2500" (printer 3) installed ***
```

Example 92:
Similar to the previous example, but this time the printer is to be automatically activated with the RPRINTER program when the workstation is started up.

Since RPRINTER is also active when you are not logged in (if the NetWare shell is loaded), you can only use the command line to include the command in the AUTOEXEC.BAT file of the workstation. In that case, the RPRINTER.EXE and RPRINTER.HLP files must be located on a local workstation (hard)disk or in the SYS:LOGIN directory of the fileserver. The AUTOEXEC.BAT file should look something like this:

```
...
IPX
NETX
F:
RPRINTER PS_001 3
...
```

By means of these commands, RPRINTER is loaded from the SYS:LOGIN directory each time the system is started up and printer 3 is allocated to the PS_001 print server.

6.6 Logging out a remote network printer from the print server

In order to disconnect a remote network printer from the print server, you must use RPRINTER in the command mode. Specify the parameter -R along with the print server name and the printer number.

Example 93:
Printer number 2 is to be disconnected from the PS-001 print server. Give the following command:

Logging out a remote network printer from the print server 249

```
RPRINTER PS_001 3 -R
```

The following system message appears:

```
*** Remote printer "EPLQ2500" has been removed. ***
```

Note: If you are working with a NetWare shell which uses the XMSNETX.EXE or EMSNETX.EXE programs to make use of extended or expanded memory, you cannot use RPRINTER with the -R option. In that case, you will have to restart the computer.

Checking the status of the remote network printer.
To do this, give the following command:

```
RPRINTER -S
```

Note: You can only request information concerning printers which are connected to your workstation.

The screen willl look something like this:

```
Print server: PS_001
Printer:       0
Printer name: PRINTER008/1
Printer type: LPT1
Using IRQ:    7
Status:       Waiting for job

Print server: PS_R008
Printer:       2
Printer name: HPLJET
Printer type: LPT2
Using IRQ:    5
Status:       Waiting for job
```

Using a remote network printer locally. If a workstation printer has been made available to others as a network printer by means of the RPRINTER program, you can nevertheless ensure that it can only be used locally. To do this, make use of the PSC program which has already been mentioned.

Example 94:
The printer which has been connected as a remote network printer to the print server PS_001 under the number 3, is to be used exclusively as a local printer.

Give the following command:

```
PSC PS=PS_001 P=3 PRI
```

The following system message appears:

```
Remote printer 3 has become private.
```

Note: This command is only implemented if you have the status of the print server manager.

In order to make the remote network printer available to other users again, give the following command:

```
PSC PS=PS_001 P=3 SH
```

The system indicates:

```
Remote printer 3 has become shared.
```

7 Communication within the network

The activities within a company now depend more than ever on a good exchange of information among the staff. The classic means of communication are the telephone, intercom, letter and messenger. If the staff are linked to one another by means of computers in a network, this provides the interesting possibility of exchanging information immediately from the place of work via *electronic post* (also often referred to as *electronic mail* or *E-mail*). The advantages are obvious:

- Less telephone costs, since information can be transported more quickly and safely via internal or external networks (including WANs, *Wide Area Networks*) than spoken messages.
- Greater efficiency, since the information is directly transmitted to the recipient regardless of personal availability or delivery times. It is immediately available for further editing in file form if required.

Unfortunately, from version 2.15 onwards, NetWare no longer has its own E-mail system, but there are functions by which messages can be sent to other users in the system. These messages are placed directly on the screen of the recipient. In addition, Novell NetWare can provide a so-called *Mail Handling System (MHS)* which supplies basic procedures to support other post products handling the exchange of messages when the network facilities are fully in use.

Owing to the growing significance of E-mail, we shall give a description of the most important facilities a program like this can provide, taking Pegasus Mail as an example. This is a *Public Domain* program, which may be freely distributed and used.

7.1 Sending messages in the network

Sending messages from the fileserver. Using the keyboard, you can send messages with a maximum of 55 characters from the fileserver (central computer) to any or all users in the network. This takes place by means of the commands BROADCAST and SEND. Both commands are used in the same way. They have the following syntax (there must be no spaces in the names or numbers):

```
BROADCAST "message" [[TO] [user_name/link_number]
[AND/,][user_name/link_number]]
```

BROADCAST	Broadcast.
message	Specify the message here between inverted commas.
[TO] user name	Specify here the name of the user who is to receive the message. If you specify several names, you must separate these by means of a comma, a space or the word AND. The word TO is optional.
link number	You can use this number instead of, or along with, the user name(s). You can gain information about the link numbers of those who have logged in using the *Connection Information* menu option of NLM MONITOR. If you do not specify any addresses (thus no user names or numbers) all users who are logged in will receive the message.

Example 95:
The users Scott and Shackleton and the users with the link numbers 34 and 56 are to be summoned from the fileserver to log out of the system. To do this, give the following command:

```
BROADCAST "Log out. Maintenance" Scott, Shackleton,34,56
```

Sending messages in the network 253

If all those who are addressed are currently logged in, the following message appears on the console:

```
Broadcast was sent to 4 stations
```

The following message appears in inverse video on line 25 of the screens of the four users:

```
>> Log out. Maintenance            (CTRL-ENTER to clear)
```

The keyboards of the workstations remain frozen until the message is cleared from the screens using Ctrl-Enter.

Note: The messages do not appear on the screen if the CASTOFF program has been activated (see section 7.2). In addition, no messages are given if an application is active in the graphic mode. The message only appears at the moment the graphic program is closed.

Example 96:
The above message is to be sent to all users. To do this, give the following command:

BROADCAST "Log out. Maintenance"

The system shows no response. The message appears on line 5 of the screens of those who are logged in.

Using SEND to send messages from the workstation. It is possible to send short messages (a maximum of 44 characters) from each workstation in the network to one or more users or groups or to the fileserver. To do this, give the following command (there must be no spaces in the user name or number) :

SEND "message" [[TO] [fileserver/][user_name/[,]
link_number],...] [CONSOLE] [EVERYBODY]

SEND	Send.
message	Specify the information to be sent between inverted commas.
[TO] user name	Specify the name of the user who is to receive the message. If you specify several names, they must be separated from one another by means of commas, spaces or the word AND. The word TO is optional.
fileserver	Specify here the name of the fileserver on which the recipient of the message is logged in. However, this is only necessary if the sender is logged in on a different fileserver.
Link number	You may specify the link number along with, or instead of, the user name. You can gain information about the link numbers of those who are currently logged in by means of the *Connection Information* menu option of NLM MONITOR. The *Connection Information* window displays a list of users currently logged in and their link numbers.
CONSOLE	If this option is specified, the message appears on the fileserver screen.
EVERYONE	If this option is specified, the message is sent to all members of the EVERYONE group. This generally includes all network users.

Example 97:

User Scott is logged in on the SERVER1 fileserver and has the link number 4. He has just received the message that the network manager is going to disconnect the link to the fileserver within a few minutes for urgent repairs. However, Scott still has to save his diary. Accordingly, he wishes to send a message to the network manager. The following command enables him to do this:

```
SEND "Snowed under with work. Wait please"
TO CONSOLE
```

Sending messages in the network 255

Novell NetWare reacts with the following message:

```
Message sent to SERVER1/CONSOLE.
```

The following message appears on the fileserver screen:

```
From SCOTT[4]: Snowed under with work. Wait please.
```

Thus, the network manager is notified from which user with which link number the message has come and can react accordingly.

Example 98:
All members of the SALES group are to be reminded of an appointment. Give the following command:

```
SEND "Reminder: meeting at 15.00" TO SALES
```

Novell NetWare responds by showing which members have received the message. For instance:

```
Message sent to SERVER1/COOK (station 3)
Message sent to SERVER1/POLO (station 4)
Message sent to SERVER1/TASMAN (station 23)
```

On the screen of the recipients the message is displayed:

```
>> From AMUNDSEN[2]: Reminder: meeting at 15.00    (CTRL-ENTER to clear)
```

The recipients are notified of the name and link number of the sender. This facilitates sending an answer.

Example 99:
A member of staff wishes to ask his colleague, who is logged in under the name OATES on the POLE fileserver, if he would like to dine with him. To make the appointment, give the following command:

```
SEND "Spare ribs by candlelight at 20.00?"
TO POLE/OATES
```

Novell NetWare confirms this message as follows:

```
Message sent to POLE/OATES (station 8)
```

Oates is perhaps delighted by the following invitation on his screen:

```
>>From SERVER1/AMUNDSEN[2]:Spare ribs by candlelight 20.00?(CTRL-ENTER to clear)
```

Sending messages using SESSION. It is also possible to send messages in a menu-driven manner using the SESSION utility program. Proceed as follows:

■ Activate the SESSION program. To do this, you only require the right (which most users have) to address the SYS:PUBLIC directory. From the *Available Topics* main menu, select one of the options shown below:

```
Available Topics
Change Current Server
Drive Mappings
Group List
Search Mappings
Select Default Drive
User List
```

■ Activate the last option, *User List*, in order to display a list of network users who are currently logged in and their link numbers (*Current Users Station*).

Sending messages in the network

- Select the user to whom you wish to send a message and press Enter. You can now choose either *Display User Information* or *Send Message*.
- Select *Send Message*.
- In the subsequent window, you can enter a message consisting of a maximum of 55 characters, minus the length of the user name. Confirm this using Enter. You will not receive acknowledgement of the message from the system. This is not required because you can only select users who are logged in, therefore the message will certainly be delivered to the destination specified. If a user has blocked the display of messages using CASTOFF, you will receive a message in a window: *The message was not sent to....*
- The message appears on line 25 of the screen of the recipient as shown previously.

The figure below indicates how a message is sent using the SESSION utility program :

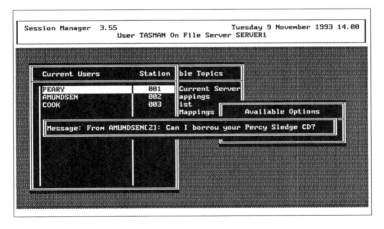

Using SESSION, you can also send a message to several users simultaneously:

- Using F5, mark the users who are to receive the message. Press Enter to activate the window in which the message is to be specified.

Sending messages using FCONSOLE to all users. If you have supervisor rights, you can also send messages using the FCONSOLE program (**F**ileserver CONSOLE). If you do not have these rights, you can activate FCONSOLE but this only allows you to request information. Proceed as follows to send messages using FCONSOLE:

■ Log in as the Supervisor or as the supervisor equivalent.
■ Activate the FCONSOLE program. The following main menu appears:

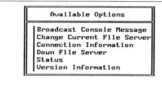

■ Select *Broadcast Console Message*. You can enter a message of a maximum of 55 characters in the window which subsequently appears. Press Enter to actually send the message.
■ The message appears on the screens of all users who are logged in, including your own. It will look something like this:

As you see, you are not notified of the sender.

Sending messages using FCONSOLE to selected users. To do this, proceed as follows:

■ Log in as the Supervisor or as the supervisor equivalent.
■ Activate the FCONSOLE program. Select the *Connection Information* option from the main menu. A

Sending messages in the network 259

window appears showing a list of all users who are currently logged in and their link numbers.
- Select the recipient of the message, or use F5 to specify several users.
- When you have pressed Enter, you can choose one of two options in the *Connection Information* menu: *Broadcast Console Message* or *Other Information* (if you selected only one user). If you selected several users, only the former option is available.
- Select *Broadcast Console Message*. You can specify a message consisting of a maximum of 55 characters in the subsequent window.
- Press Enter to actually send the message.
- The message apppears on the screens of the selected users, something like this:

Here too, the recipients are not shown the identity of the sender.

The figure below shows the FCONSOLE screen with the *Connection Information:* menu.

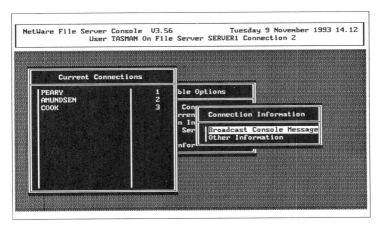

7.2 Accepting or refusing messages

If you do not wish to be interrupted by messages sent by others, you can suppress the display of messages. To do this, make use of the CASTOFF program which is located in the SYS:PUBLIC directory.

Example 100:
You wish to suppress the display of all messages sent to you from other workstations.

If a search path to SYS:PUBLIC has been installed, you only need to give the following command behind the prompt:

CASTOFF

The system reacts with the following message:

```
Broadcasts from other stations will now be rejected.
```

In other words: from now on, messages from other workstations will not be accepted. However, messages from the fileserver are excepted and this also applies to messages which are sent using FCONSOLE. This means that important messages from the network manager will get through.

The other users will notice that they cannot contact you. System messages will inform them that messages sent using SEND or SESSION are not accepted by the destination. In the case of SEND, the message will be *Message NOT sent to...*

If you also wish to suppress messages from the network manager, you should specify CASTOFF along with the ALL (or A) parameter:

CASTOFF A

The system reacts with the following message:

```
Broadcasts from the console and other stations will now be rejected.
```

Caution: From this moment onwards, no messages will be shown on your screen. You must consider the consequences of this action. It is also important to realize that the network manager cannot see that you have not received a message if he/she sends a message using FCONSOLE from a workstation or BROADCAST/SEND from the fileserver.

If you use the CASTOFF command regularly, it is advisable to include this command in the login script.

When you no longer wish to be isolated from messages from the outside world, give the following command:

CASTON

The following messages will appear, depending on the specified parameters:

```
Broadcasts messages from the console and other stations will now be accepted.
```

```
Broadcasts messages from other stations will now be accepted.
```

7.3 An example of electronic post: Pegasus Mail

Installation. The installation of Pegasus Mail is quite simple. Proceed as follows:

- Copy the PMAIL.EXE, PMAIL.HLP and NEW-

MAIL.EXE files to a directory which is accessible to all users, such as SYS:PUBLIC.
- Set the *Shareable* attribute (see section 3.4).
- In order to inform the users when they log in that E-mail is available, the system login script should be extended with the following command:

```
#NEWMAIL                                (1)
IF "%ERROR_LEVEL" > "0" THEN BEGIN      (2)
    WRITE ""                            (3)
    PAUSE                               (4)
END                                     (5)
```

(1) By means of the first command, the NEWMAIL program is activated. This registers the number of new messages for the user up until the moment of logging in.
(2) When successfully activated, NEWMAIL stores the number of new messages in the DOS variable called ERROR LEVEL. If the number of messages is larger than 0, the following commands are executed.
(3) Produces a blank line.
(4) The DOS command, PAUSE, is executed. In this way, the user has the chance to read the message displayed by NEWMAIL and to activate the PMAIL program. It is also possible to directly activate PMAIL instead of PAUSE in order to deal with incoming post immediately. In that case, replace the PAUSE command with #PMAIL.

- All network users can make use of PMAIL from now on. There are two methods of denying the use of PMAIL to certain users:

  (1) Create the NOMAIL group and place the users who may not use PMAIL in this group.
  (2) Create the MAILUSERS group and assign the users who may use PMAIL to this group.

■ In the same way, you can determine which users may send messages to user groups (GROUPMAIL group) and which users may send post via the *Internet gateway* (GW_USERS group) if available.

In this way, you have installed a well-functioning and easily-operated system for electronic mail.

Sending messages. PMAIL has its own editor for creating and sending messages, but you can also send ready-made files. The editor is largely compatible with the WordStar word processor. You can also use a different word processor if you wish. The most important options are described below:

1. Activate PMAIL using the PMAIL command. Confirm this by pressing Enter.
2. PMAIL appears with the following opening screen:

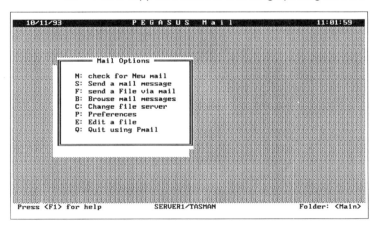

The menu options have the following significance:

N   Read new messages. This option only appears if there are new messages.
S   Send messages. Activates the text editor to create a message.
F   Send a file. A window is opened in which all the

data necessary for the transmission can be specified.
- B Look through the messages you have received or sent.
- C Change fileserver. PMAIL assumes the task of making a connection to a different fileserver and carrying out the login procedure.
- P Set the system parameters for PMAIL.
- E When you have specified a file name or have displayed a list by pressing Tab, you can edit the file in the PMAIL text editor. The file may not be larger than 32 KB.
- Q Quit PMAIL.

3. Select S in order to activate the text editor.
4. You must first specify the recipient of the message using the user name (*To:[...]*). Press F2 and Enter to select the user from the list of users. Groups can be recognized by the number sign # in front of the name.
5. On the second line *(Subj.: [...])*, you can give a short description consisting of a maximum of 64 characters.
6. Quit the second line by pressing Enter. This will bring you to the actual editor. Specify the message you wish to send.
7. If you subsequently wish to determine special conditions, you can edit the *Message Headers* by pressing F9. The figure on the following page shows the PMAIL screen containing the window for editing the message banner:

An example of electronic post: Pegasus Mail

```
┌──────────────── Send Message: Editing Screen ────────────────┐
│ To   : SCOTT                                                 │
│ Subj : New boots                                             │
│  ┌──────────────── Edit Message Headers ────────────────┐    │
│  │ Cc        : AMUNDSEN, OATES, SHACKLETON              │    │
│  │ Bcc       : POLO, STANLEY                            │    │
│  │ Reply to  :                                          │    │
│  │ Copy self : Y                                        │    │
│  │ Encrypt?  : N                                        │    │
│  │ Confirm   : [Y ]                                     │    │
│  └──────────────────────────────────────────────────────┘    │
│                                                              │
│                                                      I   1:1 │
└─ F1-Help F2-Userlist F3-Addrbook F6-Lists F9-Edit headers Ctrl-Enter-Send ─┘
```

In the *Message Headers* window, you can specify the following:

- Those who are to receive a *Carbon copy* (Cc) and those who are to receive a *Blind copy* (Bcc) of the message. The difference consists of whether the receiver is informed of the sender (Cc) or not (Bcc).
- Is the recipient to receive an address which deviates from the transmission address in order to send an answer (*Reply to:*)?
- Is a copy of the message to be included in the sender's *folder* (the default setting is Y)?
- Is the message to be coded for sending? If you select Y, you must specify a code word consisting of a maximum of 8 characters. It is self-evident that the recipient must be aware of this.
- Do you wish to know when the recipient reads the message? If so, you will receive a message concerning the date and time of reading. However, this facility can be made generally redundant for certain users. You will receive a relevant message at the time of sending.

8. When the message is ready to be sent, you can ensure transmission by pressing Ctrl-Enter which provides a direct confirmation to the subsequent question *Accept this data?*.
9. If you wish to send a file, select *F: send a File via mail* from the main menu.

10. In the *Send a file via mail* window, specify the recipient of the message in the first line. You can display a selection list by pressing F2 and Enter. You can also include a short description on the second line (*Subject:*).
11. Specify the name of the file to be sent on the third line, *File:*. Activate a selection list, if required, by pressing the Tab key. Use the keyboard to specify the directory. If you then press Tab, the required directory will be activated.
12. The *ASCII file?* option should only be set to Y if the file exclusively contains characters with ASCII values ranging between 32 and 127.
13. Quit the last window by pressing Enter and confirm the *Accept this data?* question in order to send the message.
14. The recipient of the message is informed of incoming post by a message on line 25 of the screen. This resembles the message sent by SEND:

The figure below shows the Pegasus Mail screen in which a file is defined for sending:

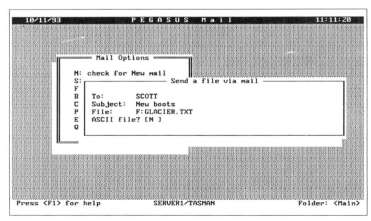

Editing incoming messages. When you receive messages, the PMAIL main menu is extended with the option *N: check for New mail*. Select this option to gain an overview of the new messages. In addition to a description and the name of the sender in various columns, you will also be informed of the date and time of sending. The figure below shows an example of this:

```
                         Folder: <New Mail> (5 messages)
 From                    Subject                            Date
 *SERVER1/AMUNDSEN       New boots                          10 Nov 93 09:50
 *SERVER1/SCOTT          Ponies                             10 Nov 93 10:13
 *SERVER1/OATES          The Outside World                  10 Nov 93 11:15
 *SERVER1/SHACKLETON     Shipping forecast                  10 Nov 93 12:16
 *SERVER1/COOK           Keel haul                          10 Nov 93 14:17
                       <       End of list       >

      →Archive Copy Dos Forward Locate Move Order Print Reply Send eXtract
              <Spc> (un)mark  <Enter> Read  <Del> Delete  <Esc> Exit
```

You then have the possibility of further editing the post received. In this, you have the choice between processing the messages one at a time or several simultaneously. A condition of the latter option is that you must have marked the appropriate messages using F5.

Reading. You can always read a message. To do this, place the cursor on the required message and press Enter. If you are dealing with a message compiled using PMAIL, the following information (for example) will be shown:

Subject:	Angle to the magnetic pole
To:	SHACKLETON
X-To:	SHACKLETON
Cc:	SCOTT, OATES
Date:	10 Nov 93 16:15:56

If this concerns a file, the PMAIL message first displays the 'envelope' containing the message. This takes place in the form of a window with information, looking something like this for example:

```
┌─────────── Message is a file transfer envelope ───────────┐
│   From     SERVER1/COOK                                    │
│   Subject  Going south                                     │
│   Date     10 Nov 93 16:39                                 │
│   File     S_DOCU.TXT                                      │
│                                                            │
│              (press any key to continue)                   │
└────────────────────────────────────────────────────────────┘
```

If you now press a random key, the entire text of the message will be displayed. You can process this as required.

Archive
You can save the files in compressed form to save space.

Copy
It is possible to include copies in other *folders*.

Dos
You can access the workstation operating system.

Forward
You can pass on a message to another user.

Locate
You can search for a certain text in all or in selected messages.

Move
Move messages to another *folder*.

Order
Change the sorting order of the messages.

Print
Print the current message. PMAIL also supports print queues in addition to local printers (see also chapter 6).

Send
Send a new message.

eXtract
If the message only consists of an *envelope* for a file, the contents of the file can be written to a separate file. This can then be adopted into the editor using the *E: Edit a file* option.

8 Archiving and protecting data

8.1 Forms of data protection

The protection of data and programs in a network deserves special attention. In previous chapters, we dealt mainly with safeguarding data against unauthorized addressing. However, this protection is not sufficient to protect the data against physical destruction. This type of destruction may be related to the condition of the hardware (such as technical defects of the server harddisk) or a power failure during data processing. It may also be caused by unintentional removal of data by a deletion command.

The network manager must ensure that the files which are saved on the fileserver are stored on a basis of logical criteria, so that if anything goes wrong, it is possible to restore the files in a logical way. Such criteria may be:

- All files in a certain subdirectory should be copied to an external disk (diskette).
- All files on the fileserver should be copied to external disks.
- The files should be copied individually to other disks.
- Saving a program and file system should take place regularly after processing by the user (for instance in a stock management system).

In principle, it is possible to archive files under Novell NetWare using the DOS command COPY, just as on a stand-alone personal computer.

Example 101:
The files in the DATA subdirectory on the server F: harddisk are to be copied to diskdrive A:. Then the files on the diskette in drive A: are to be copied back again to the subdirectory of the fileserver.

```
F:\>COPY F:\DATA\*.* A:                    (1)
F:\>COPY A:*.* F:\DATA                     (2)
```

(1) The DATA directory and all files (*.*) are specified as source.
(2) The DATA directory is again the DATA directory.

The disadvantage of this method of archiving is that the access rights and the file attributes are not saved along with the files. This is after all only the normal DOS command.

In order to also transport the access rights and the file attributes in the archiving process, you must specify the relevant Novell NetWare commands or use Novell NetWare utility programs. Early versions of Novell NetWare used the following commands to save the fileserver data:

LARCHIVE   Archives the fileserver data to local drives.
LRESTORE   Restores data stored using LARCHIVE, by means of local drives; comparable to the DOS command RESTORE.
NARCHIVE   Archives/saves fileserver data on other network drives. Otherwise identical to LARCHIVE.
NRESTORE   Writes back data stored using NARCHIVE. Otherwise identical to LRESTORE.

These commands can still be used under Novell NetWare 386. However, the NBACKUP utility program is more convenient. All functions for backing up and restoring can be executed in a menu-driven process. Accordingly, we shall confine ourselves to this utility program in the examples below.

8.2 Saving data using NBACKUP

The NBACKUP utility program for saving data is activated by typing the command of the same name. It can be activated from any position in the network as long as the user has the appropriate rights.

Example 102:
The NBACKUP utility program is to be activated by the network manager who has all rights in all directories.

- Give the command NBACKUP. The NBACKUP menu screen is activated.

The figure below shows this figure:

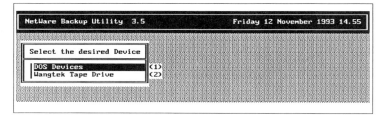

(1) We shall select the *DOS Devices* menu option for our example.
(2) Select this menu option if you have a separately installed tapestreamer of this type.

Example 103:
All files stored in the F:\DATA subdirectory on the SERVER1 fileserver are to be backed up on diskette via the A: local diskdrive after the contents of the directory have been checked. This check of the \DATA directory produces the following result:

Saving data using NBACKUP

```
F:\DATA>dir                                                          (1)

 Volume in drive F is SYS
 Directory of F:\DATA

DATA1       DAT        45   10-11-93  15:16                          (2)
DATA2       DAT        53   10-11-93  15:16
DATA3       DAT        75   10-11-93  15:17
CAPT0008    LST      2050   10-11-93  15:04
        4 file(s)       54124544 bytes free

F:\DATA>_
```

(1) Command to show the contents of \DATA.
(2) There are four files in the directory.

The data backup is to take place via a diskdrive. This is a DOS device.

■ Activate the *DOS Devices* option in the NBACKUP menu. The NBACKUP *Main Menu* appears, as shown below:

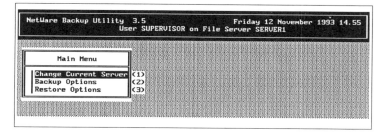

(1) The *Change Current Server* menu option can be used to select another fileserver. This function is similar to the same function in the SYSCON utility program described earlier.
(2) The data are backed up using this menu option.
(3) The backup data are written back using this option.

In order to back up the data:

■ Select the *Backup options* menu option. The *Backup Menu* window appears, as shown on the following page.

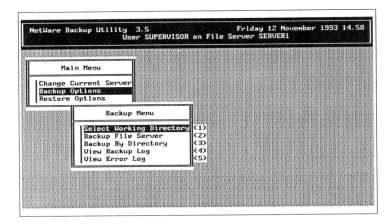

(1) This is the function to determine the working directory. NBACKUP needs this working directory for temporary storage of the protocol files which begin with the character string BACK$.
(2) This is the function to back up all data on the fileserver.
(3) This is the function to back up data in separate directories on the fileserver.
(4) This is the function to display the protocol file (logbook function) of the backup process.
(5) This is the function to display the protocol file containing the errors (Error logbook) occurring during the backup process.

Create a working directory to save the protocol files temporarily:

- Select the *Select Working Directory* menu option.
- In the subsequent window, assign the name SYS:WORK to the workdirectory. NBACKUP stores the protocol files in this directory during the backup process. BACK$ is added to the beginning of the file name.

The following figure displays this:

Saving data using NBACKUP 275

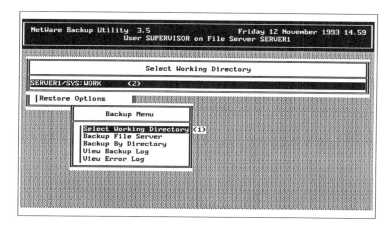

(1) The menu option used to determine the working directory.
(2) Specify the name of the working directory for the temporary storage of the NBACKUP protocol files.

- Select the *Backup by directory* function from the *Backup Menu*. Press Enter and the *Backup Options* window appears.
- Specify the parameters for the backup in the *Backup Options* window. *Yes* and *No* can be chosen by pressing Y and N. If you wish to alter certain data, such as file names and directories, you only need to press Enter at the corresponding line. The Del and Ins keys enable you to operate the input mode via a small window box.

The figure on page 277 provides an example of the result of specifying parameters:

(1) Any desired text given to describe the backup process. The text is included in the log files.
(2) Simultaneous backup of the *Bindery* system (information about users and groups). We choose the default setting here, *Yes*.
(3) Parameter *Yes:* if subdirectories also exist in the directory to be archived, these are also archived.

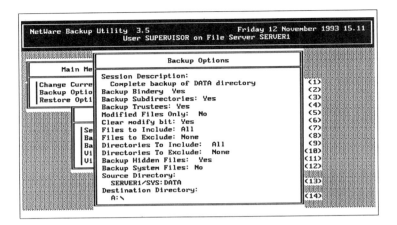

(4) Parameter *Yes:* the directory and file rights are saved in addition to the data.
(5) Parameter *No:* here you should determine whether only the modified files or all the files in the directory are to be saved. In our case, we wish to have a complete backup. Thus files which have not been altered since the last backup are also to be archived now.
(6) Clear modify bit. The *Yes* parameter ensures removal so that in the next backup, an examination can be performed into which files have been created or modified since the current backup.
(7) The *All* parameter ensures that all files in the directory will be archived. It is possible to select a certain type of file to be archived by specifying the file pattern, for example *.DAT.
(8) The *None* parameter ensures that no file is excluded from the backup process. If you specify a file pattern such as *.EXE for instance, all files with this extension will be excluded from the backup process.
(9) The *All* parameter means that all subdirectories of the specified directory are to be saved. A certain directory can be specified for archiving by pressing Enter and Ins.
(10) The *None* parameter means that, similar to point (8), no directories are to be excluded from the

archiving process. If required, specify a directory in the same way as described in point (9).
(11) The *Yes* parameter means that hidden files will also be archived.
(12) The *No* parameter prevents the archiving of system files.
(13) In our example, we specified that the DATA directory was to to be archived. Normally the server root directory is specified here.
(14) In our example, the data are to archived on a diskette in drive A:.

■ When all parameters have been specified, quit the menu by pressing Esc. In the subsequent window, you will be asked if you wish to proceed with the backup process.
■ Select *Yes*. This activates the *Start Backup Menu*.
■ If you wish to begin archiving the data right away, select the *Start Backup Now* option. Then start the archiving which will be carried out according to the parameters specified above.

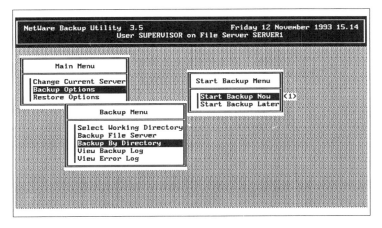

When the backup process has been completed, system data is shown in two windows. This enables you to see if the archiving has been carried out as required. The figure below displays an example of a possible result:

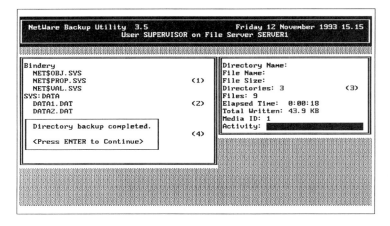

(1) Display of the archived binary files.
(2) Display of the archived data files.
(3) Protocol of the capacity information.
(4) Concluding message of the archiving process.

■ Now press Enter, as indicated in the above figure. This returns you to the *Backup Menu*.

Just to check everything, you can display the contents of the backup logbook. These include the external backup data:

■ Select the *View Backup Log* option from the *Backup Menu*. The contents of the logbook appear.

The figure below shows the protocol data of our example:

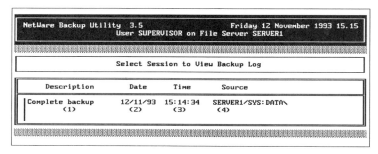

(1) Description of the backup.
(2) Date of the backup.
(3) Time of the backup.
(4) Directory from which the backup was made.

In addition to the backup log, a logbook containing backup errors is also kept. This logbook can be useful in tracing errors if, for instance, the backup process has been interrupted for any reason. The error logbook has the same structure as the backup log (see previous page).

If necessary, display the error log as follows:

- Select *View Error Log* from the *Backup Menu*. The contents of the logbook are shown.

When the archiving process has been executed successfully, quit the NBACKUP program:

- Press Esc. The *Exit NBACKUP* window appears.
- Confirm the *Yes* default setting by pressing Enter.

You will now leave the backup program. In order to check the finished result, you can display the contents of the backup diskette. Apply the command shown below:

```
F:\>dir a:                                              (1)
 Volume in drive A has no label
 Directory of A:\
BACK$000 000     45100  12.11.93  15.14                 (2)
        1 file(s)       1394176 bytes free
```

(1) Display the contents of the diskette in drive A:.
(2) The BACK$000.000 file is shown as having a size of 45,100 bytes. The data which have been archived using NBACKUP have been stored in compressed form.

Note: Keep the backup diskette in a safe place.

8.3 Restoring data using NBACKUP

When the data and programs on backup diskettes have to be restored to the fileserver, you can also use NBACKUP to do this. This can only be done, however, if these have been archived using NBACKUP.

Example 104:
The data from the DATA directory which were saved on diskette using the NBACKUP program are to be restored to the fileserver. To do this, proceed as follows:

- Activate the NBACKUP utility program by typing the program name.
- Activate the *Restore Options* option from the main menu. The *Restore Menu* appears on the screen.

The figure below displays both menus:

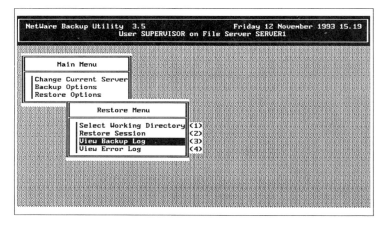

(1) The function to determine the working directory. This working directory needs NBACKUP for the *Restore* function which is analogous to the backup function.
(2) The function to restore the data.
(3) The function to display the backup logbook.
(4) The function to display the error logbook.

In section 8.2, we defined the SYS:WORK directory to contain the information required for the backup process. This directory must now be specified to the Restore program. Proceed as follows:

- Activate the *Select Working Directory* option from the *Restore Menu*.
- Type the name of the directory or let the system do the work by using the Ins and Enter keys. Confirm this using Enter. The *Restore Menu* appears again.

To check, you can display the backup data in the logbook. To do this, select the *View Backup Log* option from the *Restore Menu*. The logbook shows the data pertaining to the backup processes (see section 8.2). Now specify the directory you wish to restore:

- Activate the *Restore Session* option from the *Restore Menu*. The *Restore Session* window appears on the screen. The structure corresponds to that of the logbook. If several directories are shown in the window, select the required directory using the cursor keys.

The figure below shows the dialog window for our example:

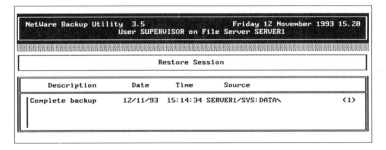

(1) Since we only archived one directory in our example in section 8.2, only one directory is shown here:

- Confirm the selected directory by pressing Enter. The *Restore Options* dialog window appears, as shown below:
- Check the parameters displayed in this window. You may need to alter some options for the restore procedure. To do this, place the cursor on the relevant line and select the required setting by pressing Enter, or enter the data directly.

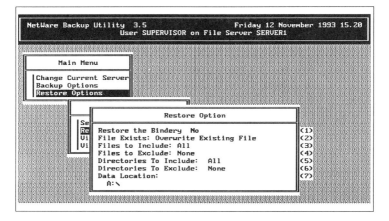

(1) If the Bindery data were also saved along with the backup, you can restore them by selecting *Yes* here.

(2) Specify here the way in which the data should be restored to the fileserver. The default setting is *Overwrite Existing File*. This means that if there are files in the fileserver directory which is to be restored, these will be replaced by the files on the diskettes. This is the most common procedure. You can alter the parameters by pressing Enter. Other options are:

> *Do Not Overwrite:* existing files on the fileserver are not replaced by files on the backup diskettes.
> *Interactive:* each file which is to be written back from the diskette is first shown on the screen.

The restoration of the file must first be confirmed.
➤ *Rename Existing File:* all files located in the directory of the fileserver receive the extension B*xx*, where *xx* represents a sequence number. At the end of the restore process, you must specify whether these files are to be retained or not. You can rename or remove them, as required.
➤ *Rename Restored File:* all files which are restored from the diskettes receive the extension B*xx*, where *xx* represents a sequence number. All files in the directory of the fileserver retain their present name.

(3) This option enables you to determine whether all or only certain files are to be restored. A possible file pattern is, for instance, *.EXE. Then only files with the EXE extension will be restored. The default setting (*All*) restores all files. This setting can be altered by pressing the Ins key.

(4) This option enables you to determine which files should not be restored. A possible file pattern is, for instance *.COM. Then files with this extension will not be restored. The default setting is *None*, meaning that no files are excluded.

(5) Similar to point (3), but now with respect to directories.

(6) Similar to point (4), but now with respect to directories.

(7) The default setting for the drive containing the backup diskette. In our example, that is drive A:.

■ When you have checked the options, press Esc.
■ Answer *Yes* to the subsequent *Save Restore* question. The *Start Restore* window appears.

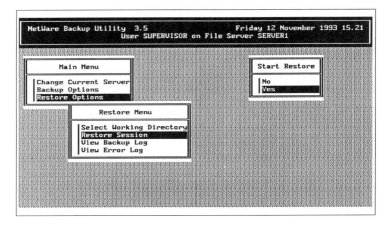

- Place the backup diskette in the workstation drive from which you wish to restore the data (see Restore Option figure above). If the backups are stored on several diskettes, insert the first diskette. The other diskettes will be requested automatically at the appropriate time.
- Activate the *Yes* option in the *Start Restore* window. The restore procedure is displayed in a file window.

The figure below shows the file window pertaining to our example:

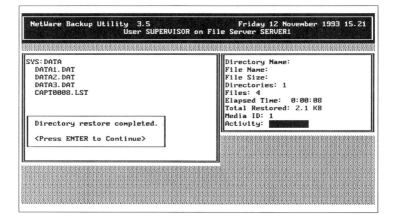

Restoring data using NBACKUP 285

The message *Directory restore completed* appears at the conclusion of the restore procedure.

- Confirm this message by pressing Enter. The main menu appears once more.
- Press Esc to quit the Restore function of the NBACKUP utility program.

9 Adapting workstations to the network

9.1 Creating and using startup files

In section 2.1, we dealt with the way in which a workstation is started up in a network. Resuming: the workstation is started up using the operating system available on the workstation. Then a connection is made to the fileserver. In order to avoid having to specify the start commands one by one, you require the CONFIG.SYS configuration file and the automatic startup file AUTOEXEC.BAT in addition to the necessary programs. Depending on the devices which are present, you can load the program and data files from a diskette, from a harddisk or from the server harddisk by means of a *boot PROM*.

Compiling a startup diskette for diskdrives. In order to activate the workstation from a diskdrive, the program and data files are copied to a startup diskette. Proceed as follows (if you do not know the DOS commands, consult an MS-DOS manual first):

1. Format a diskette and place the most important operating system programs immediately on the diskette (IO.SYS, MSDOS.SYS and COMMAND.COM).
2. Copy the COUNTRY.SYS file (date and time notation), and the HIMEM.SYS (for extended memory) and MOUSE.COM or MOUSE.SYS files (for the mouse) if required, from the system diskette or harddisk to the startup diskette.
3. Copy the NETX.COM program from the Novell NetWare system diskette to the startup diskette.
4. Copy the IPX.COM program to the startup diskette. If the program does not yet exist, you will have to generate it (see chapter 10).
5. Create the SHELL.CFG configuration file, if required, by means of a word processor and place it

Creating and using startup files 287

on the startup diskette (see sections 2.1 and 11.6).
6. Create the CONFIG.SYS configuration file and the AUTOEXEC.BAT automatic startup file on the startup diskette using the COPY CON copy command or by means of a word processor. If these files already exist on the system diskette or the harddisk, you can easily copy them to the startup diskette. However, they will probably have to be modified in this case.

Example 105:
The contents of the directory on the startup diskette are to be displayed using the DIR command.

```
A:\>dir                                                        (1)
 Volume in drive A is STARTDISK
 Volume serial number is 0F1A-E01F
 Directory of A:\

COMMAND  COM     50031 15-05-92   5:00                         (2)
CONFIG   SYS        75 14-02-93  17:50                         (3)
AUTOEXEC BAT        63 14-02-93  17:15                         (4)
COUNTRY  SYS     17078 15-05-92   5:00                         (5)
HIMEM    SYS     11792 15-05-92   5:00                         (6)
IPX      COM     24351 14-02-93  14:30                         (7)
NETX     COM     51192 29-07-92   9:32                         (8)
MOUSE    COM     31833 25-05-92  12:00                         (9)
        10 file(s)      186415 bytes
                       1197056 bytes free

A:\>_
```

(1) Command to display the contents of a directory.
(2) The command interpreter is the visible MS-DOS operating system file (COMMAND.COM, IO.SYS and MSDOS.SYS).
(3) The configuration file contains commands to activate files used to configure the computer (see below).
(4) The automatic startup file contains commands to activate other commands which are to be executed immediately after the start of the computer (see below).
(5) This is a file for the date and time settings of different countries.

(6) The data stored in this file refer to the use of extended memory.
(7) The first network shell program.
(8) The second network shell program. In the 3.11 version of Novell NetWare, this program has replaced the NET3, NET4 or NET5 programs which were used up until now. In this example, we shall not deal with the SHELL.CFG file used to configure the shell.
(9) This is the program for a Microsoft-compatible mouse.

Example 106:
By means of the DOS command TYPE *file_name* the contents of the CONFIG.SYS and AUTOEXEC.BAT files are to be shown on the screen.

```
A:\>type config.sys                                    (1)
DEVICE=HIMEM.SYS                                       (2)
DOS=HIGH                                               (3)
SWITCHES=/U                                            (4)
COUNTRY=044                                            (5)
FILES=30                                               (6)
BUFFERS=5                                              (7)

A:\>type autoexec.bat                                  (8)
@ECHO OFF                                              (9)
PROMPT $p$g                                           (10)
mouse                                                 (11)
ipx                                                   (12)
netx                                                  (13)
f:                                                    (14)
ver                                                   (15)

A:\>_
```

(1) Command to display the contents of the CONFIG.SYS file.
(2) The file for extended memory is installed.
(3) The high memory area (the extended memory between 1024 Kb and 1088 Kb) is activated for the MS_DOS operating system.
(4) This command means that the WINA20.386 file, which is necessary for the Windows 3.0 or 3.1 program, will not be sought in the root directory but in a different directory on the computer. The system extracts the search path to the directory from the SYSTEM.INI initialization file. The command DE-

Creating and using startup files 289

VICE=[[*drive*]*path*]WINA20.386 must be located in this file (refer the remarks concerning Windows 3.1 in section 5.2).
(5) The date and time notation are set to UK norms. The number corresponds to the international access number for the UK.
(6) The maximum number of files which can be open simultaneously is set to 30.
(7) The number of buffers for data exchange between working memory and an external diskette is set to 5.
(8) The command to display the contents of the AUTOEXEC.BAT file.
(9) These and the other commands do not appear on the screen during execution of the file.
(10) The prompt is displayed along with the current directory.
(11) The program for the mouse is activated.
(12) The first network shell program is activated.
(13) The second network shell program is activated.
(14) Switch to the server harddisk.
(15) The MS-DOS version number is shown.

Compiling a startup file for the harddisk. A harddisk is normally prepared for an automatic start. If that is not the case with your computer, consult the sections in your MS-DOS manual dealing with the harddisk. When using the harddisk, it is sufficient to place the programs used to make the network connection in a separate startup file or to include them in the automatic startup file.

To create a separate startup file for the connection, proceed as follows:

1. Use the COPY CON command or a word processor to create the startup file with the extension BAT (*batch*).
2. Include the startup commands used to make the connection in the file.

If you wish to make the connection immediately after starting up the computer, it is advisable to add the commands to activate the programs to the automatic startup file. Proceed as follows:

- Load the AUTOEXEC.BAT file in a word processor and add the startup commands.

Example 107:
The NETWARE directory has been created on a workstation harddisk for the network shell programs. There is also a startup file which, as a batch file, automatically makes the connection to the network. The contents of the directories and of the startup file are to be displayed.

```
C:\>dir net*.*                                              (1)
NETWARE       <DIR>       31-07-92    8:33                  (2)
NETSTART BAT           62 31-03-93   13:34

C:\>type netstart.bat                                       (3)
@echo off                                                   (4)
cls                                                         (5)
path=;                                                      (6)
c:\netware\ipx                                              (7)
c:\netware\netx
f:                                                          (8)

C:\>cd netware                                              (9)

C:\NETWARE>dir                                             (10)

.             <DIR>       31-07-92    8:33
..            <DIR>       31-07-92    8:33
IPX      COM         27797 29-07-92  18:50                 (11)
NETX     COM         51192 29-07-92   9:32

C:\NETWARE>_
```

(1) Command to display the names of directories and files which begin with NET.
(2) On the harddisk, there is one directory containing the network files and one startup file for making the connection.
(3) This command displays the contents of the NETSTART.BAT startup file. If you wish to work in the network immediately, add these commands to the AUTOEXEC.BAT file.
(4) These and the other commands are not shown on the screen during the execution of the file.
(5) The current screen contents are removed.
(6) The current search path data for the harddisk are removed.

(7) Both programs for the network shell are started using these commands from the NETWARE directory.
(8) Switch to the server harddisk.
(9) The NETWARE directory is activated.
(10) The contents of the directory are displayed.
(11) The names of the two programs for the network shell are shown.

Creating a startup file for computers with a boot PROM. If the workstation has to be started up from the server harddisk via a boot PROM, all startup files must be compiled (generated) to form the NET$DOS.SYS file and placed in the LOGIN directory on the harddisk server. To do this, Novell NetWare provides the DOSGEN and RPLFIX programs. Proceed as follows:

1. First check if the DOSGEN.COM program is located in the F:\SYSTEM directory and the RPLFIX.COM program in the F:\LOGIN directory on the server harddisk. You may have to copy the programs from the relevant Novell NetWare diskettes to the server harddisk.
2. Create a startup diskette for a diskdrive (see above).
3. Log in on the network as the network manager via a workstation with a diskdrive.
4. Activate the F:\LOGIN directory.
5. Insert the diskette containing the startup files in drive A:.
6. Generate the NET$DOS.SYS file using the F:\SYSTEM\DOSGEN command.
7. If you are running MS-DOS 5 on the workstations, the NET$DOS.SYS file must be adjusted to the operating system. To do this, give the command RPLFIX NET$DOS.SYS.
8. Assign the RO (Read Only) and S (Shareable) attibutes to the file.

The workstations with boot PROM are now ready for use.

9.2 Compiling and using menus

In order to facilitate the operation of applications and functions under Novell NetWare, it is possible to compile user-oriented menus. This enables network users to work with the applications and functions without prior knowledge of the Novell NetWare commands.

Compiling a menu. A menu consists of a title, the text of the menu lines and the commands which have to be executed when the menu line is activated. A menu can be written using the DOS command COPY CON or using a word processor. There may be no control characters in the menu text (these must have the ASCII format) and the extension of the file name in the menu text must be MNU. When compiling the menu text, you must take into account the following rules:

1. A menu title must begin with a percentage sign (%) at the first position on the line. A line may consist of a maximum of 75 characters.
2. The text of a menu line must also begin at the first position of the line.
3. The menu lines are automatically sorted according to the ASCII table. You can compel a certain order of sequence by numbering the menu lines in the required order.
4. The command to be executed must be written on the line following the menu text and must be indented by means of a tab or by one or more spaces.
5. Normally, the menu is shown centred on the screen. You can determine a different position by specifying co-ordinates. The co-ordinates are placed directly behind the menu title. They are separated from one another by spaces:

```
%menu title[,vertical,horizontal,colour]
```

> *vertical*   A number between 0 and 24 with the following significance:
> 0 = centred

	1 = top
	24 = bottom
horizontal	A number between 0 and 79 with the following significance:
	0 = centred
	1 = left
	79 = right
colour	You can specify a colour number for colour monitors. The numbers have the following significance:
	0 = standard
	1 = blue
	2 = green
	3 = red
	4 = yellow
	Numbers above 4 produce the standard setting, just as 0. The intensity of the colour and the inverse and normal attributes can be specified for the separate menu elements (frame, font etc.) using the ColorPal utility program. Activate the program by typing the program name, activate one of the colour palettes 0 to 4 and select the required setting from the available options by pressing Enter.

6. It is possible to activate submenus from a menu. The commands must be indented just as the other commands and must begin with a percentage sign. The submenus must be defined in the menu file behind the main menu.

Example 108:
A menu is to be compiled in order to activate the Word, dBASE, Multiplan and Chart applications more easily, and to be able to log out of the network simply.

```
F:\USER\MAGELLAN>copy con magellan.mnu                    (1)
%Menu,0,0,3                                               (2)
1. Word                                                   (3)
     F:\word55\word
2. dBASE IV                                               (4)
     I:dbase/t
3. Multiplan                                              (5)
     F:\MP4\MP
4. CHART                                                  (6)
     F:\CHART3\CHART
5. Logout                                                 (7)
     !Logout
^Z                                                        (8)
     1 file(s) copied

F:\USER\MAGELLAN>_
```

(1) The menu text is written using the DOS command COPY CON. In the case of large menus, it is advisable to use a word processor such as Word or WordPerfect, or even better, an ASCII editor.

(2) The menu title receives the co-ordinates 0,0. This means that the menu will be centred on the screen. These co-ordinates are not necessary for centred display, but in order to specify a red colour by means of the 3, the other co-ordinates must be specified.

(3) This is the menu line text for the Word word processor. This and the following lines have been numbered to prevent automatic sorting. This command will activate the Word program from the WORD55 directory.

(4) Menu line for the dBASE IV program. The command on the following line activates dBASE from the directory preceded by the drive letter I:. The /t parameter ensures that the screen showing the logo in the 1.1 version is skipped.

(5) The menu test for the Multiplan spreadsheet program. The command on the following line activates the program from the appropriate directory.

(6) The menu text for the CHART graphic program. This is activated from the CHART3 directory by the command on the following line.

(7) The menu text for logging out of the network. The exclamation mark for the Novell NetWare LOGOUT command ensures that all currently open files are closed in the proper manner.

Compiling and using menus

(8) Conclusion of the COPY CON command. This character combination appears if you press F6.

The figure below shows the menu at the beginning:

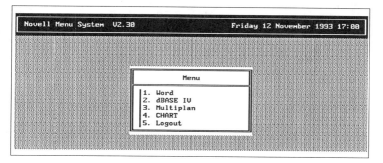

Implementing a menu. A menu like the one we have compiled above can only be shown on the screen for use by means of the Novell NetWare program MENU.EXE. Give the following command to start a menu:

```
MENU file_name[.mnu]
```

The MNU extension is not absolutely necessary. It is also possible to adopt this command into the AUTOEXEC.BAT startup file or into the login script.

Example 109:
The command to activate the MAGELLAN.MNU menu is to be included as the only command in the login script of the user MAGELLAN. Proceed as follows:

1. Start up the SYSCON utility program by typing the command of the same name.
2. Activate the *User Information* menu option.
3. Activate the user or user group.
4. Activate the *Login Script* option from the *User Information* menu. A window appears in which you can specify the commands.
5. Enter the required commands and save the data by pressing Esc.

The figure below shows a loginscript for the user MA-
GELLAN with the command to activate the menu.

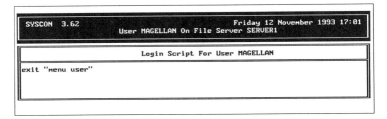

Note: When a menu is being executed, two 'help' files
are created in the directory from which you activate the
menu, GO*XXX*.BAT and RESTART.*xxx* (*xxx* represents
the start number). When you log out, these files are
automatically removed. Thus, a menu can only be executed when you have the C (Create) and the E (Erase)
rights for the directory in which you are working. In addition, a search path must exist to the directory containing
the menu files. Search paths must be created for the
programs which the menu activates or the search path
to the directory must be adopted into the command (see
the MAGELLAN.MNU example). If you activate programs via the menu, you must have at least the RO
(Read Only) and F (File) rights for the program directories.

Leaving a menu. You can quit a menu by pressing Esc
and confirming this by responding *Yes* to the subsequent question.

Example 110:
The MAGELLAN.MNU menu is to be extended with the
FILE submenu. This submenu enables you to activate
the Novell NetWare utility program FILER.

Compiling and using menus

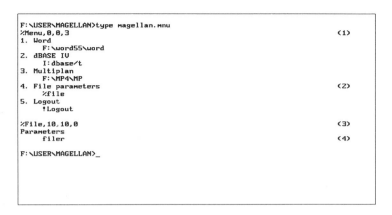

(1) The main menu is identical to the menu in the example above, apart from menu option (4).
(2) This menu option replaces the CHART option. The command to activate the submenu must be indented and must begin with a percentage sign.
(3) The submenu is defined immediately after the main menu. It is placed 10 rows from the top and 10 columns from the left-hand side. The colour is set to standard.
(4) Novell NetWare utility programs can also be activated instead of applications, such as FILER in this case.

The figure below displays the MAGELLAN main menu and the FILE submenu within this.

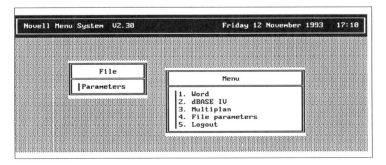

10 The installation

10.1 Installation of Novell NetWare on the fileserver

In order to install Novell NetWare on a fileserver, the following conditions have to be fulfilled:

- Prior to the installation, the server harddisk must be *low-level* formatted.
- A DOS partition with a minimum size of 2 Mb must be created and activated on the harddisk by means of the MS-DOS utility program FDISK.
- The server can be started up from drive A: using a DOS diskette or via the DOS partition on the harddisk.

Preparing the installation. Proceeed as follows:

1. Copy the following Novell NetWare files to the DOS partition:
   SERVER.EXE
   ISADISK.DSK (of *.DSK)
   VREPAIR.NLM
   INSTALL.NLM
2. Activate the SERVER program.
3. A window appears on the screen containing information. You are able to specify data here for the installation program. Type the necessary data, as shown in the following example:

Installation of Novell NetWare on the fileserver

```
Novell NetWare  V3.11 (100 user) 2/20/91                          (1)
Processor Speed: 914
(Type SPEED at the command prompt for an explanation of the speed rating)

File server name: SERVER1                                         (2)
IPX internal network number: 1                                    (3)
Total server memory: 7.7 Megabytes

Novell NetWare V3.11 (100 user)  2/20/91
(C) Copyright 1983 - 1991 Novell Inc.
All Rights Reserved.

Monday  November 1, 1993 10:12:20 pm

:LOAD ISADISK                                                     (4)
Loading module ISADISK.DSK
  NetWare 386 ISA Device Driver
  Version 3.11     February 15, 1991
  Copyright 1991 Novell Inc.  All rights reserved.
Supported I/O ports values are 1F0, 170                           (5)
I/O port: 1F0
Supported interrupt number values are E, B, F, C
Interrupt number: E
```

(1) When the server has been activated, the version number and a value for the processor speed are shown on the screen. The value shown here, 914, applies to a fileserver with a 33 MHz 80468 processor.

(2) The server must have a name consisting of a minimum of 2 and a maximum of 47 characters.

(3) The following piece of information *(IPX internal network number)* refers to the internal address which is assigned to the network. This refers to a hexadecimal number consisting of a maximum of eight positions which is not already allocated to a different network in the same configuration. The colon is the Novell NetWare prompt. This means that the server is active in the console mode.

(4) Now several NLMs (NetWare Loadable Modules) must be loaded using the Novell NetWare console command LOAD in order to effect the necessary configuration settings. The harddisk driver is loaded here. The name ISADISK applies to all computers which make use of the so-called Industry Standard Architecture (ISA) which is commonly referred to as the 'AT bus'. For computers with a Micro Channel Architecture (MCA bus), ISADISK must be replaced by ESDI, and in the case of computers with a disk-coprocessor (DCB), DCB replaces ISADISK.

(5) The valid input and output addresses (I/O ports) and interrupts are displayed on the screen. Normally, you can adopt the default settings by pressing the Enter key.

Dividing the harddisk for NetWare. When the drivers for the harddisk have been loaded, you can divide the harddisk for use by NetWare. This is done by NLM INSTALL. Proceed as follows:

1. Give the LOAD INSTALL command on the console.
2. The *Installation Options* main menu appears. Activate the *Disk Options* menu option.
3. The harddisk can be formatted using this option if that has not yet been done. The low-level formatting can also be performed by INSTALL before the installation of Novell NetWare. After confirmation of a safeguard question, all data on the disk, including for instance the DOS partition, are removed during formatting. Confirm here the default setting: no format.
4. Select the *Partition Tables* menu option in order to create the NetWare partition. The first time this option is activated, a message will appear stating that no division has yet been made on the selected harddisk. Acknowledge this message by pressing Esc.
5. Select, from the subsequent *Partition Options* menu, the *Create NetWare Partition* option in order to actually create the partition on the harddisk.

The figure on the following page displays this:

Installation of Novell NetWare on the fileserver 301

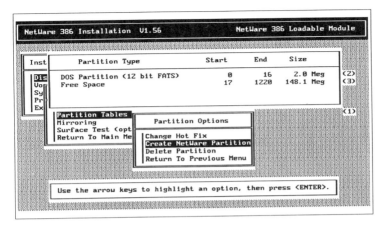

(1) The *Partition Tables* option is selected.
(2) Prior to the installation, a DOS partition of 2 Mb was specified. The fileserver is started from this partition. Thus, NetWare 386 needs DOS in order to be able to start up.
(3) The rest of the disk has not been partitioned and can be used as a NetWare partition.

6. Now specify the data as shown in the figure below. Conclude by pressing Esc and confirm the subsequent question.

The figure on page 303 shows the layout of the NetWare partition:

(1) The new partition is to be reserved for exclusive use by Novell NetWare.
(2) The entire disk capacity still remaining is shown in cylinders and Mb. By altering the number of cylinders, a Novell NetWare partition could be defined which is smaller than the space still available. However, for normal applications, the entire disk is selected.
(3) This is the setting for the *hot fix* area which is used as a reserve area on the disk where NetWare can store data if defective sectors should occur. Do not

alter these data if possible. Normally NetWare reserves 2% of the available capacity of the disk for this purpose.

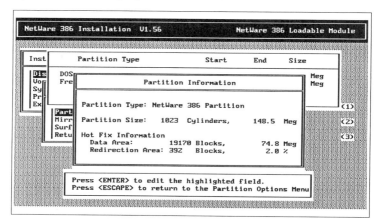

Note: In the *Disk Options* menu, a *Surface Test* option is provided. This will test the harddisk according to reliability for use in a network. In previous NetWare versions, this test could be performed using the COMPSURF utility program.

7. A NetWare volume then has to be defined. A volume represents a certain amount of storage capacity, where each volume may consist of a maximum of 32 segments which may be located on different harddisks of the server if required. NetWare 386 supports a maximum of 64 volumes. In order to define a volume, select the *Volume Options* option from the *Installation Options* menu and adopt the data shown in the following figure:

Installation of Novell NetWare on the fileserver

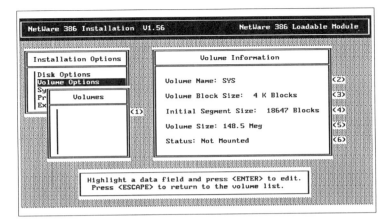

(1) Since no volumes have yet been defined, a window is displayed in which the required volumes are to be specified using the Ins key.
(2) In the *Volume Information* window, data are shown concerning the first volume (default: SYS). If you wish to assign another name, place the cursor on this field and type a new name consisting of a maximum of 15 characters.
(3) The size of the blocks determines the units in which the data is managed on the server harddisk. The default setting, *4Kb Blocks*, means that files are managed in consistent units of 4 KB. Thus, even a relatively small file of 1024 bytes (1 Kb) occupies a block of 4 Kb. The size of the block can also be increased to 6 Kb. This is convenient if database applications with large amounts of data and complex record structures are to be used.
(4) Here the number of blocks which the defined volume contains are shown. If the volume has been divided, the *Volume Segments: (Select for list)* option appears at this position. If this option is activated, a list of the segments belonging to the volume is shown. A volume may consist of various segments which may be distributed among several physical drives.
(5) The size of the defined volume is shown here.

(6) The status of the volume is shown here. A newly defined volume is always *Not Mounted*.

Activating the SYS volume (mount). Now the actual NetWare files can be copied to the server harddisk. To do this, the drive has to be activated (mounted) first. The volume is only accessible when the system has been activated. This can be done using the INSTALL program.

- In the *Volume Options* window, alter the *Status* of *Not Mounted* to *Mounted* by pressing Enter.

The same effect can be produced in a different way in the Novell NetWare console mode:

- Quit INSTALL using the Alt-Esc key combination, give the command *MOUNT [ALL]/[SYS]* and return to the INSTALL program using the Alt-Esc key combination.

This ensures that the defined volumes are ready for use (mounted).

Copying the system and utility files. The system and utility files must be copied to the server harddisk. Proceed as follows:

1. Select the *System Options* menu option. The *Available System Options* submenu appears.
2. Activate the *Copy System And Public Files* option.

The program begins to copy the system files to the harddisk. This is registered in an information window displaying appropriate messages. The program requests the relevant diskettes. If some system components do not need to be installed, a utility program for instance, the installation from the relevant diskettes can be skipped by pressing F5.

The figure below shows the installation of the system and utility files:

Installation of Novell NetWare on the fileserver 305

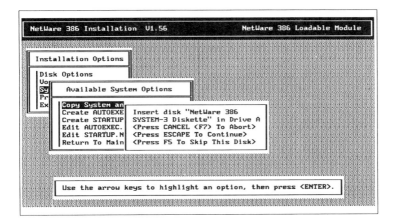

Loading the drivers for the network cards in use.
The drivers for the network cards in use now have to be loaded. NetWare 386 provides drivers for the following network cards:

- Novell RX-Net
- Novell RX-Net II
- Novell RX-Net/2 (TRXNET.LAN)
- Novell Ethernet 1000 (NE1000.LAN)
- Novell Ethernet 2000 (NE2000.LAN)
- Novell Ethernet 3200 (NE3000.LAN)
- Novell Ethernet/2 (NE2.LAN)
- IBM PC-Network (PCN2.LAN)
- IBM Token-Ring (TOKEN.LAN).

In order to load a driver for an ARCnet card, the data shown in the figure on page 307 are required.

(1) The driver for ARCnet network cards is loaded.
(2) The potential input and output addresses for this type of card are displayed. The default setting is the address 2E0. This value can be adopted by pressing Enter. If you wish to specify a different address, select one from the list shown and confirm the alteration.

```
:
:load trxnet                                                              (1)
Loading module TRXNET.LAN
Supported I/O port values are 2E0, 2F0, 300, 310, 350, 200, 250, 2A0, 3E0
I/O port: 2E0                                                             (2)
Supported memory address values are D0000, C0000, E0000, CC000, DC000, C4000,
    C8000, D4000, D8000
Memory address: D0000                                                     (3)
Supported interrupt number values are 2, 3, 4, 5, 7
Interrupt number: 2                                                       (4)
:
:bind ipx to trxnet net=4                                                 (5)
IPX LAN protocol bound to Turbo RX-Net LAN Driver  v1.12 (910107)
:
```

(3) The memory address is determined in the same way. The default setting here is D000.
(4) The interrupt number must also be determined. The default setting here is interrupt 2. However, Windows does not run smoothly under this default setting. Select the I/O address 300 and the interrupt number 3 instead.
(5) This command links the network driver and network card to the protocol used in the data transmission (see below).

Linking the network drivers to the data transmission protocol. In the following stage, the network driver and the network card are to be linked to the protocol used in data transmission (in NetWare this is mostly IPX). To do this, give the following command (see the figure above):

```
BIND IPX TO TRXNET NET=1
```

NET=1 represents a hexadecimal address for the network to which the card is connected. Each network must have its own address. If you do not specify an address for a network, NetWare will request one.

Creating the AUTOEXEC.BAT file. The AUTOEXEC.BAT file must now be created. The network commands necessary to activate the server automatically are located in this file. The file is stored in the SYS:SYSTEM directory. The file includes the following:

Installation of Novell NetWare on the fileserver

- the name of the fileserver
- the internal network address of the fileserver
- the commands to activate the LAN drivers
- the commands to load the other modules, such as MONITOR
- the parameters for the fileserver (see the SET command)
- command to activate the volume
- command to remove DOS from memory.

The first time you create this file, proceed as follows:

- In the *System* menu of NLM INSTALL, activate the *Create Options* menu. All commands which are specified during the installation in the console mode are collected here automatically. The figure below shows the window containing the data which have been recorded up until now:

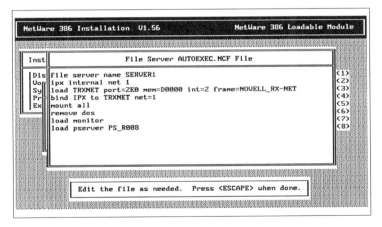

(1) The fileserver received the name SERVER1.
(2) 1 was specified as the network address.
(3) An ARCnet card has been installed in the fileserver; this has been adopted into the default settings.
(4) The TRXNET driver has been linked to the IPX communication protocol. The network card can only process data after this connection has been made.

(5) All defined volumes are to be activated.
(6) DOS is removed for memory. The memory which then becomes available is used by NetWare for *disk caching*.
(7) The NLM MONITOR is loaded.
(8) The PS_R008 print server is loaded.

Creating the STARTUP.NCF file. The STARTUP.NCF file is executed immediately after SERVER.EXE has been loaded. It must be located on the disk from which the server is activated. NetWare creates this file automatically if you select the *Create STARTUP.NCF* option from the *Available Systems Options* menu. Just as in the case of the AUTOEXEC.BAT startup file, all commands are adopted which were specified during the installation in the console mode. The command to load the driver for the harddisk should be included in any case. This command looks something like this for a standard harddisk:

```
load ISADISK port=1F0 int=E
```

If, for instance, the fileserver is equipped with an SCSI disk with an ADAPTEC controller, the command is as follows:

```
load AHA1540 port=330 int=B dma=5
```

In addition, STARTUP.NCF contains data concerning *name space support* and the maximum size of the packages which are to be transported to all networks of the fileserver.

This concludes the installation. The fileserver is ready for use and can be activated from now onwards without any information having to be entered from the keyboard.

10.2 Creating a NetWare shell for the workstations

It is possible to adopt workstations into the network by means of the NetWare shell. To do this, two programs which belong to this shell, IPX.COM and NETX.COM have to activated on the DOS workstation in order to make the connection to the fileserver. Once activated, both programs remain resident in the workstation memory and occupy roughly 70 Kb. When supplied, NETX.COM is ready for use. IPX.COM still has to be generated according to the network card being used. This is done using the NetWare utility WSGEN.

The creation of IPX can be done from a local harddisk, from a network drive or from a diskette. For our example here, we shall choose the diskette. Proceed as follows:

1. Use DISKCOPY to make a copy of the *Workstation Services - WSGEN* diskette. Insert this copy in the diskdrive and activate the drive.
2. Give the command WSGEN in order to activate the program to generate the shell. Press Enter.
3. A list of network cards supported by the drivers on the *Workstation Services* diskette appears on the screen. Use the cursor keys to select the card which has been installed and confirm your choice by pressing Enter.

The following figure displays this list:

```
           <Escape> = Cancel    <F1> = Help    <Alt><F10> = Exit
Select the driver that matches the network board in your workstation.

     ┌──────────────────────────────────────────────────────────┐
     │ 3Com 3c503 EtherLink II   v3.01EC (901101)               │
     │ 3Com 3c505 EtherLink Plus (Assy 2012)  v4.12EC (910117)  │
     │ 3Com EtherLink/MC 3C523  v2.36EC (901207)                │
     │ IBM LAN Support Program Driver  v2.60 (901031)           │
     │ IBM PCN II & Baseband  v1.15 (900905)                    │
     │ IBM Token-Ring  v2.60 (901022)                           │
     │ NetWare NE/2  v2.02EC (900718)                           │
     │ NetWare NE1000  v3.02EC (900831)                         │
     │ NetWare NE2000  v1.05EC (900718)                         │
     │ NetWare Turbo RX-Net   v2.11 (901217)                    │
     └──────────────────────────────────────────────────────────┘

        ┌────────────────────────────────────────────────────┐
        │ Highlight the correct driver; then press <Enter>.  │
        │ If the driver you want is not listed, press <Insert>.│
        └────────────────────────────────────────────────────┘
```

4. Subsequently, the configuration parameters must be selected according to the network card setting. The normal combinations appear on the screen. The combination with the number 0 is the default configuration. Adjustments to the generated IPX.COM can generally also be made using the JUMPERS utility. For instance, Windows does not run under the default setting. If you wish to run this program, select the I/O address 300 and the interrupt number 3.

The figure on the following page shows a driver configuration:

Creating a NetWare shell for the workstations

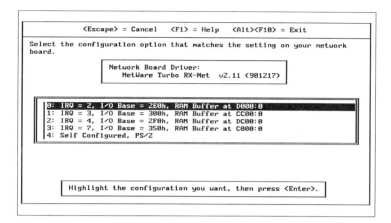

5. When you have confirmed your selection and the corresponding safeguard question, WSGEN will generate the IPX.COM driver which suits the network. In order to use this, you only need to copy the file to the startup diskette.

11 Utility programs and commands

11.1 Menu-driven utility programs

An alphabetical list of menu-driven utility programs which you can activate from any workstation is shown below. A brief description of the program is given along with the syntax of the activation.

COLORPAL *(COLOR PALette)*
Alters the colour of the NetWare menus; defines new colour combinations.
Activate: COLORPAL

COMCHECK *(COMmunications CHECK)*
Checks the communication line between fileserver and workstations.
Activate: COMCHECK

DSPACE *(Disk SPACE)*
Restricts the available disk space on a volume or the size of a directory.
Activate: DSPACE

FCONSOLE *(File server CONSOLE)*
Utility program to check the activities in the network (connection information, sending messages, selecting a different fileserver, switching off the fileserver, information about the network version).
Activate: FCONSOLE

FILER
Management of files and directories (removing, copying, rights, attributes).
Activate: FILER

JUMPERS
Alters the configuration of the network driver (IPX), in as much as the driver used in this process allows this.
Activate: JUMPERS

MAKEUSER
Creates or removes one or more users simultaneously.
Activate: MAKEUSER

NBACKUP *(Netware BACKUP utility)*
Archives and restores files on the fileserver and on local drives.
Activate: NBACKUP

PCONSOLE *(Print CONSOLE)*
Installs a print server, deals with print operation in the network, provides information about print processes in the network.
Activate: PCONSOLE

PRINTCON *(PRINTjob CONfiguration)*
Determines print options used by CAPTURE, NPRINT and PCONSOLE.
Activate: PRINTCON

PRINTDEF *(PRINTer DEFinition)*
Determines printer definitions and print forms.
Activate: PRINTDEF

RCONSOLE *(Remote CONSOLE)*
Gives access to the fileserver console from a random workstation (REMOTE and RSPX must be loaded on the fileserver).
Activate: RCONSOLE

RSETUP *(Remote SETUP)*
Creates a custom boot-diskette for a remote fileserver.
Activate: RSETUP

SALVAGE
Examines and recalls deleted files.
Activate: SALVAGE

SESSION
Utility program to switch fileserver, to examine and alter the mapping and search drives, to examine the list of users and user groups and to send messages to users.
Activate: SESSION

SYSCON *(SYStem CONfiguration)*
Displays information about, and alters, user rights; creates and alters login scripts.
Activate: SYSCON

UPGRADE
Adopts system settings (user environment) when transferring from NetWare 286 version 2.*xx* to NetWare 386.
Activate: UPGRADE

USERDEF *(USER DEFinition)*
Installs various users using ready-made templates containing the profiles of the users to be installed.
Activate: USERDEF

VOLINFO *(VOLume INFOrmation)*
Displays information about each volume installed on the fileserver.
Activate: VOLINFO

11.2 Utility programs on the command line

An alphabetical list of the non-menu-driven utility programs which can be activated from any workstation is shown below. A brief description of each program is given, along with the syntax of the activation.

ALLOW
Sets a template for the inherited rights of a directory or file *(Inherited Rights Mask)*.
Activate: ALLOW [path] [TO INHERIT] [list_of_rights]

ATOTAL *(Accounting TOTAL)*
Calculates the user accounts.
Activate: ATOTAL

ATTACH
Enables access to a different fileserver.
Activate: ATTACH [fileserver/[user_name]]

BINDFIX *(BINDery FIX)*
Reorganizes the Bindery files if problems arise.
Activate: BINDFIX

CAPTURE
Redirects the print output from the local port to a network printer.
Activate: CAPTURE [parameter]

CASTOFF
Suppresses the display of messages on the bottom screen line.
Activate: CASTOFF [/All]

CASTON
Allows the display of messages again.
Activate: CASTON

CHKDIR *(CHecK DIRectory)*
Displays information about a directory.
Activate: CHKDIR [pad]

COMCHECK *(COMmunication CHECK)*
Checks the communication between fileserver and workstations.
Activate: COMCHECK

DCONFIG *(Driver CONFIGuration)*
Alters the configuration of the IPX.COM network shell.
Activate: DCONFIG [volume:]file [parameter]

DOSGEN *(DOS remote image file GENeration)*
Creates startup file (boot image file) to boot remote workstations.
Activate: DOSGEN

ECONFIG *(Ethernet CONFIGuration)*
Adapts the IPX.COM network shell to the Ethernet II standard.
Activate: [drive1:] ECONFIG drive2: IPX.COM SHELL: parameter

ENDCAP *(END CAPture)*
Terminates the redirection of output to a network printer.
Activate: ENDCAP [parameter]

FLAG
Displays and alters file attributes in the currently active directory.
Activate: FLAG [path] [TO INHERIT] [attributes]

FLAGDIR
Displays and alters directory attributes.
Activate: FLAGDIR [path [attributen]]

GRANT
Allocates access rights for a file or directory to users and user groups.
Activate: GRANT rights [FOR path] TO [USER/GROUP] user_name [/parameter]

HELP *(network HELP)*
Activates the NetWare online help program.
Activate: HELP [command]

LISTDIR *(LIST DIRectories)*
Displays the directory structure and assigned rights.
Activate: LISTDIR [path] [parameter]

LOGIN
Logs in on a fileserver.
Activate: LOGIN [/parameter] [fileserver/[user]] [script_parameter]

LOGOUT
Logs out from the fileserver.
Activate: LOGOUT [fileserver]

MAP
Displays and alters the logical drive allocations and search drives.
Activate: MAP [drive:]   (display)
                MAP [drive:]=[drive:|path]   (alter)

MENU
Activates a menu for a specific user.
Activate: MENU [path]file

NCOPY *(Network COPY)*
Copies files while retaining NetWare attributes.
Activate: NCOPY [path1]file [TO] path2 [/parameter]

NDIR *(Network DIRectory)*
Displays the contents of directories and precise information about directories and files.
Activate: NDIR [path] [/parameter]

NPRINT *(Network PRINTer)*
Prints files via a network printer without activating an application.
Activate: NPRINT path [/parameter]

NVER *(Network VERsion)*
Provides information about the NetWare version used on the fileserver and workstation.
Activate: NVER

PAUDIT *(Print AUDIT trail)*
Displays the account data of a user on the screen.
Activate: PAUDIT

PSC *(Print Server Command)*
Management of network printers and print servers.
Activate: PSC PS=ps P=number parameter

PSERVER *(Print SERVER)*
Loads a print server on a dedicated workstation.
Activate: PSERVER [fileserver] print_server

PURGE
Removes deleted files definitively; creates disk space.
Activate: PURGE [file|path] [/ALL]

REMOVE
Removes access rights for a file or directory from a user or user group.

Activate: REMOVE [USER|GROUP] name [[FROM] path] [parameter]

RENDIR
Renames a directory.
Activate: RENDIR path [TO] directory_name

REVOKE
Revokes access rights for a file or directory.
Activate: REVOKE rights [FOR path] FROM [USER|GROUP] name [parameter]

RIGHTS
Provides information about the effective rights for a file or directory.
Activate: RIGHTS [path]

RPRINTER *(Remote PRINTER)*
Connects a local printer as a remote network printer to a print server.
Activate: RPRINTER [print_server printer_number] [-R]

SECURITY
Checks the fileserver security system.
Activate: SECURITY

SEND
Sends short messages to one or more users or groups.
Activate: SEND "message" [TO] [USER|GROUP] [fileserver/]name [[AND|,] [fileserver/]name]

SERVER
Installs Novell NetWare 386 and *boots* it later on the fileserver.
Activate: SERVER [parameter]

SETPASS *(SET PASSword)*
Alters one's own password.
Activate: SETPASS [fileserver] [/user]

SETTTS *(SET Transactional Tracking System)*
Configures programs which do not work correctly with

TTS (Transactional Tracking System).
Activate: SETTTS [number [number]]

SLIST *(Server LIST)*
Displays the available fileservers in the network.
Activate: SLIST [fileserver]

SMODE *(Search MODE)*
Determines the use of search drives.
Activate: SMODE [path [mode] [/SUB]]

SYSTIME *(SYStem TIME)*
Displays and adopts the fileserver date and time as the workstation system time.
Activate: SYSTIME

TLIST *(Trustee LIST)*
Displays access rights for a directory or file.
Activate: TLIST [path [USERS|GROUPS]]

USERLIST
Displays the names of the users currently logged in on the fileserver.
Activate: USERLIST [fileserver/][users] [/A|O|C]

VERSION
Displays the version numbers of the NetWare utility programs and NLMs.
Activate: VERSION [path] file

WHOAMI *(WHO AM I)*
Displays information about the user ID under which one is currently logged in on a fileserver.
Activate: WHOAMI [fileserver] [parameter]

WSGEN *(Work Station GENeration)*
Creates the IPX.COM network shell.
Activate: WSGEN

WSUPDATE
Replaces the files on a workstation with more up-to-date versions from the fileserver.

Activate: WSUPDATE [source_path] [destination_drive:file_name]/parameter

11.3 Console commands

An alphabetical list of the commands which you can use from the fileserver console is shown below. A brief description of the command is given along with the syntax of the activation.

ADD NAME SPACE
Enables the storage of other than DOS files, for instance Macintosh files, on the fileserver.
Activate: ADD NAME SPACE name [TO [VOLUME]] volume_names

BIND
Connects LAN drivers to a communication protocol and to a specific network card in the fileserver.
Activate: BIND protocol [TO] LAN_drivers I network_card [driver_parameters] [protocol_parameters]

BROADCAST
Sends messages to one, several or all users currently logged in.
Activate: BROADCAST "message" [[TO] userIconnection_nr] [[ANDI,] userIconnection_nr...]

CLEAR STATION
Logs out a workstation from the fileserver.
Activate: CLEAR STATION connection_number

CLS
Clears the console screen.
Activate: CLS

CONFIG
Displays the fileserver configuration.
Activate: CONFIG

DISABLE LOGIN
Revokes the rights of users to log in on the fileserver.
Activate: DISABLE LOGIN

DISABLE TTS
Deactivates the Transaction Tracking System.
Activate: DISABLE TTS

DISKSET
Configures an external harddisk with DCB (Disk Coprocessor Board).
Activate: LOAD [path] DISKSET

DISMOUNT
Switches off a volume on the fileserver.
Activate: DISMOUNT

DISPLAY NETWORKS
Displays all accessible networks with all network addresses.
Activate: DISPLAY NETWORKS

DISPLAY SERVERS
Displays the accessible servers.
Activate: DISPLAY SERVERS

DOWN
Restores the cache memory prior to switching off the fileserver.
Activate: DOWN

ENABLE LOGIN
Allows users to log in on the fileserver.
Activate: ENABLE LOGIN

ENABLE TTS
Activates the Transaction Tracking System.
Activate: ENABLE TTS

EXIT
Switches to MS-DOS when the fileserver is shut down.
Activate: EXIT

INSTALL
Utility program to install Novell NetWare.
Activate: LOAD [path] INSTALL [parameter]

LOAD
Adopts NetWare Loadable Modules (NLMs) into the operating system.
Activate: LOAD [path]loadable_module [parameter]

MODULES
Displays the NLMs (NetWare Loadable Modules) adopted in the operating system.
Activate: MODULES

MONITOR
Loads MONITOR to check the efficiency of the network.
Activate: LOAD [path] MONITOR [parameter]

MOUNT
Makes a volume available to the users.
Activate: MOUNT volume_names|ALL

NAME
Displays the name of the fileserver.
Activate: NAME

OFF
Clears the console screen.
Activate: OFF

PROTOCOL
Requests the normal communication protocol or registers a new protocol.
Activate: PROTOCOL [REGISTER protocol frame id_number]

PSERVER
Activates a print server on the fileserver.
Activate: PSERVER

REMOTE
Prepares access to the fileserver console from a work-

station (see also RCONSOLE).
Activate: LOAD [path] REMOTE [password]

REMOVE DOS
Removes MS-DOS from the fileserver working memory.
Activate: REMOVE DOS

ROUTE
Submits data packages to a Token Ring network.
Activate: LOAD [path] ROUTE [parameters...]

RS232
Initializes the fileserver serial port in combination with REMOTE.
Activate: LOAD [path] RS232 [communication_port] [baud]

RSPX
Prepares access to the fileserver via a workstation (see RCONSOLE).
Activate: LOAD [path] RSPX

SEARCH
Defines search directories on the fileserver for NLMs (NetWare Loadable Modules) and NCF files (default SYS:SYSTEM).
Activate: SEARCH [parameters]

SECURE CONSOLE
Regulates the addressing of system routines.
Activate: SECURE CONSOLE

SEND
Sends messages from the fileserver console.
Activate: SEND "message" [[TO] user|connection_nr] [[AND|,] user|connection_nr]

SET
Examines and alters operating system configuration parameters.
Activate: SET [parameters]

SET TIME
Sets the fileserver date and time.
Activate: SET TIME [month/day/year] [hours:minutes:seconds]

SPEED
Displays the processor speed.
Activate: SPEED

SPOOL
Examines and determines the default print queues for NPRINT and CAPTURE.
Activate: SPOOL number [TO] [QUEUE] name

TIME
Displays the fileserver date and time.
Activate: TIME

TOKENRPL
Enables remote booting of workstations without diskdrives using Token Ring network cards.
Activate: LOAD [path] TOKENRPL

TRACK OFF
Suppresses the display of data transmission between various networks.
Activate: TRACK OFF

TRACK ON
Displays data transmission between various networks.
Activate: TRACK ON

UNBIND
Removes the communication protocol from a network card driver.
Activate: UNBIND protocol [FROM] LAN_driver [parameters]

UNLOAD
Removes NLMs (NetWare Loadable Modules) from the operating system and releases the working memory for the cache.

Activate: UNLOAD

UPS
The Uninterruptible Power Supply on the fileserver.
Activate: LOAD [path] UPS [type I/O port discharge recharge]

UPS STATUS
Checks the status of the Uninterruptible Power Supply on the fileserver.
Activate: UPS STATUS

UPS TIME
Determines the period of usage of the fileserver with reference to the UPS battery and the charging time of the batteries.
Activate: UPS TIME [discharge recharge]

VERSION
Displays the NetWare version and copyright.
Activate: VERSION

VOLUMES
Displays the list of currently logged-in fileserver volumes.
Activate: VOLUMES

VREPAIR
Non-destructive correction of smaller data fields on the server harddisk.
Activate: LOAD [path] VREPAIR

11.4 List of the login script commands

An alphabetical list of all commands which may be included in the system login script or in the user login script is given below. The valid syntax is shown, occasionally with an explanatory example and description. Some commands can also be used in combination with system login variables. A list of system login variables in given in section 11.5.

- Executes a program (external)

Syntax:

```
#[directory/]program,parameters
```

This command activates a program. The first character must be a number sign (#). A directory can then be specified, if required. The name of the program will then be shown along with the extension (EXE or COM). In contrast to the case with EXIT, no batch commands with the extension BAT can be activated using this command. Specify the parameters behind the prompt as you would do at DOS level. It is obvious that the # command is always at the end of the login script, after all the MAP commands for the user have been executed. See also EXIT.

ATTACH - Logs in on a different fileserver

Syntax:

```
ATTACH [fileserver_name/[user_name]]
```

Example: ATTACH SERVER1/POLO

You can log in on different fileservers at one time by means of the ATTACH command. A precondition of this is that you have used LOGIN to log in on at least one fileserver. You can display a list of available fileservers using SLIST. If you only specify the command name, a dialog will take place concerning the name of the server and the user. You may also have to specify a password. The ATTACH command does not execute a login script.

BREAK OFF/ON - (Dis)continues a login script

Syntax:

```
BREAK OFF/ON
```

List of the login script commands 327

If the BREAK ON command is placed in the login script, it is possible to discontinue the runthrough of the login script by pressing the key combination Ctrl-C or Ctrl-Break. The BREAK OFF command does not permit this.

COMSPEC - Determines the search path and file name for the DOS command interpreter

Syntax:

```
COMSPEC=drive:\file_name
```

The drive may be:

- a logical drive, such as F:
- a search drive, such as S3:
- a network drive, number *n*:

Example: S2:\COMMAND.COM

By means of the COMSPEC command, the search path and the name of the DOS command interpreter are defined in the login script. In larger networks, it is often necessary to load different command interpreters. The appropriate choice for the workstation can be made in the login script in combination with the command IF...THEN.

DISPLAY - Displays the contents of a specified file

Syntax:

```
DISPLAY [directory/]file_name
```

Example: DISPLAY SYS:PUBLIC/INFO.TXT

If, for instance, information must be given to the user during the login procedure, the message can be edited in the INFO.TXT file in the PUBLIC directory first. Each user who logs in using a login script containing the DIS-

PLAY command receives the text from the INFO.TXT file on the screen, line by line.

DOS BREAK OFF/ON - (Dis)continues DOS programs

Syntax:

```
DOS BREAK OFF/ON
```

Just as with BREAK, the interruption of DOS programs can be allowed or prevented after the execution of the login script. The default setting is DOS BREAK OFF.

DOS SET - Sets DOS environment variables

Syntax:

```
DOS SET name="value"
```

By means of the DOS SET command, you can set a variable to a certain status, just as in the DOS environment.

Example: DOS SET PROMPT="PG"

Note: In the login script, the part behind the equals sign must be placed between inverted commas, in contrast to the DOS command SET.

DOS VERIFY ON/OFF - Switches on/off the DOS verify option

Syntax:

```
DOS VERIFY ON/OFF
```

This command enables you to submit the VERIFY option to the MS-DOS operating system via the login script (see the DOS manual).

DRIVE - Switches to a logical drive

Syntax 1:

`DRIVE drive letter:`

Drive letter represents a letter from A to Z.

Syntax 2:

`DRIVE drive number:`

If you, as a user, always switch to the same logical drive after logging in, you can include the DRIVE command in the login script.

EXIT - Discontinues the login script and returns control to the operating system to activate a program

Syntax 1:

`EXIT`

Syntax 2:

`EXIT file_name`

In the former case, the runthrough of the login script is discontinued and MS-DOS reassumes control of the workstation. In the latter case, the login script is also discontinued but this time the *file_name* program is activated. This may be a menu program for instance. A batch file may also be activated here. See also # at the beginning of this section.

FDISPLAY - Displays the contents of a specified file (without control characters)

The FDISPLAY command is similar to DISPLAY, except that any control characters or other non-printable characters will not be shown.

FIRE PHASERS - Produces PC tones

Syntax:

```
FIRE PHASERS n
```

n = number of repetitions

This command enables you to produce acoustic signals at the workstation.

INCLUDE - Activates a sub-login script

Syntax:

```
INCLUDE [directory_name/]file_name
```

This command enables you activate text files with executable login script commands. The commands in these subfiles are then processed one by one. Recursive and nested commands to a maximum of 10 levels are allowed.

IF ... THEN - Branching in the login script

Syntax:

```
IF condition THEN command
```

Analogous to the DOS programming of batch files, the execution of commands with branching can be operated in login scripts.

Example: IF DAY_OF_WEEK = "SUNDAY" THEN EXIT

The answer 'Sunday' to the question regarding the day of the week, leads to the discontinuation of the login script. This can be used, for instance, to prevent working in the network on Sundays.

The following relational operators can be used in programming:

relational operator	significance
=	equal to *or* is
<>	does not equal *or* is not
>	is greater than
<	is less than
>=	is greater than or equal to
<=	is less than or equal to

MACHINE NAME = "name"

The computer can be given a name by means of this command. This can also be done using the login script variable *%station*.

Example: MACHINE NAME = "%station"

In the example, the station number is specified as the name of the computer.

MAP - Defines and/or displays search paths and logical search drives

Syntax 1: MAP DISPLAY ON/OFF
Switches on/off the display of drive allocation on the screen.

Syntax 2: MAP ERRORS ON/OFF
Switches on/off the display of errors in the drive allocation on the screen.

Syntaxis 3: MAP
Displays all current drive allocations on the screen.
Syntax 4: MAP drive
Displays the allocation of the specified drive.
Syntax 5: MAP drive:=pad
Allocates the directory to the specified drive.
Example: MAP G:=\PROGRAM\WORD
Syntax 6: MAP drive:=drive:
Two drives are allocated to the same directory.
Example: MAP F:=G:
Syntax 7: MAP search path:=pathname
Allocates a search path. A maximum of 16 search paths are possible, S1 to S16.
Example: MAP S1:=\DATA\DRAKE
Syntax 8: MAP INSERT search path:=path name
Allocates the next available search drive.
Example: MAP INSERT SEARCH1:=\PROGRAM\WORD
Abbreviated notation: MAP INSERT S1:=\PROGRAM\WORD
Syntax 9: MAP DEL drive
Removes drive allocation.
MAP REM drive
Removes drive allocation.
Syntax 10: MAP ROOT drive:=path name
Allocates a pseudo root directory.
In this way, a user who is not the Supervisor can gain access to a root directory if required. This is not permitted to normal users under normal circumstances.

PAUSE - Interrupts the login script temporarily

Syntax:

PAUSE

List of the login script commands 333

The PAUSE command forces an interruption of the login script runthrough. The message *Strike a key when ready* then appears on the screen. The runthrough of the login script is continued when you press a key. This prevents information on the screen disappearing too quickly for the reader.

PCCOMPATIBLE - Sets a parameter for an IBM-compatible PC

Syntax:

```
PCCOMPATIBLE
```

If there are problems with the *Exit file* command, this command may provide the solution. This command must be placed directly in front of the EXIT command in the login script.

REMARK - Comment line in the login script

Syntax:

```
REMARK [text...]
```

The REMARK command defines the subsequent text as being exclusively comment text. You may also use the asterisk (*) or semi-colon (;) instead (thus, *[text] or ;[text]).

WAIT - Discontinues the execution of the login script

Syntax:

```
WAIT
```

This command is identical to PAUSE.

WRITE - Displays text on the screen

Syntax:

```
WRITE [text;...login_variable;...text;...]
```

This command enables you to display text and/or the contents of variables on the screen. The text and the variables must be separated from one another by a semi-colon. The text must be placed between inverted commas. The valid login script variables are listed in section 11.5. The following characters have a special function:

- \r   to the beginning of the line
- \n   to the beginning of a new line
- \"   inverted commas which are to be displayed
- \7   acoustic signal

11.5 List of login script variables

NetWare provides system information via system variables in combination with the login commands. These variables are used in the login script to run the login procedure. The variables are also often used in combination with IF...THEN routines. In that case, you must specify the variable names using the % sign, for instance %LOGIN_NAME.

%1-%19	Parameter specification in combination with the LOGIN command (maximum of 19 parameters)
AM_PM	Time notation.
DAY	Day number, from 1 to 31.
DAY_OF_WEEK	Day of the week, Monday to Sunday.
ERROR_LEVEL	Error code: 0 = no error, not 0 = error has occurred.
FILE_SERVER	Name of the fileserver
FULL_NAME	Full name of the user, as defined via SYSCON or MAKEUSER.

List of login script variables

GREETING TIME	Contains time of day in the form of *Morning, Afternoon* or *Evening*.
HOUR	The hour as a number between 1 and 12.
HOUR24	The hour as a number between 1 and 24.
LOGIN_NAME	User name.
MACHINE	The computer description of the workstation corresponding to the shell definition.
MEMBER_OF_GROUPNAME	Name of the user group.
MINUTE	The minute as a number between 0 and 59.
MONTH	The month as a number between 1 and 12.
MONTH_NAME	Name of the month, January to December.
NETWORK_ADDRESS	Network address of the fileserver.
NDAY_OF_WEEK	Day of the week as a number between 1 and 7 (Sunday is 1).
OS	Operating system used on the workstation, for instance MS-DOS.
OS_VERSION	Operating system version.
P_STATION	Physical address of the logged-in station.
SECOND	The second as a number between 0 and 59.
SHORT_YEAR	Contains the last two numbers of the year notation, for instance 93 for 1993.
STATION	The logical number of the workstation.
SMACHINE	Short computer name.
USER_ID	User identification number.
YEAR	Current year (for instance 1993).

11.6 List of the configuration commands for SHELL.CFG

A list of all commands which the IPX, NETX and NETBIOS programs use via the SHELL.CFG configuration file is displayed below.

Setting parameters for the IPX program

CONFIG OPTION
This option enables you to temporarily alter the configurations made using SHGEN or DCONFIG. This means that the alterations are only effective in the current workstation working memory and have no influence on the IPX.COM file itself.

INT64=ON/OFF
If interrupt 64h has to be supported, this parameter must be set to ON. This is the default setting.

INT7A=ON/OFF
As under INT64.

IPATCH=*byte-offset,nn*
This parameter enables the patching of addresses from the IPX.COM program.

IPX RETRY COUNT=*nn*
The maximum number of transmission attempts per package which may be executed at the workstation may be set to *nn*. The default setting is 20.

IPX SOCKETS=*nn*
The number *nn* determines the maximum number of sockets which the IPX.COM program may open. The default setting is 20.

SPX ABORT TIMEOUT=*nn*
This parameter determines the maximum time one will wait for an answer from another workstation. When this

limit is exceeded, the session is discontinued. *nn* is specified in ticks. The default setting is 540 ticks (roughly 30 seconds).

SPX CONNECTIONS=*nn*
Determines the maximum number of SPX connections at *nn*. The default setting is 15.

SPX LISTEN TIMEOUT=*nn*
This parameter determines the delay before data packages necessary for the maintenance of the connection are retrieved. The default setting is 108 ticks (roughly 6 seconds).

SPX VERIFY TIMEOUT=*nn*
This parameter determines the time interval after which SPX informs the other side of the connection that the workstation is still connected. The default setting is 54 ticks (roughly 3 seconds).

Setting parameters for the NETX program

ALL SERVERS=ON/OFF
This parameter determines whether all available fileservers are to be informed that a task has been concluded or only those fileservers which are directly involved. The default setting is OFF.

CACHE BUFFERS=*nn*
This determines the number of buffers for the user station in terms of blocks (1 block is 512 bytes). The default setting is five blocks.

EOJ=ON/OFF
This parameter automizes the *End Of Job*, so that files can be closed in the proper manner. The default setting is ON.

FILE HANDLES=*nn*
The maximum number of files which may be open simultaneously. The default setting is 40.

HOLD=ON/OFF
This parameter ensures that files are not closed automatically. The default setting is OFF.

LOCAL PRINTERS=nn
nn determines the number of connected local printers at a workstation.

LOCK DELAY=nn
nn determines the delay in ticks until the shell reattempts to create a lock. 18 ticks represent 1 second. The default setting is 1 tick.

LOCK RETRIES=nn
nn determines the number of attempts to create a lock.

LONG MACHINE TYPE=name
Specifies the computer name. This name is also included in the login script variable %MACHINE. The maximum length of the name is 6 characters.

MAX CUR DIR=nn
This parameter influences the length of the directory name to be displayed. nn can range from 0 to 255 characters. The default setting is 64 characters.

MAXIMUM TASKS=nn
This parameter determines the maximum number of active tasks. The value may vary between 8 and 50. The default setting is 31.

MAX PATH LENGTH=nn
This parameter determines the maximum length of the path name. The default setting is 255 characters.

PATCH=byte-offset,nn
This parameter enables the patching of addresses from the NETX.COM program.

PRINT HEADER=nn
This parameter determines the size of the buffer for the escape sequences in combination with the beginning of

a print job. *nn* is specified in bytes. The default value is 64.

PRINT TAIL=*nn*
This parameter determines the size of the buffer in combination with the end of the print job. *nn* is specified in bytes. The default value is 16.

READ-ONLY COMPATIBILITY=ON/OFF
This parameter blocks the disk addressing of a file with the Read Only attribute. The default setting is OFF. This parameter is geared to older versions of Novell (2.1 and previous).

SEARCH MODE=*nn*
If certain executable program files require additional program modules (such as overlays), the search path can be supplemented using this parameter (similar to the DOS command APPEND). The following settings of *nn* are possible:

0   The search procedure is not fixed. The user specifies the procedure.
1   If no search path has been determined in advance, the operating system first examines the current directory and then defined search paths (MAP) for availability. This is the default setting.
2   The system does not support search paths.
3   Search paths are only supported in the addressing of Read Only files.
4   Free.
5   A check is performed for availability, firstly in the current directory and then in all defined search paths (MAP).
6   Free.
7   A check is performed for availability, firstly in the current directory and then in all defined search paths (MAP). In this case, however, it is only done if the file is to be dealt with as a Read Only file.

SHARE=ON/OFF
This option determines whether follow-up procedures

may adopt the file settings of the first process in the same way. The default setting is ON.

SHORT MACHINE TYPE=_name_
Analogous to LONG MACHINE TYPE but with a maximum of only 4 characters and in combination with the %MACHINE login script variable.

SHOW DOTS=ON/OFF
In order to adapt to DOS conventions, this parameter ensures that the directory names for the current directory and the parent directory are displayed. The default setting is ON.

TASK MODE=_nn_
This parameter determines the settings for the separate tasks. The default setting for _nn_ is 1.

Setting parameters for the NETBIOS program

NETBIOS ABORT TIMEOUT=_nn_
As under SPX ABORT TIMEOUT.

NETBIOS COMMANDS=_nn_
Determines the maximum number of commands in NETBIOS. The possible values range from 4 to 250. The default setting is 12.

NETBIOS INTERNET=ON/OFF
This parameter ensures more rapid data transmission within NETBIOS. The default setting is ON.

NETBIOS LISTEN TIMEOUT=_nn_
As under SPX LISTEN TIMEOUT.

NETBIOS RECEIVE BUFFERS=_nn_
Determines the number of buffers to store data. The possible values range from 4 to 20. The default setting is 6.

NETBIOS RETRY DELAY=nn
The maximum time in terms of ticks which may elapse until confirmation of the data transmission. The default setting is 10 ticks.

NETBIOS SEND BUFFERS=nn
Determines the number of buffers for sending data. The possible values range from 4 to 20. The default setting is 6.

NETBIOS SESSIONS=nn
Determines the maximum number of sessions which NETBIOS supports at one time. The possible values range from 4 to 400. The default setting is 10.

NETBIOS VERIFY TIMEOUT=nn
As under SPX VERIFY TIMEOUT.

NPATCH=byte-offset,nn
This parameter enables patching of NETBIOS addresses.

Index

ABort 236
access control 97
access rights 55, 83, 90
accounts 122
accounts, restricting ~ 129
adapting workstations to the
  network 286
ALLOW 61, 95
applications, installing ~ . . . 141
archiving data 270
ATTACH 24
attributes 83
Autoendcap 170
AUTOEXEC system file . . . 132
AUTOEXEC.BAT 20, 286
AUTOEXEC.BAT, creating ~ . 306

backup 270
Banner 172
boot PROM 286, 291
booting 16
BROADCAST 252

CancelDown 239
CAPTURE 168, 173
CASTOFF 260
CASTON 261
CD, change directory 33
CHKDIR 45
CHKVOL 44
commands, configuration ~ . . 336
  console ~ 320
  login script commands . . . 325
  utility program ~ 311
CONFIG.SYS 286
console commands 320
console operators 133
Copies 171
COPY 72, 270
COPY CON 289
CReate 171

data protection 270
dBASE IV 143
dedicated mode 13
dedicated print servers 167
dedicated workstation 241
DEL 54, 77
DIR, display directory 33
directories, access rights for ~ . 55
  changing names of ~ 52
  creating ~ 52
  displaying ~ 30, 45
  effective rights 58
  removing ~ 52
  rights 48
directory name as drive letter . 53
directory tree 31
drivers 305

E-mail 251
effective rights 38
ENDCAP 168, 178
ERASE 77
error logbook 137

FCONSOLE 25, 258
file access rights 83
file attributes 83
file locking 142
FILER 41, 75
files 36
files, changing name of ~ . . . 75
  copying ~ 71
  creating ~ 69
  deleting ~ 81
  displaying contents of ~ . . . 77
  moving ~ 75
  provisional deletion of ~ . . . 77
fileserver 20, 40
fileserver information 126
fileservers, allocation of ~ . . 204
FLAG 86

Index

FLAGDIR	87	Modify	83
Form	171	mount	304
FormFeed	172, 238	MOuntForm	238
full name	110	Multiplan	161
		NAMe	172
GRANT	65, 93	NARCHIVE	271
		NBACKUP	271
Inherited Rights Mask	48, 61	NCOPY	72
installation of Novell NetWare	298	NDIR	37
IPX	336	NETBIOS	340
		NetWare shell	309
Keep	172, 236	network print routines	225
		network printer configuration	205
LARCHIVE	271	NETX	337
LISTDIR	59	NEWMAIL	262
Local	170	NoAutoendcap	170
logging in	14, 20	NoBanner	172
logging in, ~ to several fileservers	24	node-address	40
logging out	20, 22	NoFormFeed	172
login attempts	134	NoNOTIfy	169
LOGIN directory	19	NoTabs	171
login script	112	NOTIfy	169
login script commands	325	Notify List	209
login script variables	334	Notify List, altering ~	233
login script, displaying, editing		NPRINT	180
system ~	135	NRESTORE	271
editor	136		
system ~	22	partitioning the harddisk	300
user ~	22	password	21
login security	25	password, assigning, altering a ~	26
login time	120	changing user ~	110
LRESTORE	271	pathnames	34
		PAUse	236
Mail Handling System (MHS)	251	PCONSOLE	185
MAP	36, 54	Pegasus Mail	251, 261
MArk	237	print commands, inserting ~	
MD	52	in print queue	187
menus, compiling and using ~	292	parameters	181
quitting ~	296	print forms, defining ~	217
messages, accepting or		print job	167
refusing ~	260	print job configuration	219
editing ~	267	print job configuration, copying ~	224
reading ~	267	removing ~	224

print jobs, options for ~ . . . 218	REN 75
removing ~ 189	RENDIR 52
print modes 213	Restoring data 280
print queue 167, 187	REVOKE 93
print queue, allocation of ~ to	RIGHTS 59, 90
printer 228	rights, altering ~ 60
changing status of ~ . . . 193	equal allocation of ~ 117
installing ~ 197	extending ~ 63
operators 192	RPRINTER 206, 245
users 190	
print routines, installing ~ . . 195	SALVAGE 77
print server 180, 196	SEND 252
print server, activating a ~ . . 241	server 12, 17
determining features of ~ . . 204	server, activating a different ~ . 125
installing ~ 200	SET 240
range of application 201	SETPASS 27
starting the ~ on fileserver . 244	SHared 239
switching off ~ 228, 245	SHELL.CFG 336
print status 226	SHow 168
PRINTCON 218	SLIST 40
PRINTDEF 211	SORT 38
printer configuration, altering ~ 209	SPOOL 199
printer definitions, exporting ~ . 216	stand-alone 11
printer features and forms . . 211	standard configuration 12
printer functions, defining ~ . . 213	STARt 237
printer mapping 195	startup diskette, compiling a ~ . 286
printers 166	startup file, compiling a ~ for
printers, local network ~ . . . 167	harddisk 289
local ~ 166	STARTUP.NCF 308
remote ~ 167	STOp 236
removing allocation of ~ . . 208	Supervisor 14, 97
printing from applications . . 167	SYS volume (mount) 304
PRIvate 238	SYSCON 26, 98
PSC (Print Server Command) . 234	
PURGE 77, 81	time restrictions 131
	TImeout 169
Queue 171	TLIST 57
	TREE 31
RD 52	Trustee Rights 56
record locking 142	
remote network printer,	UNLOAD 245
activating a ~ 245	user group management . . . 100
logging out from printserver . 248	user groups 102
REMOVE 94	

Index

user groups, adding
  members to ~ 102
  adding membership of ~ . . 110
  adding ~ 107
  directory rights for ~ 104
  displaying members of ~ 102, 110
  removing members from ~ . 102
  removing ~ 107
  revoking membership of ~ . 112
  subdirectories for ~ 105
user login script 112
user management 98, 108
user name 14
user rights 107
user work environment . . . 128
USERLIST 46

users, adding ~ 108
  displaying list of ~ 108
  restricting ~ 118
utility programs and commands 311

VOLINFO 42

WHOAMI 29, 57
Windows 156
Word 5.5 148
work environment 128
workgroup manager 15, 114
workgroup manager, specifying ~ 138
workstation 12
workstation, displaying information 28